freedom
for all of us

Matthieu Ricard
Christophe André
Alexandre Jollien

freedom
for all of us

A Monk,
a Philosopher,
and a Psychiatrist
on Finding Inner Peace

Translated by Sherab Chödzin Kohn

Abridged English Version

sounds true
BOULDER, COLORADO

Sounds True
Boulder, CO 80306

Sounds True is a trademark of Sounds True, Inc.

Published by special arrangement with Allary Éditions in conjunction with their duly appointed agent 2 Seas Literary Agency

Published 2020

Cover design by Lisa Kerans
Book design by Kate Kaminski, Happenstance Type-O-Rama

Printed in the United States of America

Library of Congress Cataloging-in-Publication Data

Names: Ricard, Matthieu, author. | André, Christophe, author. | Jollien,
   Alexandre, 1975- author. | Chödzin, Sherab, translator.
Title: Freedom for all of us : a monk, a philosopher, and a psychiatrist on
   finding inner peace / Matthieu Ricard, Christophe André, Alexandre
   Jollien.
Description: Boulder : Sounds True, 2020.
Identifiers: LCCN 2020028204 (print) | LCCN 2020028205 (ebook) | ISBN
   9781683644828 (trade paperback) | ISBN 9781683644835 (ebook)
Subjects: LCSH: Peace of mind. | Liberty—Psychological aspects. |
   Self-realization.
Classification: LCC BF637.P3 R5713 2020 (print) | LCC BF637.P3 (ebook) |
   DDC 170/.44—dc23
LC record available at https://lccn.loc.gov/2020028204
LC ebook record available at https://lccn.loc.gov/2020028205

10 9 8 7 6 5 4 3 2 1

The outward freedom . . . that we shall attain will only be in exact proportion to the inward freedom to which we may have grown at a given moment.[1]

—*Mohandas Gandhi*

Contents

Preface

"We're not going to work!"

This is what all three of us decided. We had planned to get together for a few days in midwinter, as we have in previous years. "We're not going to do any work; we're just going to get together for the fun of it—talk, laugh, enjoy the fresh air." Our dear friend Delphine had invited us to her mountain chalet, high up in the heart of the Alps. Everything was set for a week of vacation in this peaceful haven. We planned no more than roaming about in the snow, enjoying a few cheese fondues, a little reading, and a relaxed time. But then . . .

By the end of the first afternoon, we found ourselves in the pine-paneled sitting room with its views of the surrounding summits. In a good mood, sitting by the fire, listening to the flames crackle, we picked up our discussions again as if they had never been interrupted. Within the sweet warmth of unconditional companionship, serious subjects started coming up along with our jokes and laughter—subjects like how to deal with states of dependency and how to stay on course when "sad passions," or heavy depression, seem to be pushing us headlong into despair.[1]

Once more an urge to keep track of what we were saying, to share with others, started coming up. We were soon saying that it would be a shame to let all these ideas just go down the drain, that we should save them at least for ourselves, keep some record of these exchanges of ours that we ourselves were finding so rich and engaging. So our indefatigable Matthieu put a microphone on the table "just in case, so we won't be sorry later, so we don't forget anything." His two accomplices did not object.

Though it didn't seem like a big deal, knowing the microphone was there was stimulating. It kept us from spacing out while our companions were talking; it pushed us to develop our thoughts more coherently. In the end, it reminded us of our readers—their hopes, their expectations, and their legitimate needs. Then it was as though our readers were there with us, sitting beside us on the couches. And little by little we got caught up in the whole thing.

The question of freedom presents itself as an invitation to look into things deeper, to drill down, to develop a more appropriate approach to life, to create appropriate tools. It calls on us to shake ourselves out of our state of automatic pilot, to break free from the prison of habitual patterns, to try to achieve something more. It is a huge question that requires us to go back over things in order to look in a new way at what is really one of the great challenges of life.

From moment to moment, we are called upon to undergo a complete conversion—to deal with our mental toxins, drop our conditioning, and go deeper within ourselves in the direction of our true nature, which is freedom. Since human beings are not born free but may become so, a whole process of mind training is necessary. This is the area of endeavor the three of us were attempting to explore on the basis of our experience. Getting beyond our concern for what others might think of us, getting beyond any form of narcissism, beyond the egoism that drags us down—these were a few of the challenges involved in our commitment to the total ecology of being that we wanted to sketch in these pages.

A word of caution about the significance of our remarks: they might seem like teachings, but they are only the musings of three friends in search of inner progress—three friends who are interested in sharing their experiences, successful or unsuccessful—the efforts they have made, and their way of looking at things. The remarks we have transcribed in these pages are a faithful reflection of the exchanges we had. Spontaneous and imperfect as they may be, they are sincere and in keeping with the choices we have made in our lives. In editing them down, we simply passed them through the sieve of the following questions: Is what we are saying clear enough? (No jargon—we hate that.) Is it helpful? (What interests us is real change, not just talk.) Is it accessible to everyone, not just to a few sages or intellectuals?

The Greek philosophers created a very beautiful concept: *metanoia*. Metanoia is a way of working on oneself. It requires an intimate conversion, a radical self-transformation leading to a way of life that saves us from the sad passions, from impulsiveness, from egoism, from the prison of habitual patterns. Advancing spiritually, making inner progress, shedding what weighs us down, liberating ourselves for our own sake as well as for the sake of the entire world — those are the things that make up the great challenge that is at the heart of this book.

We hope that our humble dialogue may encourage our readers to take up this challenge as well.

Introduction

What Is Inner Freedom?

MATTHIEU The word *freedom* mainly evokes the aspiration of all beings to lead a life free from imprisonment, oppression, and deprivation of basic rights. But what we would like to talk about here is inner freedom. We are, nearly all of us, the plaything of our whims, our conditioning, our impulses, our inner conflicts, our wandering thoughts, and our afflictive emotions. This servitude of ours is at the root of much that torments us. How do we free ourselves from the prison of these mental mechanisms, in the face of which we often feel helpless, even resigned?

The main difficulty here comes from a lack of insight. We are not able to identify these mental mechanisms or to spot the types of thoughts that enslave us. Wisdom, the lucidity and competence that would allow us to regain our freedom, is too often lacking. Inner freedom could be achieved though better comprehension of how our mind works and through clearer understanding of the mechanisms of happiness and suffering. Developing this type of insight is a matter of training—training that permits the mind to manage afflictive mental states with ease and intelligence.

It is our hope that this book will clarify the means for freeing ourselves from the causes of suffering. Inner freedom brings us great strength and makes us less vulnerable to our own thoughts, which sometimes arise as enemies. It also makes us less vulnerable to external conditions, which are always changing. We feel less vulnerable, we are less centered on ourselves, and we are more open to others. Inner freedom naturally expresses itself as an increase in compassion. Bottom line: everybody wins.

ALEXANDRE   As I consider the spiny question of freedom, a memory comes to my mind. Father Morand, the chaplain at the institution for handicapped people where I lived from age three to twenty, gave me a weighty tome that I leafed through with a sense of awe. It was a manual of philosophy, whose yellowed and worn pages had an imposing presence. I was fourteen years old; I was lugging around a heavy load of complexes and neuroses, and I was taking my difference—my singularity—very hard. Realizing that I was never going to be like other people and being subject to a nameless panic, I was trying to find something I could hold on to. I needed a compass, some sense of direction. And quite appropriately, this large volume had a chapter on alienation, bondage, and the sad passions. And how did the author describe the victim? As a stone in free fall. Quite the metaphor!

My battered brain went on full alert—battle stations, battle stations! All my questions from all sides came together into one. What is freedom really? Is it doing what you want? Giving free rein to your desires? Encountering no hindrances, zero obstacles? But what I was really asking myself was what room for maneuver there might be for a cerebrally motor-impaired kid who was already fleeing from a set destiny—rolling cigars in a workshop for the handicapped. How could this confused, mixed-up kid escape from this inner prison, this avalanche of diagnoses, this whole litany of labels? Was there such a thing as fate? Was everything written in stone?

I was up to my ears in total chaos—complexes, defense mechanisms, fear of being rejected, ill-identified desires. All of this led to a more or less robotic life. Poleaxed by uncertainty, maximally insecure, I was trying desperately to put a little clarity and joy into a life that seemed just a wee bit rough.

Then, for the first time, something spoke to me. Benedict de Spinoza, in his famous letter to G. H. Schaller, proposed a thought experiment and drew the following conclusion: "A stone, being conscious merely of its own endeavor and not at all indifferent, would believe itself to be completely free and would think that it continued in motion solely because of its own wish. This is that human freedom, which all boast that they possess, and which consists solely in the fact that men are conscious of their desire, but are ignorant of the causes whereby that desire has been determined."[1]

As a teenager, I happened to see a TV program in which a professional philosopher was hesitating to answer a question that had been put to him: which is more important—freedom, happiness, or wisdom? Was he supposed to choose, put a check next to the one he preferred? Establish a hierarchy where there really is no choice? At the time I wanted everything—wisdom, happiness, freedom. I surmised that one couldn't reasonably expect happiness without a minimum of inner freedom. How can we advance toward wisdom when inadequacy, fear, and a host of attachments, conditionings, and habits hold us in thrall?

In this area, Spinoza remains a wondrous healer. His method is supposed to be clearheaded and effective: we confront what weighs us down psychologically, what imposes its influence on our way of being and alienates us. In short, we track down the deterministic elements and forces that drive us to be attached, to love, to hate, to fear, and to eternally temporize.

Listening to you, Matthieu, I understand that wisdom and freedom move forward together, hand in hand. And could their first step be to calmly spy out and expose the automatic-pilot approach that lays its dead hand on our daily existence? And by so doing to rediscover and renew a lucid and joyous relationship with ourselves and the world, stop being a puppet, stop putting the remote control that governs our state of mind into the hands of circumstances or of the first person who comes along?

If so, the challenge of the spiritual life lies in boldness: daring to move forward calmly yet at the same time full speed ahead, to develop a state of freedom that has nothing to do with the caprices of the "I" or with the dictatorship of the "they" that often force us to cave in to the norm, to yield to oppressive standards. Spinoza, Nietzsche, Freud, and many others lavish healing teachings on us: Freedom doesn't just come along; it has to be constructed, discovered in the midst of the alienation and illusions that shut us up in our own world, far from reality. In order to benefit from it, we are invited to engage in a process of "liberation," to start moving forward, to say goodbye to our preconceptions and drop our projections as well as the heap of expectations that have us by the throat. Let us hasten to imitate Epictetus. When asked who he was, the sage replied not disingenuously,

"I'm a slave on the way to being free." Yes, this is our big job! It involves nothing less than advancing toward joy and peace with the resources at hand, in the midst of our chaos. The ancient philosophers saw themselves as *progredientes*, progressives, progress makers.

With the help of ascesis (self-discipline), working with others, and a hefty dose of good luck, we can cut our moorings, cast off, and set sail. On this voyage some have to row harder than others. Even if there is such a thing as equal rights—the inalienable dignity of every human being—we still have to acknowledge that we don't all start out with the same chances. Some of us definitely have a heavier ball and chain to drag. Hence the multitude of injustices and the outrageous pervasiveness of hardship and suffering in the world, which we must perceive as an urgent call to commit ourselves to help others.

Thus, it is along with our traumas, wounds, inner dysfunction, deficiencies, and inadequacies, but also a great unsuspected reserve of inner resources, that we must set out in the direction of freedom. The chess player knows how to take limitations into account. He can't move his pieces just as he pleases; nevertheless, conforming with the rules and excelling at his art, step by step, he can win the game. In the same way, trials, defeats, and frailties are perhaps not ultimately brakes on our progress; rather they constitute the ground, the foundation, on which we can build an existence without psychodramas, without "mind-forged manacles."

In getting started on this immense task, let's take stock: to whom or to what have we handed the remote control of our life? To anger, resentment, fear, jealousy? To the best part of ourselves? What occupies the center of our daily lives? Who are we attached to by love, to use Spinoza's words? What are the great desires and profound aspirations that structure our inner life?

CHRISTOPHE Montesquieu said that freedom is the right to do what the laws allow. Outer freedom is that of the body and the speech. It is the right to do what one wants, while remaining within the limits defined by laws. Inner freedom, that of our minds, follows other laws, the laws of our brain in particular. It's the brain that might well shut us up in our habits and our automatic patterns, our negligence, our fears, our emotions. Therefore, we must learn as much as possible about how our mind works.

Listening to you, my friends, I thought to myself that for us caregivers, the question of the freedom of our patients is the hidden thread behind our efforts, even if our ostensible mission is to restore their health. Health is a great facilitator of freedom; without a doubt, when we are sick—whether it's the flu or a migraine or other more serious ailments that are painful or debilitating—our freedom of movement is constrained. But our inner freedom, the thing that might save us, is also threatened, first by the suffering that turns us back on ourselves and closes down our world, then by the fear (of not recovering, of dying) that absorbs the energies we need for all the other aspects of our life. Our quest, therefore, must be not only to regain our health, but also to regain our freedom, inner or outer, which is threatened by illness. How can we remain free to act, to hope, to be happy? Without a doubt, we the caregivers must take more care to speak to our patients in a way that preserves the areas of freedom within them.

As a psychiatrist and a psychotherapist, I have often perceived certain pathologies as obvious losses of freedom. Phobias restrict our freedom of movement; depressions stifle our freedom of decision and action; addictions enslave us. But all these losses of external freedom have their root in a loss of inner freedom. Our sufferings and our fears are invisible prisons that we have the greatest difficulty in escaping from.

However, illness is not the sole cause of the restriction of our freedom; everyday life also harbors many traps. There is the trap of habit and ritual; we always think, act, and live in the same manner. And there's the trap of everyday occupations and preoccupations; we devote the main part of our mental and physical energy to necessary but trivial tasks, neglecting what gives meaning to our lives.

This last loss of freedom is a very important one, as I see it. Studies on the content of our thinking show that the main part of our inner life is composed of "trivial" thoughts about our personal activities, such as paying the rent and taking out the garbage, and about our professional activities, such as replying to emails or setting up meetings. Setting time aside to focus our inner life on something else—such as contemplating nature, reflecting on our ideals, meditating on gratitude or compassion, being happy to be alive—requires a personal decision. That decision is not so difficult, but it's one we make too rarely. That freedom, the freedom to choose to remain a human being and not turn entirely into a worker-consumer, is the inner freedom I have to bring to life in myself. In working on this question of one's inner life, I have discovered to what extent our contemporary lifestyles externalize us, exile us from ourselves, and restrict our freedom.

We are talking about a universal need here. It would be an error to believe that this discussion concerns only the well-to-do people who enjoy greater material and political comforts and want to coddle their sweet little inner freedom as in a cozy cocoon, whereas those who are externally subordinate for economic or physical reasons couldn't draw any profit from it. This seems to me to be slanted thinking that impoverishes reality. Inner freedom is a concern for everybody.

Not Splitting Human Beings in Half

MATTHIEU   Under no circumstances and in no way should our reflections on inner freedom minimize the importance of external freedom. So many people are still the prisoners of totalitarian regimes or for some other reason are not free in their movements, speech, or action. And too many others are prisoners of poverty and limited access to health care and education. We should do everything in our power to come to their aid. How would it be if we were to say to the galley slave, "Keep on rowing and at the same time cultivate your inner freedom. Everything is going to be okay!" Considering outer freedom and inner freedom to be opposites makes no more sense than opposing physical health and mental health; they are complementary, and they influence each other. Therefore, it is perfectly possible to undertake bringing both of them to an optimal point. Moreover, many of us are already doing that by joining programs for inner liberation with activities promoting external freedom, particularly within humanitarian organizations.

There are people who enjoy favorable external conditions but who, inside, feel like prisoners of their minds. On the other hand, I have seen many hermits who radiate tremendous inner freedom, but who externally may look like tramps. I have also met Tibetans who have undergone years of detention in forced labor camps or in Chinese prisons and who say they survived because of the inner freedom they cultivated. Ani Pachen, a Tibetan princess who became a nun and a prominent member of the Tibetan resistance, was kept prisoner by the Chinese for six months in a dark room. She depended on the singing of birds to tell night from day. The same is true of the Dalai Lama's doctor, Tenzin Chödrak, who found in a kind of inner freedom the strength to bear imprisonment and torture. Both Pachen and Chödrak affirm that not succumbing to hating their jailers was what saved their lives.

I'm not trying to advocate resignation or sacrifice, but rather to emphasize the importance and the necessity of an inner path. Inner freedom is not the prerogative of the wealthy or the privilege of those upon whom fortune has smiled. It is the concern of every human being, both in joy and sorrow.

CHRISTOPHE What I learn from these stories of exceptional human beings is that maintaining just a small area of inner freedom (e.g., "don't let despair, hatred, and fear take command of your mind," "you must overthrow their dictatorship") can make it possible for us to resist the waves of distress connected with helplessness and the loss of outer freedom. It might seem ridiculous to be searching for some piece of inner territory that can serve as an island of resistance, but it is vital. In any case, that is what absolutely all survivors of dire ordeals tell us.

We should take heed of that lesson and begin training immediately. What are the minor woes that afflict us at this moment? An illness, a family conflict, money problems? Whatever they are, I should ask myself what area of freedom I am striving to cultivate within myself despite them. What area I am reserving for happiness in spite of everything ("I have problems, but I'm alive"), for hope and optimism in spite of everything ("a solution will surely come, whether from myself or from around me")? Let's be wise enough to begin this inner work without waiting for life to embroil us in some serious ordeal.

ALEXANDRE We don't have our inner freedom on one side and injustice, inequality, and oceans of suffering on the other. Everything is connected, interdependent—everything. We simply have to roll up our sleeves and get to work. Since we are social beings to the very tips of our nails, since we live communally, let's build our happiness together, with one another.

Expounding on inner freedom, talking about working on ourselves, should not distract us from making a robust commitment to a more just, more equitable, more generous world, just as you said, Matthieu. On the contrary, emancipation from the self, joyous detachment, brings us a freedom that expresses itself in relationship, in giving.

Relieved of the chaos of our passions, we can work toward everyone being able to enjoy equality of opportunity, political and social freedom, and having the resources necessary for working on oneself. Ultimately, everyone can attain inner peace. But frankly, if they have to slave away night and day or have to deal with severe illness without support, it becomes more difficult.

In *The Passions of the Soul*, René Descartes defines generosity as the consciousness of being free joined with the desire to make good use of being free. Making good use of freedom is freeing ourselves from everything that weighs us down, removing our chains, then offering our hand to others, giving our support, living with others as teammates. So let's get on with it!

To begin a process of ascesis, we should begin by detecting the sparks, the advance signs, the harbingers of anger or other emotions that cause us to lose ourselves. Imagine a man like Gulliver, bound to the earth. If he randomly yanks and pulls this way and that, he exhausts himself, and he has no chance of getting loose. His only hope is to identify the bonds on his limbs one by one so he can cut them one by one.

The Feeling of Freedom

CHRISTOPHE There is also the subjective dimension of freedom. Sometimes in looking at my life, I have slight bouts of uncertainty. I think I'm free, I feel free, but am I really? "Men are deceived in that they think themselves free," says Spinoza.[2]

It is very important that our illusion of freedom, because it is fundamentally incomplete and fragile, should not dissuade us from working tirelessly on ourselves. As our common friend, the philosopher André Comte-Sponville likes to say, "We are not born free; rather, we become that way, and it is a never-ending process."[3] The work on this project is perpetually ongoing. We are forever drawn to work for the preservation or restoration of our freedoms, whether they are inner (freeing ourselves from our fears and habits) or outer (liberating ourselves from our excessive attachments and dependencies).

Ultimately, the question of whether or not I am totally free doesn't interest me that much. It is clear to me that I will never be totally free (as far as I'm concerned anyhow). But what makes me happy is all the times I see that I have freed myself from thus and such anxiety, dependency, or habit. I can then look at the constraints and fetters that remain, saying to myself that I have freely chosen them and taken them on, as with various familial and professional commitments.

As for my other bondages, yes, I'm still working on them! But at least I'm aware of them, and I don't torment myself about them too much. We should work on our freedoms, stay lucid about our areas of nonfreedom (attachments and habits), and not forget to rejoice in being alive.

ALEXANDRE   The supergenius Chögyam Trungpa is clear on this point: the spiritual journey can never resemble a guided tour. We can forget about itineraries, guidebooks, and instruction manuals. Our daily life calls on us to improvise, initiate, try unheard-of approaches, to go forward with the means at hand. A thousand times a day, the *progrediente* screws up, takes wrong paths, stumbles, gets discouraged. The challenge? The essential? Stay on course. Dare to maintain at least a somewhat contemplative attitude so you can observe your inner battlefields without losing your composure. Notice the forces that have you by the throat, the chaos that pervades you, and make them into a kind of playing field, a school of life. Why fatalistically associate the process of liberation with forced labor, a process of sacrifice, when it's really about enjoying yourself and finding joy in the process all along the way?

MATTHIEU   The Dalai Lama said that a lot of us consider ourselves free when we're really like a screw turning in its hole without ever getting out of it. He was referring to the illusion of freedom that we maintain as we pursue our daily round without ever trying to free ourselves from our conditionings and without trying to liberate ourselves from the causes of our suffering, from the more or less fetal state that prevails in our mind. We cannot be free unless we extricate ourselves from the fog of mental delusion and ignorance that creates a distorted view of reality.

CHRISTOPHE What's difficult about freedom is that it is a concept, and we're not clear how this concept translates into daily life. There is the *feeling* of freedom that we have sometimes—we have the joyful feeling that no limitation, no constraint is weighing on our life—or that we miss at other times when we are more aware of our obligations and constraints. But even at those times, we can always recall that it is possible to inhabit those constraints differently.

For example, when I get home from the hospital after a tiring day of working with patients and their sufferings, or if my wife tells me that thus and such a person has phoned me and that they're not in good shape and it would be good if I were to call them back, my first reflex is to heave a sigh of complaint and think, "Here is an additional burden I don't want to bear." I feel not at all free to do what I want to do: "Not only was I a prisoner of my job all day, but here I am now a prisoner of my friends. I'm sick and tired of being a psychiatrist day and night." However, I try to see the absurdity in this situation, and I give myself the advice that there's no need to now add a lack of inner freedom to my lack of external freedom. Not that I should feel obligated, but I should choose to engage in what I have to do, not because I have chosen it, but because it makes sense.

So I make the effort to go through a second phase that consists in telling myself, "Remember, this person needs you. It's important to him." And in a third phase, I whisper in my inner ear, "Remember that with joy." I do what I can to re-inject a sense of freedom and joy into this situation that I didn't choose freely. Before making this phone call, I say to myself, "Even if this conversation only lasts ten minutes, be genuinely present and don't hold back."

All this is to say that I freely accept certain servitudes, provided that they are transitory and, even better, if they serve others to suffer less or be healthier.

ALEXANDRE Spiritual exercises—ascesis—apply here and now. Freedom implies a whole series of mini-acts repeated again and again from moment to moment. It's easy to ramble on about perseverance and effort, but doing the job, progressing, is quite another matter. Peace, acceptance of the real, makes its territorial gains step by step.

Part I

obstacles to inner freedom

MATTHIEU While working to achieve our external freedom and contribute to that of others, we should by no means neglect progressing in the direction of inner freedom, which is what allows us to face the ups and downs of life with equanimity and, at the end of the spiritual path, to free ourselves from ignorance and the causes of suffering.

We would now like to discuss the obstacles to be met on the path toward inner freedom and the means of cultivating, increasing, and deepening inner freedom to the point where it can become our real way of being.

1

Akrasia: Weakness of the Will

Recently, I had to resign myself to going on a diet. Aflame with good intentions, I rushed headlong into a bookstore with the avid hope of uncovering some book that would give me all the answers about how to do it. Back home with a mountain of books, I was soon sprawling in front of the TV devouring a huge bag of chips. Having delegated the responsibility for my weight loss to the authors of the how-to books, I could munch away, feeling completely free.

Here was a nasty divorce between my deepest desires and the nagging demands that were threatening to spoil my life, a yawning abyss between my intentions and my deeds. Where was I going to find the force to resist the sirens that were seducing me away from the path of good sense, reason, and wisdom? Yes, gobbling up that bag of chips was like shooting myself in the foot. I knew it perfectly well, but I went right ahead and did it anyhow. How could I overcome that force of inertia, those habit patterns, those conditionings?

Once in a hospital, a man gave me an inspiring lesson. He was suffering from cancer and was dragging an IV trolley behind him. Puffing on a cigarette, he remarked, "You know, I'm a goner anyhow, so why not?" How can one defeat absolute pessimism, fatalism that has already given up the game, and introduce a note of freedom in the very midst of the desires and appetites that rule us? A joyful and marvelous challenge!

—Alexandre

ALEXANDRE Leading one's life under the sign of freedom means above all making progress, advancing, making one's daily life a part of a dynamic process. A lively movement toward the peace, happiness, and love that end aberrant behavior, illusions, and discouragement—this is the voyage we are talking about. But what conflicting winds we face! Everything seems to be conspiring to sink this puny little ship of ours: the sad passions, anxiety, illness, physical impairments, as well as all our inner conflicts, our wavering will. Are there a number of different helmsmen fighting over the wheel? Aren't they ever going to come to an agreement on a course that will bring us safely to port?

What Is Akrasia?

ALEXANDRE The Greeks developed a very illuminating concept to describe this battlefield, this arena of inner conflicts raging within our hearts: *akrasia*. Etymologically, *acratos* means "inability." We could also translate this term as "weakness of will." Saint Paul summarizes these conflicts that can rage deep within us: "For I do not do the good I want to do, but the evil I do not want to do—this I keep on doing."[1] From this comes a feeling of civil war, of fragmentation into a hundred pieces and endless frictions. Impotent, the will points out a direction, but our impulses, emotions, fears, and fits of temper just do their own thing. Who among us has never experienced this kind of alienation? It leaves us helpless. It's stronger than we are.

Akrasia can inject a kind of rot into many areas of our lives. It can bring on alcoholism, drug addiction, and other addictions. In short, all our areas of inner conflict can rise up and show us how hard it is to go with the best in ourselves. Our inability to change pervades many realms. I may know perfectly well that a certain relationship is harmful, but nevertheless I go ahead and wallow in it up to my ears. How do we escape the workings of these gears, cease to maintain these hell-bent mechanisms that make us lose touch with ourselves and reduce our efforts to nothing? Not to mention the guilt that gnaws at anybody who stands helplessly by and watches himself open up a huge gulf between his life ideals, his convictions, his higher aspirations, and his actual behavior!

At this point, there is an absolute need for ascesis, for an inner process of pacification that dares to be wholesome and to throttle the tyrants of impulse. Matthieu, you often talk about coherency, about the perfect harmony that prevails within the sage. The intention and the act proceed from the same source. No falsehood, no illusion can survive. For the progressive, the *progrediente*, somebody advancing toward freedom burdened with a heap of conflicts, there is a formidable obstacle: discouragement, the feeling of total impotence, perhaps even of inauthenticity. How is it possible not to give up the struggle when one experiences oneself as the weak puppet of desires that are bigger than oneself, and when from morning till night one is bumping around in a gigantic spin dryer, completely washed out?

Following Chögyam Trungpa, in this chaos you try to take the approach of an auto-body repairman: don't bother feeling guilty or blaming yourself; just relate to the job at hand. Even the most sincere altruistic intentions can yield to fear, fantasies, or a sense of deprivation. And the best will in the world may not be up to the job of destroying egocentricity or liquidating narcissism. So undertake a cheerful process of ascesis: note the damage without flinching. Like the repairman in a body shop, fearlessly contemplate the dings and scratches in your heart and soul.

CHRISTOPHE From a practical point of view, *akrasia* means the inability to keep one's commitments or live up to one's resolutions. For example, I would like to be kind and compassionate more often. I'd like to eat fewer desserts. I'd like to get more exercise. But I just don't get there. I would say that akrasia involves what one *is capable of doing* but does not do even though one sees doing it as desirable. (If it's beyond one's abilities, then we get into a different category, which we'll talk about later in relation to addiction.) Three dimensions are in play here: I want to, I can, but I don't.

Sometimes I get caught in this kind of a trap: I'm in front of my computer, I'm having trouble getting through writing an article, and I let myself escape by reading my emails or doing some vague surfing on the internet. I turn away from my work, I immediately take the bait of these distractions, and at the same time I find fault with myself and tell myself I'm wasting my time. But a big part of me, the akrasic part, has no inclination to go back to the hard work.

Quite clearly, one is rarely akrasic by choice, but most often just through one's inability to work with the problem at hand. Or also through habit. If you give akrasia too much space, it's quick to make you prey.

MATTHIEU In Buddhism, akrasia is a deadly contradiction between what would be good to do and what one actually does, and it corresponds to one of three kinds of laziness. The first consists in doing as little as possible and just taking things easy. The second is rejecting the task at hand before even starting on it, by saying, "Hey, that's not for me. I'll never be able to do it." It's not because one is really incapable of doing the task, it's just because one doesn't feel like making the effort. Here, stagnating in the status quo of our habitual tendencies is a kind of inertia that forces us to keep repeating the same behavior.

The third form of laziness consists in knowing what is really important and nevertheless engaging in a hundred other less useful things rather than getting down to the essential job, all while having a little voice in one's ear, saying, "Hey, watch it! This is not smart. You're just making things worse, aggravating your suffering, perpetuating the very torments and dependencies you're trying to get rid of." Moreover, the attractive, seductive guise that these tendencies present themselves under is sometimes really quick to suck us in. "I can resist everything except temptation," Oscar Wilde said.[2]

Why Akrasia Is a Trap

CHRISTOPHE These "artificial and ephemeral paradises" you're talking about are very common in our materialistic environs. We live in a world of temptations, superficialities, destabilizations. We have to navigate it the best we can, going back and forth between necessary distrust and indispensable indifference.

Sometimes I think that our societies could be described as "akrasio-genic" because of the contradictions they harbor: they provide us with lots of information about what we need to do to live well, but at the same time they allow companies to deluge us with temptations (bad food, sex, tobacco, alcohol, etc.).

There is also a way of viewing our psychology that is still too widespread and turns out to be very discouraging and demotivating. According to this view, we are manipulated by an unconscious that is swarming with insatiable desires, and it is impossible to block this natural activity without causing a backlash and having it come back twice as strong.

We often find ourselves alone facing temptation. It seems to me that formerly there were more social relationships and "oversight" by close friends or family. Not only were we less exposed to temptations — no commercials, no screens — but we were also nearly always surrounded, in the middle of a group, and not solitary and left to ourselves, like a child in front of a jam jar. Akrasia feeds on our distress and our solitude like a vampire.

Finally, keeping resolutions is quite simply hard to do! Dealing with akrasia often consists of putting the kibosh on certain behaviors (smoking, eating too much), certain emotions (anger, stress), and certain thoughts (negative thinking or pessimism). At the same time, akrasia consists of starting different behaviors (eating more vegetables, tidying up more often), different emotions (being more compassionate), or different thoughts (cultivating positive thinking). So all at the same time you have "less" and "more," which perhaps explains the difficulties we have getting results here, because the two involve different brain circuits.

The work of Olivier Houdé, professor of psychology at the Sorbonne (University of Paris), on learning and on what he calls "free thought" is very interesting. He shows that to get our judgment and behavior to evolve, we have to activate certain psychological abilities (such as flexibility, logic, and detachment), and at the same time inhibit certain others (such as prelogical reasoning, automatic behavior, habits, and prejudices). The inhibitory function is located in the inferior prefrontal cortex. Working with this psychological "resistance" is fundamental for all learning (in children) and all psychological evolution (changes of opinion or behavior in adults).

ALEXANDRE The philosophical tradition calls the moderation of desires "temperance" (sophrosyne in Greek). But how do we make progress in that area? How do we learn the right balance? How do we tame affectivity, sexuality, the heart? In order not to become completely enslaved by them and completely alienated from oneself, we must undertake an ascesis—develop an art of living.

When you speak of self-control, Christophe, you point to the powers of the sage—his capacity for self-determination, his self-mastery. For the progressive on the path, it's another thing altogether! What is the challenge here? Withdrawing from cupidity, ceasing to lose oneself in one's emotions, welcoming sensuality as the perfect opportunity for freedom, generosity, giving of oneself.

To put an end to discouragement, it helps to point out that akrasia is more or less regional. It invades certain areas of our existence and doesn't trouble others. It injects its rot into our daily lives at certain moments, but it does not alienate our entire being. As Nietzsche says, we remain wholesome in our totality. Shouldn't we scout out where our vulnerabilities are and turn them into points of special vigilance?

Spotting the akrasic regions of our being, the behavior patterns and tendencies that are too strong for us, isn't that already treading on the path of freedom? From going overboard in the bookstore to acts of violence, to alcohol abuse, to craving for affection—these could be the areas. There are a thousand opportunities for the will to throw in the towel. Without necessarily blaming or condemning, why can't we proceed in total humility to open our eyes to our weaknesses, our deficiencies, our wounds? The voluntarist approach, which believes everything is in our power and all we have to do is snap our fingers to make a 180-degree about-face, is an illusion that never liberated anybody. No, the intemperate person doesn't need a kick in the butt or any form of reproach. To liberate oneself, it's always a matter of understanding, exposing the mechanisms in play, and taking action to get out of these prisons by developing healthy habits that can open up a new life to us.

MATTHIEU You're right. Kicking someone who's in chains and telling him to get a move on is not the best way to go. It works better to show him how to free himself from the chains. It's of no use either to give lessons to others if one has not oneself achieved the freedom one is advocating. There's a tale about a mother, accompanied by her little son, who one day came to see Mullah Nasruddin, a mischievous wise man whose exploits have been told for centuries in the Middle East and India. The mother asked Nasruddin to tell her child to stop eating sweets, hoping that his word would have more effect than hers. Nasruddin paused for a while and then told the mother, "Come back in two weeks." Two weeks later, the mother brought her son back to Nasruddin, who looked the child straight in the eyes and said in a very loud voice, "Stop eating candy!" The child, on whom this made a big impression, timidly nodded his head. The mother couldn't help asking the mullah why he hadn't told her son that two weeks earlier. "Because I wanted to check for myself to see if it was possible to stop eating sweets," he said.

In addition, not being able to is different from not wanting to. If a task is beyond our ability initially, we have to go step by step. The fact that the journey might be long should not discourage us. The important thing is knowing that we are going in the right direction.

ALEXANDRE Progressing toward freedom is more a marathon than a sprint. And the will in this adventure is more a rudder than a motor. It indicates a direction; it helps us stay on course and persevere. But if we overdo relying on our will alone, we end up completely washed out, riding on our rims, drained.

CHRISTOPHE Couldn't we also regard will as a fuel? The rudder would be our values, our ideals, our goals.

MATTHIEU Without fuel, you can't move. My uncle, the solo sailor Jacques-Yves Le Toumelin, was becalmed in the doldrums off the Galápagos Islands for three weeks without a breath of wind. His sailboat didn't have a motor. In such a situation, you can swing your rudder in whatever direction you want, but you won't move an inch. Personally, I would say that our motivation is the helm of the boat. By controlling the rudder, it determines the direction of our journey. The will is the wind that fills the sails and enables us to arrive safely in port.

ALEXANDRE   In the long run, the obstacles that prevent us from getting on with our life—from cruising freely on life's ocean—rob us of our vitality. Here's where the sage, like a good doctor, arrives to resuscitate us. Far from condemning us, he confirms that our approach to life is possible, that the things that torment us are not fixed by an unyielding fate. Light and playful, he dances with life, quite apart from its psychodramas. He doesn't aggrandize the sole power of will; he doesn't obstruct the life and joy that pervade him. He just is.

MATTHIEU   Yes, from the moment you have eroded the habitual tendencies that underpin and maintain your sufferings, all your manifestations of thought, speech, and action become a benefit to yourself and others. You act with ease, flexibility, and freedom, without having to force yourself to laborious effort. You are in perfect harmony with your deepest values. The sage is a teaching all by himself, just from what we can experience of his way of being. The messenger himself becomes the message.

It's Total Bedlam, but What's the Problem?

CHRISTOPHE   I often feel that what leads to akrasia is not just weakness of the will, but intolerance of uncertainty, discomfort, and suffering.

Let's take what we might call "emotional akrasia." If I have just found out that I am suffering from a serious illness, I try to tell myself, "This is real. You have to accept it as it is. Don't despair. And above all, it's not a good idea to dwell on it. Do what you have to do to get right back to your happy life. That's where your salvation lies." But uncertainty is so unbearable that I prefer to dwell on negative certainties and pessimistic scenarios: "I'm completely done for. I'll never get over this." And at that point, what appears to be a lack of will is, in fact, only an inability to stand up to uncertainty and suffering. Perhaps we lack the will to continue to apply the strategies that we know will do us good—it's just that it's so difficult to go toward that good.

And when one has trouble controlling one's emotions, I think it may not so much be weakness of the will as temporary inability. I am sucked in by my painful and negative emotions, and when surveying the field of battle I say to myself, "Okay, wait, stay calm. Stay on course. It'll all calm down. The situation will evolve. Just hold steady and don't lose it."

ALEXANDRE   You're doing a good thing by recalling the transitory, ephemeral quality of our struggles and battlefields. What kills us, it seems to me, is forgetting that everything passes—even roof tiles landing on our heads, fits of emotion, torments of the soul. It's crazy the way catastrophic scenarios just burst loose on us. It's really hard, in the middle of mental torment, not to believe that emotion is going to eat us up alive. Immediately, the litany of conceptual mind kicks in: "I'm screwed. I'm done for. I don't have the strength. This is one blow too many." In the midst of akrasia, remembering that everything is transitory, impermanent, lets you flow with it, lets you welcome the chaos.

A friend of Matthieu's helped me a lot in this area. When we were getting back from Korea, right while we were moving and I was a complete bundle of worries, she let me have it: "It's total bedlam, but what's the problem?" That's become a keeper for me, my mantra. Whenever I'm passing through a turbulence zone, I say to myself, "This truly is total bedlam, but what's the big deal?" Our conceptual mind, this gigantic machine for churning out worries, is conditioned to exaggerate. Without feeding an exaggerated optimism, it can help to realize that there are two kinds of suffering, two layers if you will: the tragic side of life (illness, earthquakes, physical impairments, death, a certain loneliness) and the whole big heap of psychodramas fabricated entirely by the ego. Fortunately, we can slay these inner dragons, progressively do them in, and thus stop allowing ourselves to be totally taken in by all the false prophets living inside us.

How to Beat Akrasia

CHRISTOPHE   The fraudulent activities of the conceptual mind that you're talking about, Alexandre, sometimes take form as an inability to keep from harming oneself. For example, if patients have eczema, they might scratch themselves violently, which makes their skin lesions even worse and increases their urge to scratch. This can degenerate to the point of provoking serious abrasions, which creates a whole new set of complications. The ideal would be not to start scratching (just as, psychologically, the ideal would be not to start chewing continually on certain thoughts). But this is too hard and, moreover, letting oneself go and scratching provides a few seconds of relief. We know perfectly well the relief is not going to last, but we scratch anyhow. So the question posed by akrasia becomes: how not to scratch, or where to find the strength not to scratch?

MATTHIEU   It is a relief to scratch, but the real ideal would be for the itching to stop. This leads us to the idea of an antidote that entirely dissolves habitual tendencies instead of just pacifying the symptoms.

Akrasia is also related, it seems to me, to a lack of consistency and to various forms of cognitive dissonance between our ideals, our values, and our behavior. We have seen officials in charge of the struggle against tax evasion putting their money into Swiss bank accounts to avoid taxes, or politicians and clergymen putting themselves forward as champions of the dignity and rights of women though they have committed sexual violence themselves. We know that supposedly good family fathers carried out the role of executioners in the concentration camps.

Habitual tendencies result in an accumulation of thoughts, emotions, and behaviors. If you place a large weight for a few weeks on the middle of a long, unsupported plank, at the end of a certain time the plank will bend and remain bent even after you take the weight away. It becomes impossible to flatten it out again, and if you force it too much, it will break. You have to turn it over and hang a weight that corrects the curvature from it; after many days, it will be able to hold its original form. We have to show this same kind of perseverance to gradually wear away our habitual patterns. This is indeed the point where willpower and perseverance apply. The Buddha often said, "I have shown you the path, but it is up to you to travel it." The Buddha cannot tread the path in our place, and he will not bring us to enlightenment and liberation from suffering like someone throwing a stone up onto the roof of a house. He shows us the way, explains it, and gives the advice we need to travel on it without obstruction. It is essential to be confident that we are persevering in the right direction. A traveler who has lost his path, without reference point, feels helpless and gets discouraged.

Cognitive dissonances cause us to be out of sync with our values, with what we think is right, and that inevitably leads to a feeling of malaise. Therefore, it is desirable to undertake a process that will put us in harmony with ourselves. Such a process requires effort, but such an effort will be supported by the enthusiasm that sees the benefits that lie at the end of the path. Knowing that there is always the possibility of change, we have to set in motion the causes and conditions that can make our situation evolve.

ALEXANDRE   That bit about the warped plank is ingenious, brilliant! Since it takes time to harden in our habits and develop this nasty warping, getting back up the slippery slope also isn't going to happen overnight. It's going to take infinite patience.

Spinoza reminds us that a human being is not an empire within an empire. We are embedded in nature, caught in circumstances we have not necessarily chosen, and we certainly are not in possession of plenipotentiary, imperial powers. Our first step has to be to identify our sad passions, the forces that shape us, the reflexes and conditionings that weigh on the course of our lives. With infinite compassion, we must keep our eye on the areas of our life where we are fragile and develop vigilant attention toward them. Food, alcohol, sensuality, sex, the thirst for recognition — these are the areas that call on us to make an effort to improve, become freer, lighter, less enamored of ourselves.

In order not to collapse along the way, we have to identify the resources at our disposal for moving in the direction of peace. We have to look at what is happening within us with the attitude of a good mechanic. Stay very factual and objective; don't call in the hordes of blame and guilt. What is presently going on with me? Where do I stand with regard to the big challenges in my life? What are the qualities of the storm that is raging here and now? The traditions of the East advise us to adopt the posture of a witness. We must slow down, allow ourselves time, survey the field of battle without insisting on an emergency intervention. It's bedlam all right, but what's the problem? It's a mess, but why lose confidence and abandon faith? Life goes on, and the challenge is not to make a federal case out of it when the walls begin to shake a bit.

The ingenious healer Spinoza also provides us with an extremely powerful tool: find out what really brings us joy. The art of finding fundamental joy no matter what the circumstances is the essential sustenance needed for any spiritual journey. Fighting against akrasia is not a mere matter of will or self-control. If from morning till night we do nothing else but resist temptation, our daily life will quickly go sour on us. We have to attempt an ascesis that is playful and light. Spinoza is right a hundred times over: It is not self-deprivation that leads to detachment; rather it is the joy that is very close to freedom. It's true: only a light, playful, and merry heart can gladly give up the crumbs of feeling good, say no to the drug fixes of oblivion, and gather the happiness that lies beyond all mirages.

There is a strategy for beating akrasia: regionalize, look into the precise details of how the problem occurs, demarcate your akrasic areas. Nobody can be reduced to their weak points. You can be a good family father even if you totally lose it at one particular moment in your life. You can practice altruism and still remain a seriously debilitated, fragile, vulnerable, incapacitated person. Gentleness toward oneself is not only a balm but also a tonic that empowers us with a sense of perseverance and helps us keep our head above water.

"We Can't Really Change": Another False Idea

MATTHIEU   Some people say that in the end we can't really change. Of course, if we continue to maintain and even reinforce our bad habits, our character traits will remain generally stable or will get worse in the absence of major upheavals in our life. On the other hand, if we acknowledge that there are points that need improvement in our way of being, and we decide to apply ourselves to the task, it is completely possible to evolve.

We now know that neuroplasticity—that is, the capacity of the brain to modify itself in interaction with our experience—allows us to change at any age. This plasticity can be set in motion by a change in external conditions and also through training our mind and the development of our abilities that have hitherto remained in a latent state. We can learn to read, juggle, and play chess; we can also learn to cultivate essential human qualities like attention, emotional balance, and compassion. But in all cases, without training, there's no change.

We are not attempting here to come up with some kind of self-help manual in five points and three weeks. Rather, what we want to do is share a body of knowledge that has accumulated over two millennia of exploring how the mind works—knowledge that has been corroborated by contemporary cognitive science and neuroscience.

Moreover, experience shows that many people who started off in an unsatisfactory or painful state have successfully traveled the path that leads to greater inner freedom. Resilience in particular is a quality that is acquired through experience but can also be cultivated through mental training. In addition, there are sages who have gone still further and have freed themselves entirely from all forms of mental delusion; they enjoy irreversible inner freedom. And since history has shown that this kind of transformation is possible for others, why should it not be possible for us too?

We must distinguish between the pessimist who says to himself, "I'm hopeless. I don't have the capacity to improve. That's the way it is, and there's nothing I can do about it," and the person who observes, "Yes, I have weak points, but I also have good qualities, especially willpower. I have one painful wound, but the rest of my body is healthy, and I think that if I take care of this wound it will heal in the end." The optimist is more realistic than the inveterate pessimist; he knows that change is possible, that there are all kinds of opportunities to take advantage of and all kinds of pathways to explore. The enthusiasm born from contemplating the benefits of change can get us out of akrasia. The way to do it is to define a series of specific tasks, limited quite precisely, that can easily be accomplished one by one. Otherwise, we are in danger of concluding that the job taken as a whole is way beyond our means.

Toolbox for Dealing with Akrasia

ALEXANDRE

Don't make a huge drama out of your struggles, relapses, and mistakes. Every January 1, I come up with a list of resolutions that are impossible for me to keep in the long run. Discovering freedom is first of all seeing where all our fetters are, taking stock of our resources, and dissolving our psychodramas one by one.

We have our work cut out for us, but the situation is never hopeless. The spiritual path is more like a marathon than a sprint. Along the way, we might stumble or take a beating. On this great journey, we have to know what will cheer us up, console us, reinvigorate us. A marathon runner who takes steroids or painkillers can't hold up in the long run. Wisdom requires identifying what nourishes us fundamentally. The art of being cheerful, no matter the circumstances, comes from a sense of unconditional joy.

Decentralize. Dealing head-on with our inner struggles definitely means crashing right into a wall. So prudence requires us to decentralize a little and to stop setting up our problems right at the center of our existence, yet at the same time, not evading them altogether. In concrete terms, when things are not going well for me, nothing keeps me from calling up somebody else who is also struggling with akrasia to give them some support, to express solidarity with them, to listen to them.

MATTHIEU

The first step. Buddhist practice recommends that we begin by identifying the mental states and afflictive emotions that affect us the most and that we are most vulnerable to. Then we have to identify the appropriate antidotes and put them to work. We must also understand that what is tormenting us does not come from a single cause but from many causes and conditions that all activate each other interdependently and must also be taken into consideration.

One step at a time. Shantideva, the great Indian Buddhist master, said that there are no big difficult tasks that cannot be divided up into little easy tasks.

Motivation. If training one's mind by appropriate means makes it possible to become less prone to anger, anxiety, and arrogance, then this method is without a doubt worth exploring. If you break your leg, rehabilitation will take some effort, but that's better than walking on crutches for the rest of your life. Look around you—hundreds of people have done this successfully.

CHRISTOPHE

In praise of resolutions. Akrasia is fed by the absence of projects. Certainly weakness of the will can hamper and complicate the process of decision-making, but envisioning and making decisions is a profitable thing to do. Studies show that a great number of our resolutions are helpful: 40 percent are still being kept after six months and 20 percent after two years. On the other hand, if you don't make any resolutions, you get a zero-percent result.

In praise of nonjudgment. Very simply, we have to accept that there is going to be a certain amount of failure in keeping our resolutions and not attack ourselves or put ourselves down for that.

In praise of discernment. It's up to us to see if the problem of akrasia is momentary (because we're tired or too exposed to temptations), or if it's ongoing (perhaps then the goal is too difficult for this moment in our lives, or else we have to review how we're going about it).

2

Dependency

I don't think I'm that prone to dependency. But once I had an addictive experience that showed me how quickly the loss of freedom can set in and that it can affect anybody, even people who are in a quite good state or a pretty good state.

I was on vacation at my brother's place. After dinner, toward nine o'clock, my brother suggested we try a video game called Civilization. *It involved creating and directing a civilization from the Stone Age all the way up to modern times. It was so fascinating that when I looked at my watch for the first time, it was already three in the morning! I went to bed still struggling with my urge to keep going "a little while longer."*

The following day during dinner, I only had one thing on my mind— getting back to the game. Despite my wife's admonitions, I plunged back into the game several nights in a row.

As we were leaving, my brother proposed giving me the game. "Definitely not!" I replied. Since that time, none of those games has been allowed under my roof.

I remember an ad from one of the makers of these addictive games, saying, "You won't be able to resist!" This slogan was at once a challenge—who's stronger, the game or you?—and the promise of dependency. What better motto for dependency could there be than "You won't be able to resist"?

—Christophe

CHRISTOPHE   Medically speaking, being dependent is being unable to do without a substance (alcohol, tobacco, drugs), a relationship (emotional or sexual dependency), or a behavior (dependency on the esteem of others or on flattery). There is such a thing as normal dependency: we all depend on water, oxygen, sun, other human beings. But what we're going to talk about here are the dependencies that make us suffer.

The reasons dependency is problematic are that it creates suffering for oneself and others, and it has an uncontrollable side to it. All activities that bring us intense or quick pleasure can lead to dependency. Primary examples are activities related to sex, alcohol, and food. If the dependency consists in drinking a glass of wine every evening, we could say it's just a behavioral problem. But as long as it does not reach a level of habituation, where we feel we have to increase the dose if the pleasure obtained is not sufficient, it's not a pathological problem. Rather we are in the realm of habit, a form of minor dependency on comfort and pleasure that we can still pass up at the cost of a little discomfort.

Toxic dependency, on the other hand, reduces our freedom significantly. The dependent lives only for the next fix. He suffers an impoverishment of his view of life. As I see it, this is the worst kind of self-alienation. Going from akrasia to dependency, there is a further loss of freedom. In the case of akrasia, we know what we should do and it's within the limits of our current capacities, although we don't consistently succeed in doing it. In the case of dependency, we know what we should do, but it is impossible for us to accomplish it. Sometimes, deep down we don't even really want to. (We all know that at that stage it's very difficult to help dependent persons.) "I just can't resist" is the motto of the dependent.

MATTHIEU   We could describe dependency as an accumulation of indulgences and delusions that in the end pushes us into the abyss of addiction. I'm not saying this by way of finding fault; it's simply a clinical observation. The work of the mind in this case is to free itself from the chains it itself has forged. In the brain, dependency, just like the training of the mind that helps to free us from it, will modify the neuronal networks that are implicated in addiction.

ALEXANDRE That's where we need a major dose of patience. It takes time to climb out of that hole.

The Cerebral Mechanisms of Addiction

MATTHIEU Being dependent is desiring something in spite of oneself or continuing to desire something one no longer likes. A few years ago, I was struck by the findings of a professor of neuroscience named Kent Berridge, whom I met several times, mainly at a conference organized by the Mind and Life Institute. At one point, we spent five days discussing the question of desire, need, and addiction.

Berridge's studies show that there are different neuronal networks in the brain for *liking* and *wanting*. When one likes something that gives one pleasure—for example, a warm shower after a hike in the snow, or a delicious dish of some kind—the neuronal networks activated are not the same ones as are activated when one wants this thing. The pleasure one feels from certain experiences, often sensual in nature, is very volatile, and the activation of the corresponding neural networks is also labile. It can transform very quickly into indifference, disgust, or even revulsion. One cream cake is delicious; five of them make you nauseous.

Berridge and other researchers have shown that by repeating pleasurable experiences, we strengthen the cerebral networks that make us desire and want these experiences. The changes in these networks are much more stable. There comes a time when we no longer feel pleasure. And yet we continue to desire this experience again and again. So the desire, the craving, is much more stable than the pleasurable sensations, which are by nature ephemeral. As a result, intense pleasures are rarer than intense desires. When desire becomes powerful and constant, and we become hypersensitive with regard to it, we can speak of dependency or addiction. In the end, we find ourselves in the sad situation of not being able to prevent ourselves from desiring something that no longer brings pleasure—and might even have begun to disgust us.

Berridge describes an extreme situation: it is possible to induce a rat to desire something that has never caused it any pleasure and that it has hitherto found repugnant. If one repeatedly activates the regions of the brain connected with desire at the same time as one gives a rat water that is as salty as the Dead Sea (three times saltier than other bodies of saltwater), one rapidly arrives at a point of conditioning where as soon as the desire region is activated, the rat immediately abandons a lever that gives it access to sugar water and goes to the lever that gives excessively salty water and activates that one instead. Before this conditioning, the rat had systematically avoided that lever.

We see what a vicious situation this is — it's pointless to say to the person suffering from a dependency, "You just have to consider alcohol, the drug, or addiction to sex as something repugnant," because quite often the subject is already disgusted by the object of his dependency. Thus, it is not enough to consider something undesirable to stop wanting it. Some subjects tell us that they can't resist going toward the object of their desire even though they detest their addiction to it. It seems to me that there are important lessons to be learned from this research.

CHRISTOPHE Some people criticize neurobiological exploration of our desires, dreams, and fantasies — of our psychological machinery. They say our approach is reductionist, that human beings cannot be reduced to their biology. That's true. But I nevertheless find it comforting to know that if I am a victim of dependency, it is because of dysfunctional mechanisms that have established themselves in my brain and because I have abandoned myself to these compulsive mechanisms without regulating them. That makes me responsible — no one is going to work on my brain for me. But it doesn't find me entirely guilty — I'm not an indolent person who chose to become dependent. There is a biological element that I didn't choose to put in place but which I have to rouse myself to counteract.

Moreover, this biological dimension accounts well for the dissociation that we experience: on one hand, we go toward the thing that brings us pleasure, and on the other, we know perfectly well that there are serious downsides to this: medical downsides, because addiction harms our bodies; psychological downsides, because we see ourselves as weak, inadequate, and have the sense of having lost our free will in a certain area of our life;

and relationship downsides, because addiction gradually isolates us. So at best, we feel a sense of self-deception and unworthiness. At worst, we have a feeling of existential emptiness: I'm in the grips of a desire that brings me no benefit and that eventually ends up depressing me and ruining my life. And I'm helpless to prevent it.

MATTHIEU   Yesterday we saw wild animal tracks in the snow. We could say, "A rabbit passed by here, or a fox or a weasel." In the same way, in studying the brain we see the tracks left behind by various kinds of thoughts, our habitual tendencies, our emotions, our confusion, or our wisdom. Analysis of these tracks can be quite revealing. Some might say that this kind of analysis takes the poetry out of human life; for me, these scientific studies had a revelatory effect that crystallized an intuition of mine. Understanding the dissociation between what we like and what we want provides the tools we need to free ourselves from deadly dependency and to shape our intervention against it more effectively. We know that mind training can remodel our neuronal connections through the process of neuroplasticity. Therefore, we have to reverse our conditioning thought by thought, emotion by emotion, in order to gradually weaken the cerebral networks associated with the habitual tendencies that cause us endlessly to desire what is harmful to us.

CHRISTOPHE   What's striking about studies of the cerebral machinery of dependency, of whatever kind, is that the pleasure circuit is fragile and unstable. It disintegrates rapidly, whereas the cerebral circuit of addiction is much more stable and resists dissolution over time. Being dependent gradually gets us hooked on something that no longer brings us pleasure—only pain and fear.

Why Is It So Difficult to Overcome Addiction?

MATTHIEU   Freeing oneself from addiction is a real challenge. Experience, corroborated by the neurosciences, shows that in addition to exertion of the will and having to maintain this exertion over a long enough time, there are four obstacles.

First, it turns out that it is more difficult to activate the regions of the brain linked with the will in victims of dependency. These victims are handicapped on the level of the willpower that they need so badly.

Second, addiction modifies the brain in a stable fashion to make it more responsive to stimuli that trigger addictive behavior. This sensitizing of the brain makes us react more readily and more strongly to factors that trigger consumption of a toxic substance or that lead to turning on a video game.

Worse yet, in any training (such as meditative practice or learning to play the piano), neuroplasticity, the transformation of certain bundles of neurons in specific regions of the brain, occurs mainly in the region of the brain known as the hippocampus. And we know that the activity of the hippocampus is inhibited by depression, which makes change more difficult. By contrast, activity in the hippocampus is stimulated by learning to juggle, learning to meditate, or engaging in sports. Unfortunately, the hippocampus is also inhibited in dependents. Thus, a person suffering from addiction ends up with less willpower and decreased capacity for change.

So there is a quadruple obstacle: reinforcement of desire, a high level of responsiveness to addictive stimuli, weakening of the will, and inhibited activity in the region of the brain that can actualize change. This is precious knowledge for someone attempting to overcome dependency. We have to mobilize the willpower we have left to the maximum possible extent and patiently strengthen it day after day.

ALEXANDRE   As the philosopher Simone Weil points out, there is such a thing as an asceticism for the passionate. It's crazy what we are willing to do, to sacrifice, to relieve a yen, to obey a desire.

Basically, there are perhaps two types of liberation. One of them is radical, abrupt, the famous click, or epiphany: I realize that I'm at an impasse, I see the abyss that I'm pushing myself into, and I find the energy and strength to bid *adieu* to the bad habits, to change my life. And then there's the longer and more arduous conversion: step by step you have to end the inner civil wars, to pacify and unify your inner life. But let's avoid absolutizing either one of these approaches. Every person achieves freedom and makes progress starting from the particular point they happen to be at and depending on what their particular strengths and weaknesses are.

At a time when I was weighed down by a massive emotional dependency, one distinction helped me profoundly: pleasure and desire should not be confused with each other. Matthieu, you gave me a wonderful tool with that. Thanks to you, I understood that the cerebral zones linked with pleasure were unstable, changing, fluctuating, while the regions of the brain responsible for desire were tenacious, solid, and stable. Concretely, I might feel an immense pleasure in the company of a certain person and have a good time with them, easing my loneliness. But the bad thing here occurs if I reach the point of desiring this person and the circumstances I share with them but no longer get the least pleasure out of it. From that point on, a desire—a compulsion running on empty that is never satisfied—turns me into a slave. Incapable of any satisfaction and reduced to a state of need, I become a sad little puppet.

And this is where a redeeming question comes in. What really gives me pleasure? Deep down, what really brings me fulfillment? Moralism is not what heals us. There's no point in demonizing dependency when what is really needed is to descend into the depths of our fundamental nature, our ground of grounds, and heed the inner compass that points to what really brings us joy. Spinoza is right again: joy is what makes us free. Joy gives us the strength to go whistling on by the counterfeit pleasures we have been talking about.

CHRISTOPHE   We have to keep in mind that our efforts have to be geared to the long term, because what we are going to do here is reconfigure the circuits of our brain. In freeing ourselves from our dependencies, the difficulty comes from having to combat these deeply rooted mechanisms. Any progress is regularly followed by relapses and regressions, which we should definitely not regard as proof of our inability to change, but rather as a sign that we have stumbled on the path and have to start walking again.

This model of psychological change has still not been established in our minds. We're still going by the model of an epiphanic change, as if everything became okay the moment we understood the situation. Change really happens through a new learning process that counteracts the old one or through learning new abilities. It's vital to get the message here: most psychological changes that take place in our minds, up to 90 percent, are the fruit of regular, patient, and constant efforts. The movie version — I understand something, and *poof*, through some leap of salvation, the change happens instantly and forever — is sexier, but much less realistic.

MATTHIEU Knowing that our suffering comes from traces left behind in our brains by our bad habits shows also that nothing is written in stone and we can reverse this process.

CHRISTOPHE That being said, my understanding is that it is incredibly difficult to get out of situations like dependency. We know that we should not expect immediate results, that we have to commit ourselves firmly, telling ourselves, "Make a lot of little efforts, and you'll get there." But we don't know when that's going to happen. And in the meantime, we suffer. That's why the easiest way out often consists in indulging fully in what one is hooked on. There are substance dependencies, but there are also people hooked on complaining and worrying. It's tempting to moan, to tell ourselves how unfortunate we are, how unlucky. And paradoxically, this is a solution we inadvertently adopt in order not to have to keep maintaining an effort. We get to be experts in complaining.

MATTHIEU This is what Eckhart Tolle has called "the pain-body." When ego fails in its quest for victory, it reconfigures its identity and becomes a victim. This permutation permits it to crystallize a new way of continuing to exist and of distinguishing between "I" and "other." It says to itself, "Everybody is against me," and in that way creates a niche for itself that it can entrench itself in, an identity it can hang on to.

The Tipping Point

MATTHIEU There is another situation that is both fascinating and hard to understand. Many people tell us that having tried many times to break out of dependency, at a given moment, they arrive at a tipping point. All at once, they're out of it, once and for all. They remain vulnerable to a drug or to alcohol for the rest of their lives, and they're quite aware of that, but they never touch it again. It's all or nothing. You have to stop completely. Because once you start again, it's a slippery slope.

A friend told me how she had become an alcoholic in an effort to palliate her daily anxiety and agoraphobia attacks. "I knew," she said, "that alcohol would not resolve anything, but it gave me more euphoria and oblivion than tranquilizers did. It only reduced the anxiety for a few hours, and the anxiety was faithfully there for me at its post the following morning—along with the bonus of all the physical discomforts of alcohol, which my body did not tolerate well. Over the years, I went into decline; I became a liar, and I was very ashamed of myself. One evening I 'saw myself.' I understood with sudden clarity that I was losing my husband, my family, my dear friends, my job—and myself. That night I decided never to drink another drop of alcohol. It was rational and emotional all at the same time, a clear and powerful 'vision' of reality. It was a lightning bolt that shook me profoundly. It was as if I could see the past, the present, and the future at the same time, along with what was waiting for me if I kept going downhill. I held up in my resolve, even though it wasn't easy. Of course, the anxiety problem doubled, but I fought it barehanded, without tranquilizers and without illusions. The experience I had had sustained me through all the temptations. It's more than twenty years now that I have been abstinent. I can be confronted by a table full of all the fashionable elixirs; they no longer tempt me a bit. Better yet, I'm completely indifferent to them."

ALEXANDRE In Zen, you find advocates of both the gradual path and the sudden path. For the gradualists, enlightenment comes progressively, whereas the sudden-path people see it as coming all at once. Why do we want so much to categorize, to speak in universal terms, when in reality every person has to find his or her own way, overcome suffering with the means they have available? Telling a junkie who's into it up to his neck to drop his habit overnight might very well have the opposite effect; it might heighten his sense of needing the drug and create a terrible panic. The challenge is to ask in a concrete way what could help me here and now to take a firm step toward greater health, to drop my dependencies one by one.

CHRISTOPHE It's problematic and perilous to hit people with ultimatums. I think that only works if you're talking to yourself.

It is sometimes said that you have to hit bottom in order to change, not for the pleasure of hitting bottom and hurting yourself, but because in cases of extreme dependency, life becomes so empty and arid that you reach a point where you are receptive to an event, even a simple and ordinary one, that forcefully opens your eyes and produces a specific state of enlightenment in your brain. Just as there are states of enlightenment due to grace, there are also states of enlightenment due to suffering and distress, whether they are those of others or one's own. And these states are not just intellectual observations. When you are dependent, every day you see that you're going downhill. You see your weakness and the stupidity of your hang-up. Generally this is only an intellectual thing, and you know deep down that you are going to fall back into it. But moments of revelation can happen, and in such moments there is suddenly a cerebral illumination, a complete reconfiguration of mind and body.

MATTHIEU From what I have understood, our points of view and our decisions result from a collaboration between many different areas of our brain. But this collaboration is a dynamic state that is subject to sudden reconfiguration into a new state that represents an equilibrium different from the preceding one. These states are the result of interaction between the regions of the brain connected with the major mental states (attraction, repulsion, pleasure, displeasure, fear, disgust, anger, joy, surprise, etc.) as well as other regions involved in regulation of these mental states, notably in the prefrontal cortex.

The image that comes to mind is of flocks of starlings or schools of fish. The animals move, synchronized by the thousands, like a single cloud, which can suddenly change shape and direction when chased by predators. In the brain, everything can change suddenly from one state of concordance to another one that is very different from the one before. In certain cases, the new attitude becomes stable and irrevocably fixed for the rest of our lives, which is something I find fascinating.

CHRISTOPHE   All the contemporary studies show that at times our brains institute a decision-making process before we are even aware it is taking place or that we even wanted such a thing. And we can do nothing at that point but go along with it. It's a kind of revelatory state coming from our depths. We say to ourselves, "I can't go on like this!"

MATTHIEU   According to neuroscientist Wolf Singer, it is unpleasant to experience a situation of conflict and indecision corresponding to an incomplete process on the level of cerebral activity. Resolution of this inner conflict through making a decision is experienced as a relief.

CHRISTOPHE   But unfortunately I think a state of comfort, or rather a habit of discomfort, can also develop when the state of indecision has lasted overlong. Then from this kind of habituation one passes on to resignation, a sense of giving up. One follows the path of least resistance, even if it is painful and leads in a bad direction. One prefers the easy way and predictability—even if it's destructive—to difficulty and the unknown.

ALEXANDRE   For somebody struggling with addiction, it is tempting to fill the void, to manage the need, by whatever means available, even if that means is fairly worthless. When we're prey to these unfortunate mechanisms, as we are, how can we possibly emerge from this abysmal suffering? The drug addict who smokes a joint and the sex addict who watches an X-rated film know full well that this kind of fix will bring only a very brief respite. Fleeing the world means risking a very hard landing. It is a singular paradox that behind addiction an urge toward self-mastery may lie hidden: grabbing the bottle and gulping down a shot is still somehow trying one's best—for lack of knowing any better way—to calm one's distress, get rid of suffering, and anesthetize oneself. Everybody does what they can to get through the pain that is gnawing at them, sometimes through recourse to expedients that make them sink even lower. How can we abandon these counterproductive measures and try other means that might actually help in the long run? Consuming, giving ourselves over to addictive behavior, is always a way of trying to find some kind of consolation, some relief. In this direction lie only stopgaps, crumbs, which miss out completely on something much better: freedom, profound joy.

How can we really move forward, undertake ascesis, and find pleasure elsewhere than in toxic behavior patterns? Perhaps 180-degree changes are a utopic illusion. The spectacle of our daily life shows us the difficulty of breaking free of the habits, reflexes, and images that keep us stuck in the same loop. At the beginning we might well choose ineffectual means that we hope might bring some relief, fill the void, and soothe our wounds.

CHRISTOPHE It's true that these stories of sudden transformation perhaps don't represent the most usual way of breaking out of dependency. But studying and understanding them might provide us with some new weapons. The question is, what happens on the way to the transformation? Is there an incubation period, a period of preparation? Is it possible for the "click" — the epiphany in which one says to oneself "This can't go on like this" — to occur if one hasn't made any effort beforehand? Or is this moment generally preceded by a period of distress lasting a few weeks or several months, and a progressive evolution in awareness of the situation?

MATTHIEU The friend of mine who told me her story, indicated that this sudden epiphany is the culmination of continuous efforts and progressive moments of recognition and awareness, small steps that amount to many mini-breakaways from the object of addiction. There is an incubation period, during which the intensity of the distress increases in relation to the pleasure of the addiction (as dulled as it may have become). When it becomes clear that the downsides of continuing with the addiction are intolerable, the tipping point is reached. It's a bit like a ripe fruit. If you try to pick an apple that is still green, you break the branch, and the apple is inedible. When the fruit is ripe, you barely have to touch it, and it falls in your hand.

Emotional Dependency

ALEXANDRE   Since humans are open and sensitive creatures of relationship, they are not self-generating—for better or for worse! The worse side is perhaps the dependency, the emotional need, the projections, the misunderstandings, the disappointed expectations. A sense of relatedness with others can sometimes turn to vinegar. Not to mention the toxic relationships that downright spoil our lives.

In connection with this, a friend of mine gave me a precious lesson. As soon as he starts thinking of visiting his mother in an old-age home, he prepares himself for, as he puts it, "descending into the contaminated pit at Chernobyl." And he adds, "I expect to get gobsmacked by a ton of negative waves, a heavy load of reproach, a truckload of criticism." And God knows he loves his mother, which is why he was doing everything in his power to avoid spoiling the relationship. He had the courage to attempt to introduce a note of freedom into the midst of this ghastly mess. How many times in our lives do we attach ourselves to people who give us only a few crumbs of affection, without ever fulfilling our heart's need? Worse, we are capable of tying ourselves, gluing ourselves to women or men who do nothing but drag us down.

Swami Prajnanpad summed it up well: A dog will always come to his master with the hope of getting his dish of food, even if he has an evil owner who beats him instead. Through fidelity and necessity, the poor beast is ready to take the nasty blows, get injured over and over again, and bind himself irrevocably to his torturer. What aren't we willing to go through to fulfill our needs and finally get the pittance we miss so very much? In the absence of being totally fulfilled through unconditional love, you can bet that some of us—and myself the first among them—will crawl on our knees to pick up a few crumbs. This is where the serious danger of dependency and alienation lies.

Fortunately, there are a thousand and one roads that lead out of this prison. Why should we confer on anyone the right of life or death over our happiness? What is the point of delegating our inner peace to somebody else? Spinoza (again!) warns us away from charlatanism. The way to overcome a sad passion, he writes, is by means of a greater emotion. To do away with a toxic attachment without exhausting ourselves in the struggle, we must embrace a greater, vaster aspiration—for example, the desire to get out of that toxic relationship and surround oneself with genuine relationships and tread the path toward enlightenment. This joyous ascesis, one way or another, will get us out of what you described so well, Matthieu, that kind of desire that has become autonomous, has acquired a life of its own, those patterns that run in an endless loop.

Relating to one's body is essential. If we can't stand ourselves, if we hate our own guts, how could we avoid running to the first person who comes along, hoping that they'll turn out to be an automatic dispenser of rewards, of Band-Aids? And in this case, it is not the other I love, but rather an idealized image, a phantom.

Apropos of the dog's food bowl and the crumbs, I can't help but bring up a comical episode I recounted in my book *La Sagesse espiègle (Playful Wisdom)*. Just back from living in Korea, I became besotted with some guy to the point of losing the faintest sense of freedom. Every day at 3:00 p.m. I called him up on Skype. That was my daily dose, my fix. I wanted to become this guy, to steal his silhouette with its graceful, broad shoulders; he was so handsome, so well built. To the exact degree that I despised myself, I adored my idol. Completely disoriented, not knowing which way to turn, I had to make use of quite a few expedient means to free myself from this persistent addiction. Aided by the writings of Chögyam Trungpa, I naturally tried to adopt the attitude of the objective auto-body repairman so I could relate to the total mess I was in without sinking entirely into a sense of guilt or believing that I was forever damned, forever screwed. Also, thanks to you, Matthieu, I was able to take a head-on look at this relationship, which was no longer giving me the least pleasure and was having a withering, ruinous effect on my daily life.

In order to regain my basic health, in the end I had to try all kinds of ways to break down the monopoly of this infatuation and discover within myself the ability to take a positive attitude toward having a handicapped body, toward the tragedy of life—the ability to dare unconditional love that can receive and give affection on every hand.

Yes, there are a thousand and one ways to achieve liberation, to take leave of our prisons. And the wounds we bear should never be a source of shame.

MATTHIEU It is essential not to stigmatize psychological problems—addiction and depression in particular—as defects or faults for which we are entirely responsible. Instead we should relate to them as ailments or dysfunctions connected with the innumerable factors—social, environmental, genetic, physiological, and cerebral—that actively participate in the formation of our makeup. "It's an illness," wrote my father, who suffered from alcohol dependence, "whose ravages one has to learn to contain through the use of a whole slew of stratagems." The most effective countervailing force is to "have in oneself a desire that is stronger than the desire for alcohol and is incompatible with it." For him, it was the desire to write. Discriminating intelligence and the will to utilize our potential for transformation with perseverance are key elements in liberating ourselves from these ills.

CHRISTOPHE Emotional dependencies are by no means rare. They take the form of a need for continual contact (phone calls, texts), hypersensitivity to any form of separation or distance, intolerance of any form of criticism, fear of being abandoned, and extreme need for signs of affection or love, which have to be repeated endlessly. Like all dependencies, emotional dependencies are normal needs we lose control of.

No one is perfectly and totally autonomous and independent on the emotional level. That is something that simply does not exist within the human species. Humans are social animals who cannot survive properly in isolation. They must surround themselves with numerous relationships. We are all dependent on each other; we are all co-dependent, but in a regulated way!

We need strong and supportive emotional relationships with those around us. But these dependencies are partial and not total: we don't have to share *everything* with one person. These dependencies are flexible and not rigid: we can tolerate periods of temporary emotional separation without feeling in distress or danger. And above all, these dependencies are multiple: we don't burden one single person with all our expectations; rather we have a number of objects of attachment.

Rousseau wrote in *Èmile, or On Education*: "Every affection is a sign of insufficiency; if each of us had no need of others, we should hardly think of associating with them."[1] Thus, we are dependent because we are inadequate. That's why we have to love and help each other, but not suffocate each other, as in the case of emotional dependencies, where the fantasy of the dependent person is fusion, permanent satisfaction of his emotional needs.

People who suffer from emotional dependence lose the dimension of freedom — their capacity to appreciate the richness of the world and draw nourishment from it. They have only one source of consolation and reassurance: the object of their attachment. Everything else is secondary — indeed, totally without interest as far as they are concerned. This is what makes it an addiction.

ALEXANDRE   The cause of the tenacity of emotional dependency is perhaps to be found in the belief that the other has the ability to fulfill our visceral need for solace, to satisfy our needs. The addict, thus enchained, becomes prey to an overwhelming series of negative secondary effects and is subject to unthinkable maltreatment. It is by no means certain in such cases that cold reasoning and willpower alone will cure him. It is not enough to create an Excel spreadsheet of the pros and cons of a given relationship and see that you are getting nothing but a few crumbs out of it. This will not halt your downfall; you will not cease to be walled in or Scotch-taped to the other.

CHRISTOPHE   This is an essential dimension of emotional dependency. It doesn't take long for victims to realize that the disadvantages (loss of freedom, fear of abandonment) far outweigh the advantages. But the advantages are related to a fundamental need: the need for love and security. For that we might be willing to give up our freedom and dignity.

ALEXANDRE   What can complicate dependency even more is the kind of semi-secret life that develops. Who has the brass to come right out and confess, "I'm completely dependent. I've got to have the bottle" or "I can't stand it anymore. I'm mad for that guy, that woman"? How can we not fear the reactions of the people around us? How can we stop hiding the illness we are carrying around inside us from our friends, from people in general, from the doctor, from ourselves?

This is where those who love us unconditionally could become the agents of an inner cure. But how can they do their work if we hide our wounds from them? The first step is perhaps to dare to be transparent, to drop embarrassment and shame: "Look, I'm completely strung out on this person. I'm crazy about her. Help me!" And it's a definite sign: as soon as you start telling little fibs, lying, pretending nothing's up, or hatching little cover-up schemes, it's a sure sign that danger is lurking. Not to mention the sense of guilt that prevents us from confronting the real problems, which holds up our progress.

Matthieu, you often remind us of our true nature, the "original goodness" that lies deep within us; you evoke a large-scale dynamic that dispels despair, fatalism, and resignation. When we are fully in a state of dependency, we can completely forget that we all have a buddha nature shining within us that arises out of inconceivable freedom. Moving toward greater health and pulling ourselves out of addiction initially requires having the courage to see things clearly, to be transparent, to quit lying, to quit telling fibs. Being aware of the dissociation you mentioned between pleasure and desire is tremendously liberating. "This guy makes my head spin," "I dream about this woman," "I need this tranquilizer, this drug" — and I don't get any pleasure out of any of it. In vain I try to satisfy my craving by every means available, to the point of screwing up my whole life along the way. That is why it is urgent for us to observe this chaos objectively and come up with a diagnosis; we must identify the work on ourselves that our lives are calling on us to carry out.

CHRISTOPHE   But what makes clear seeing and sharing difficult is that dropping your mask and talking to others about your dependency means displaying your weakness, showing yourself completely naked. That's a tall order! That requires no small effort!

Now, as Matthieu explained, one of the problems of dependency is that we have great difficulty making efforts to change the way we are.

MATTHIEU   Where does that feeling of need come from? Generally, it can be triggered when one's basic needs (food, drink, sleep, etc.) are not being satisfied. The state of need experienced by someone who is deprived of a substance on which he or she is dependent is brought about at least in part by physiological reactions. As for the state of need that makes a person intensely desire a situation or a person—the case of emotional dependency—that is connected with a sense of being unfulfilled, which also does not happen without physiological interactions. The feeling is that we lack something without which it is inconceivable we can ever feel lasting satisfaction.

In this case, we are victims of an illusion that makes us believe a state of fulfillment would be the result of an accumulation of objects, situations, or persons that are indispensable to some imaginary happiness. Actually, fulfillment does not require that we be "full" of things of all kinds. It is, rather, a feeling of profound harmony and satisfaction that is "full" in itself.

This is the very essence of inner freedom: a feeling of peace and unity, free from attraction and repulsion, from dissatisfaction. This is the freedom that meditators work toward over many years of practice. But well before reaching that freedom, it is certainly possible to experience moments of fulfillment walking in the forest with dear friends, sitting by a mountain lake or by the fire listening to sublime music, standing at the top of a mountain pass looking out on an immense landscape, or being in other circumstances in which mental agitation ebbs away and leaves room for the natural simplicity of the mind. Being able to taste freedom of this sort depends on our level of familiarization with the way our mind works and also on our ability to free ourselves from the automatic mechanisms of thought. Once inner freedom is achieved, nothing is lacking anymore.

The Power of Solidarity in Working with Addiction

ALEXANDRE   One of my acquaintances owes his salvation, his freedom, to Alcoholics Anonymous (AA). What a boost it is—what a joy!—to be able to kick the habit through the support of our friends in the good, who, instead of reproaching us heavy-handedly, work with us and offer a hand! All of us need to have the courage to offer our support to people working with akrasia. Our big challenge is to overcome our more-or-less congenital absence of compassion, our cruel inability to offer our life to others without reserve, to love unconditionally. In addiction, we face not only the weight of habit, but also the dictatorship of "they" — the fear of rejection, the fear of others' looks, the misery of being considered worthless and useless. Only love can overcome these formidable obstacles!

MATTHIEU   One of the strengths of Alcoholics Anonymous and other group therapies is precisely that in those groups, persons in a state of dependency no longer have to hide themselves and can share their ordeal with others. They are all in the same boat and know how they got there. This is not the time to pretend anything or tell phony stories. The shared goal is to beat the habit by helping each other and by accepting to be guided in the process. In the absence of this, the suffering of loneliness and blame is added to the suffering of dependency.

CHRISTOPHE   From my point of view as a caregiver, I have always been impressed by the results Alcoholics Anonymous (AA) can achieve for certain patients — even if everybody does not agree with their approach, which is very personal and intrusive. Listening to you, I was thinking that the AA program has three very powerful elements: nonjudgmental understanding, social support, and spirituality.

No matter what state patients arrive in, even drunk, they are accepted, which is not the case in our group-therapy programs. No matter what you say, no matter what you do, no matter what state you're in, you are listened to. The important thing is not being sober at that very moment but being sincerely motivated by the desire to stop drinking alcohol. And this is a desire that most alcoholics have. It's going on to the next step, actually doing something about it, that is hard for them.

Social support is another pillar. People in AA programs help each other a lot. Each person has a sponsor who is always on call, night and day, with whom they can talk about the suffering and temptations they face.

And then there is the spiritual aspect, which is very important in AA. Early on, as a therapist, this scared me a little, and then I gradually understood that this was an integral and important part of their program, which refers overtly to this spiritual dimension, talking about a "higher power" that one can call God, fate, guardian angel, or good star. There is often great solace for patients in imagining a compassionate presence, because they know for sure that they have the malevolent forces of dependency hovering over them. Today I'm more comfortable with the need certain patients have for spirituality, and I understand better the help that brings them. Spirituality allows us to have a vision of what we are going to put our faith in. In extreme situations, we put our faith in bad things, bad people, bad expectations. Alcoholics Anonymous has a system, whether we approve of it or not, that supplies the spiritual dimension that some people need in order to keep on with their struggle and to believe that a solution is possible in their particular case.

In any struggle against dependency, we need to be sure that we have people around us who can understand and listen to us nonjudgmentally.

Toolbox for Working with Dependency

CHRISTOPHE

Accept the fact that a single, simple solution does not exist. Quite frequently the people we're working with underestimate the complexity of the strategies that have to be put in place to free themselves from dependency. It's not just a question of willpower. In other words, it's not just a matter of mind over emotion or mind over instinct. It is, in fact, an immense effort that involves working on three levels:

- The psychological level. How can I fight addiction? How can I strengthen myself by enriching my life, opening myself to other interests?

- The environmental level. What is it in my environment that keeps drawing me back into the same mistakes? What in my environment could help in my struggle?

- The relationship level. Who can I turn to for solace? For information?

Think about temptation reappearing. We have to realize that one day or another we will be exposed again to whatever triggers our addiction (alcohol, drugs, tobacco, sexual images, etc.). How will we react then? It is worthwhile to consider this question in advance, even to do some preparatory training. In certain kinds of cases and situations, behavioral experts in addiction have their patients do exercises with them. For example, they have them spend time in the presence of a bottle, sniff the wine, take a mouthful and spit it back out, and empty the bottle into the sink. Having actually acted this out with them increases their chances of being able to do the same thing later on their own.

Realize that addictions are powerful. They only develop in the area of your basic needs. You don't get addicted to a pair of shoes or an electric lamp! You get addicted to alcohol, love, sex, sugar—things related to satisfaction of your basic needs. As a result, you often cannot simply do without them, because by abstaining you are depriving yourself of a basic need. Therefore, you have to reorient yourself to different ways of feeding the needs in question. You have to ask yourself, what is it I'm trying to get in this dependency? What other ways of satisfying this need should I make the effort to explore? What would a life be like in which I didn't have this dependency but in which I was still happy and in which this basic need was still satisfied?

Never forget that life is the most effective therapy. Despite being a therapist and believing in what I do, I must acknowledge that life itself can do as much good—even more good—than psychotherapies and medications because life brings us everything we need for our nourishment all at once. The example I often give is vitamin C. We can get it from pills, but it's also found in kiwis, oranges, and many other fruits. And the vitamin C we absorb from eating fruit is much better because it is accompanied by many other nutrients not found in pills but that can heighten vitamin C's effect. In the same way, in life there are turning points and circumstances that simultaneously bring about new encounters with people, new sources of enjoyment, changes in environment, and new emotions. Suddenly all these elements, supported by our efforts, fall harmoniously into place and help us go in the right direction. Thus, we should do our best not to isolate ourselves, but rather stay engaged in ordinary life, activities, excursions, get-togethers, and new experiences. Life itself is the mother lode of solutions and resources!

MATTHIEU

Avoid activating factors. Refrain from triggering the addiction by exposing yourself to factors that set off that irresistible desire. Stay out of the visual field of substances, images, and all other things or objects related to the addiction. If that is not possible, get some space, get away from everything. Take a ramble in nature with some friends, long enough to allow you to recover your strength and resilience.

Address the critical moment. Research shows that the critical moment is the instant you are confronted by the stimulus: you see the white powder or the bottle, either in reality or as a forceful mental image. That is the point at which things very quickly become unstoppable. If you let the process take hold, it gathers so much strength that it becomes very difficult to cut off. You can't tell yourself, "Okay, I'll take just a little bit, and then I'll stop." A meditative practice could help by expanding the temporal space of this moment of confrontation, giving you more room to maneuver. By directly contemplating the thoughts engendered by the mental image of the object of desire and letting your mind rest in the present moment, you give these thoughts the time to lose their intensity and vanish by themselves. It's like a drawing on water that disappears as you draw it. If you succeed in suspending the process of the afflicting thoughts for a long enough time by remaining in the present moment, you can avoid getting caught up in the chain reaction that leads to your losing control.

Observe the compulsion in the space of awareness. The great Buddhist sage Nagarjuna said, "It feels good when we scratch, but it's better yet when the itch goes away!" To this end, it is recommended that we look at the itch with the eye of awareness for a long enough time for it to fade away and for us to feel free of it again. Some people can scratch themselves till they bleed. But if we stop the scratching, although it is certainly difficult to tolerate the itch for a few moments, it will eventually disappear.

If we apply this metaphor to the context of dependency, it means that we have to muster enough determination, or strength of mind, to let this nagging compulsion fade out by itself, like a fire that we stop adding wood to. The fire will get weaker and weaker until it finally goes out. That's the way things work.

ALEXANDRE

Follow Spinoza's advice. Open yourself to identifying what really brings you happiness, what really nourishes you deep down in your ground of grounds.

Break the monopoly. Vary your pleasures, or better yet find joy in everything. Life is hard. We have endless doubts, persistent discontent, trials, misfortunes, physical deterioration, and bereavement. With all that, for us to grasp at any straw that offers momentary oblivion—it doesn't take much. To beat addiction—and God knows it's easier said than done—you have to break free from the exclusive control of anybody or anything. Never hand someone a remote control that can send you straight to hell. Nobody and nothing should be allowed to become anybody's everything.

Dare to be transparent. Ask for help, acknowledge your inner hurts, and never forget that no person is a *causa sui*—an impenetrable, separate, autarchic entity. There are surely other ways of relating with human beings that don't require you to weigh yourself down with fear, jealousy, and attachment.

 Learn to tell the difference. Learn to distinguish between what you are running after day and night and that which you genuinely, fundamentally desire in your deepest nature. Listen to yourself so you can identify the needs and pleasures of your heart.

3

Fear

In Korea, I had the opportunity to do a Zen retreat in the country for three months. The first weeks went by trouble free. It was paradise on earth. One day my wife and children came to visit. We had a wonderful time together roaming around the woods, sliding down hills, and so on. When the time came, they went back to Seoul.

Then right away old memories started popping up. I began remembering those horrid Sunday nights when I virtually lost my parents and had to go back to the institution. I don't know what got into me, but I started pounding away on my keyboard, surfing the internet. I discovered that in the past there had been a case of rabies in the neighborhood [that the retreat center was in]. That's all I needed to unleash a total panic attack. I was terrified of the idea of having accidentally sat on a rabid raccoon. I remember certain meditation sessions where I was so tortured by fear I had to bite my lip to keep from screaming out loud.

I tried everything—meditating, taking walks, watching movies. Nothing brought relief from this ongoing panic. On the verge of going completely batty, I happened upon a video that recommended a bizarre exercise: you were to imagine turning up the volume of your anxiety by calling up terrifying images. So I imagined that one of my children had forever perished as a result of being bitten by a rabid animal. After ten minutes, the video recommended doubling the level again in order to observe your unpleasant bodily symptoms (pains, sweats, cramping, etc.).

This exercise, which was counterintuitive to say the least, helped me a lot. I realized that if I was capable of turning up the volume on my anxiety, I was also capable of not feeding it anymore. The exercise had another virtue: it showed me that my torments were entirely created by my mind.

—Alexandre

CHRISTOPHE In psychology, *fear* refers to the various reactions of the body and mind to a present danger. We distinguish it from its cousin, *anxiety,* which refers to the various reactions to the *possibility* of danger—that is, impending or imagined danger. Panic is fear without an object—without an actual and present object—but it is not without reality because it possesses our body and mind.

Fear in all its forms is without a doubt one of the emotions that most inhibits freedom. It affects external freedom by often driving us to flight or evasion. It affects inner freedom in that it pollutes our thoughts and drives us to keep a watchful eye on our environment so as to anticipate all possible dangers and to calculate in advance how to provide maximal security for ourselves and those close to us. Our brain is transformed into a machine for keeping watch, evading, and planning.

Even an imaginary risk is capable of invading and possessing our mind—like the rabid raccoon, Alex, that put you into that state. Under the influence of that improbable projection, your vision of reality became twisted, and your universe shrunk. You lost all flexibility, all means of envisaging other possibilities or even an action you might take.

Fear is the most archaic emotion. Even in primitive organisms, there are two more or less reflexive basic movements: approaching (seeking resources and pleasure) and avoiding (protection from danger). Thus, we can consider fear to be the mother of all the other painful emotions: shame comes from the fear of how we are regarded by others, sadness from the fear of long-lasting want, anger from fear of failure or humiliation. If you really think about it, we are always harboring one or several fears about one thing or another, no matter what our age is or what phase of life we are in.

Panic Attacks

CHRISTOPHE   The constant in panic attacks includes projections of virtual dangers, of improbable catastrophic scenarios, and the feeling of being on the edge of insanity—and thus having the fear of going mad. We lose control of ourselves, and the mind inflicts on us all kinds of suffering that we are aware, deep down, is absurd and self-created. But the body believes in it—it makes no distinction between the virtual and the real. For the body, it's all true and it panics, like somebody at the movies panics even though he or she is well aware that it's only a horror film.

ALEXANDRE   Phantom rabid raccoons drove me to a state of helplessness. I was completely powerless to fight off these ideas, these fantasies, made out of nothing. In the face of panic, reasoning has no traction. Why does logic have no power of persuasion, even though the facts should prevail? People try in vain to defuse irrational fears through whatever rational means they can come up with: "Look yourself over from head to foot! Do you see any trace of a bite?" Again we see the pitiful helplessness of rational demonstrations to counter the madness of the racing conceptual mind.

MATTHIEU   Why doesn't reasoning have any effect on these extravagant fears? The supposed cause of the panic—having accidentally sat on a rabid raccoon—just doesn't hold up. But telling yourself that isn't enough. So what has to be done is to identify the real cause of the panic that took the form of a rabid raccoon. When we encourage people to analyze and dissect their fears, we find that the main element is generally the fear of death. If we succeed in identifying the fundamental cause, we can try to remedy it one way or another, even if it's far from being easy.

If we are not able to remedy the fundamental cause directly, we can try what we call a decompression technique for fear. For example, we can take the afflicted person to a place that is clearly devoid of danger—a vantage point that overlooks a vast mountain landscape or a calm ocean—and encourage that person to take some deep breaths, and then to mingle their mind with the vast and luminous sky—with the landscape extending into infinity—and let their disturbing thoughts dissolve in that space. Doing this can make the basic suffering fade away more easily.

If this is not possible, the person can visualize these landscapes or other peaceful environments in which the mind can temporarily escape from the shrinking and narrowing effect of fear and the self-alienating state of urgency that it engenders.

CHRISTOPHE Most of the time, we don't realize that the person suffering from anxiety attacks has left our world behind and entered another world that does not follow the same rules. Information is treated in a completely different way in this virtual world. Even if the supposed danger represents only one chance out of a billion, one gets caught up in this miniscule possibility. This is no longer the same logic that applies for a person not suffering from anxiety. And the only efforts one can make to help these people is to bring them back to reality—sometimes by quite dumb and basic means. Taking a walk, contemplating nature, working, going out, doing things, talking with friends—all those things help the person to get re-grounded in reality.

That's why the panic attacks that get us in the middle of the night are often the most severe ones: you are alone and you can't protect yourself by means of action or distraction. Happily, meditation also helps, which is not surprising because meditating is not thinking with one's eyes closed; rather, one's whole body is implicated. When you meditate, you pay attention to your breath, reconnect with your body, and listen to the sounds around you. The body, even when crazed with panic, is always in reality, never in a virtual world.

In your case, Alex, you were in retreat, cut off from possibilities of action and interaction. I have quite a few patients who have had panic attacks when they were doing spiritual or meditative retreats. Formerly, when special protocols for patients (like Mindfulness-Based Cognitive Therapy, or MBCT, and Mindfulness-Based Stress Reduction, or MBSR) did not exist yet, many of our patients suffering from anxiety or depression wanted to meditate and do Zen or vipashyana retreats. One out of three of them blew up in mid-flight! That's because Zen or vipashyana masters are not therapists and are sometimes very hard and demanding.

But how did you get out of it, Alexandre? At what point did you have the feeling you were back to reality?

ALEXANDRE   I couldn't find the inner resources to defeat this panic. Once again, salvation came from the outside. I woke up our good Matthieu in the middle of the night, and he convinced me that the chances of me inadvertently sitting on a rabid raccoon were about the same as getting hit in the face by a meteor.

On that occasion you gave me a very profound teaching: contemplate nature and stop considering it an enemy, a hostile presence, or a permanent danger. That definitely calmed me down a lot.

MATTHIEU   Sometimes the whole world arises as a potential enemy. In fact, it's our mind that becomes our worst enemy. "At times that imaginary lake around him expands to such a point," writes Charles-Ferdinand Ramuz, "that he can't cross it anymore."[1]

ALEXANDRE   The madness of conceptual mind, as it spins its wheels, always comes up with some logic to countervail the voice of reason. It's a truly diabolical process that can put up pretty heavy resistance to people who are trying to reassure a fear-stricken person. Nevertheless, we would be wrong to give up. I remember with tremendous gratitude Dr. Olivier, a good friend of mine whom I would call up and who would provide me with scientific facts to counter the delirium of my imagination.

How to Free Oneself from Panic

MATTHIEU   I have a friend, a very balanced and calm person in everyday life, who told me that she sometimes wakes up in the middle of the night with a persistent anguish that doesn't necessarily have an object.

It's a sort of vague, diffuse, existential angst. She still retains the ability to observe this anxiety, and she sees that it is devoid of actual existence, that it's nothing more than a powerful fabrication of her mind, resembling a big storm cloud.

With a little bit of training in meditation, one could look at this anxiety straight on and deconstruct its apparent power. The part of our mind that is observing the anxiety is not anxious; it is just aware. Of course, when it's acute, it is not easy in the midst of a panic attack to access the unpanicked part of the mind that is observing the panic, but this possibility exists. In this case, there is a space within our awareness that is not under the influence of the panic. It's like a foot in the door that keeps it open. If one manages to sustain this observation, the state of freedom naturally takes on increasingly greater proportions, and the door opens wider and wider. Some level of anxiety will still be there — it's not going to suddenly disappear — but it gradually loses its power, becomes less real, less in control, and then it finally disappears from our mental landscape.

CHRISTOPHE Meditation has taught me a tremendous amount, both for helping my patients and for dealing with my own panic. When you feel that you're about to be gripped by panic, you can take the position of observing what is happening, re-anchoring yourself in the breath, in the body, watching your thoughts, watching everything that is in the process of developing. You can imagine yourself on the bank of a river, watching the raging current of panic carrying everything along with it. From time to time, you slip back into the current; you have to pull yourself back out and begin again.

After giving therapy and treatment to our patients with anxiety (and depression) during periods of crisis, we teach them how to do mindfulness meditation, and almost all of them then succeed in keeping their further panic attacks at bay — if the attacks do come back (for example at moments of fatigue or when life problems rear their heads). Almost all of them then succeed in keeping their panic attacks at bay; if by chance the attacks do come back (for example, at moments of fatigue or when life problems rear their heads).

MATTHIEU That's exactly the reaction I had from a person, about twenty years old, who didn't dare to look within himself because he was afraid of what he might find. Nevertheless, this is the only means of getting to the heart of the problem and learning to recognize the pure awareness within which thoughts form and dissolve. Tibetan Buddhism is very rich in techniques that allow us to deconstruct the thoughts that take us over and let them fade away by themselves. These thoughts that overtake us so strongly, are they like a blazing fire? Like rocks tumbling down a mountainside that are going to crush us? Nothing like that. They are mere fabrications of the mind. Recognizing this is already taking a step toward freedom. If it's the mind that fabricates all these thoughts, it can also provide the remedy for them. We soon draw the conclusion that there is nothing irremediable about this situation and that with patience and through using the appropriate means, the mind itself has the ability to free us from the torments it itself has created.

ALEXANDRE *Joyful Wisdom*, the book by Yongey Mingyur Rinpoche, might well be a big help in eliminating fear and dispelling anxiety. Without a doubt, it is a help in unmasking the mechanisms that torture us. Fear puts an extra layer over reality, a fog; it puts a layer of fallacious interpretations over the facts. Ascesis consists of contemplating the haze of emotions that you have been describing and dispelling them. The Zen tradition guides us in the direction of naked awareness: observe what is happening without coloring or touching up your experience of your projections, your expectations, and the categorizations of your ego.

Mingyur Rinpoche suggests a very simple exercise that will definitely dispel the fog of conceptual mind. Over the course of a day, we come up with all sorts of mental comments. In the bathtub, in front of the mirror, Mental FM starts playing: "You look like death warmed over this morning! And those bags under your eyes. . . ." Living this experience without adding anything—that is the challenge Mingyur Rinpoche makes!

In this regard, Zen teaches us to distinguish perception from conceptualization or from our inner sales pitch. What is it I actually have before my eyes? What are the facts? I look in the mirror; I meet with Matthieu and

Christophe. Why must we always add another layer of comparison — "This is better," "This is fine," "This is bad"?

The example of Mingyur Rinpoche's practice particularly touches me, because this wise person, as he tells us, passed this way himself. He also experienced fear before he freed himself from the sad passions and afflictive emotions. He is a forerunner for us, who confirms for us that another way of life is possible.

MATTHIEU   In his childhood, he had great difficulty managing his panic attacks. For him, also, they were connected with the fear of death, the fear that the house would fall down, that lightning would strike him, that his heart would stop beating, or that he wouldn't be able to breathe.

Starting at the age of six, without telling anyone about it, Mingyur would occasionally go to a cave near his house in the Nubri Valley of Nepal. He would sit and meditate, even before anybody had ever given him meditation instruction. This calmed him down, without solving the problem, however. Then at the age of thirteen, at his own wish, he went on a contemplative retreat of three years. He absolutely wanted to meditate. (This is obviously a rather exceptional case.) At the end of a year, he was suffering constant panic attacks. One day he said to himself, "That's enough. I'm going to shut myself up in my room, and I'm going to apply to the hilt the teachings on the nature of mind given to me by my father (Tulku Urgyen, a very respected spiritual master). I'm not going out until I solve this problem." So he put those instructions to work methodically, and in three days, he had gotten rid of his panic once and for all. He does acknowledge having had a few more episodes, but he now knew how to resolve them, as he tells us in his books *The Joy of Living* and *Joyful Wisdom*. Today, he emanates a sense of joyful freedom, which is quite contagious, as well as manifesting an impressive level of wisdom.

In particular Mingyur Rinpoche advises us not to consider panic as an enemy, which would create additional tension (fear that the panic might come back), but rather to try to make friends with it ("Hello, panic, welcome!"), and he counsels us to use panic to progress toward inner freedom. More precisely, he proposes four strategies: begin by observing the panic attentively, in particular the physical sensations it sets in motion. Do this in the manner of a spectator observing a rushing river with a higher-than-usual water level. In your case, my dear Alexandre, it would likely be anxiety; for others it might be jealousy or despair.

If instead of diminishing, the panic increases, the second strategy is to concentrate on something else—the sounds around us, the coming and going of the breath, or a landscape before us. We can also concentrate on another afflictive emotion. In his case, Mingyur Rinpoche artificially created anger and then concentrated on it. That approach makes it possible to become familiar with managing the afflictive emotions and train with one of those emotions—anger in this case, which is less invasive than panic. It is easier to work with because the anger you have created is less afflictive than the anxiety that is your principal problem.

If that still doesn't help, the third method is to step back and look at what is hidden behind the panic: fear of the panic, aversion toward the panic, resistance to the panic. Finally, if nothing else works, the last option is to take a break: take a walk, take a shower, play with your children, go see some friends.

ALEXANDRE Mingyur Rinpoche also provided a fabulous tool: panoramic vision, that immense inner availability that is close to the big mind put forward in Zen. In anxiety, through a strange optical illusion, awareness fixates; it focuses on one point, on the worry du jour, forgetting everything else. At that point, the exercise consists in becoming aware of what is around you *besides* the anxiety and opening yourself to the world that is much bigger than your agitated ego.

CHRISTOPHE Learning to deal with these attacks and no longer fearing their return is essential. However, that is not something you can just decide to do; it's something you have to work on. The applicable Latin proverb is, *Si vis pacem, para bellum* (If you want peace, prepare for war). If you want to live happily and you are anxiety prone, you have to be capable of dealing with waves of anxiety in such a way as to no longer drown in them. This involves real training. What you have just described is one of the means of working with anxiety: you work on the muscle of your attention. All the scientific studies show that the more anxious you are, the more attention is focused on the object of your anxiety. And you ignore everything else. The kind of vision that we should prioritize in our lives in general, and especially in periods of anxiety, is the opposite of that: panoramic vision. See the problem or the possibility of the problem, but also see all the available alternative resources, everything that also exists and is not the problem.

This is what positive psychology tries to do; it is also a psychology of alternative resources. It suggests that we should regularly attempt to expand our view and appreciate what is going right in our lives, what is working well, what is helpful, and what gives us strength. If fear appears, these resources will allow us to put up a better fight against adversity with its multiple aspects: its real aspect (anxiety-prone people also have real problems like everybody else), its overblown aspect (people with anxiety see their problems in an amplified way), and its imagined aspect (people with anxiety often trip out on their improbable catastrophic scenarios involving rabid raccoons and who knows what else!).

At the end of the day, people suffering from anxiety don't do so badly against real and concrete difficulties, but they exhaust themselves trying to deal with the rest because the anxiety-stricken brain treats the imaginary danger like a reality, with all the earnestness and energy such a reality requires. Since the threat exists, I react as though it were real, because my brain is focused point blank on the fear. What might help us here is to accept letting the fear have its space but not letting it take up *all* the space. And then we should invite our mind to engage all the rest: pay attention to the breath, to the body, to sounds, and take a good look at our environment. In short, we should ground ourselves in what is real and tangible. Then, starting from there, we should look at our thoughts the same way, with distance and perspective; we should let our thoughts pass just as we let our outbreaths pass. And each time we see our mind tightening up again, shrinking back onto the fear again and again, we should reopen our attention to everything that is there rather than letting it dwell exclusively on the fear.

There are a whole lot of other techniques, but what anxiety sufferers should realize is that these techniques cannot be applied right in the midst of the storm. It's not when the plane is crashing that we start learning how to use a parachute.

If we assume the principle that the human condition implies regularly experiencing moments of anxiety or despair, a kind of training in life is necessary. This is a psychological undertaking, in my opinion, that we should not shirk. If we do not prepare, we risk being ravaged by panic attacks when they strike us or by becoming dependent on tranquilizers, alcohol, or some other substance to get relief.

Trust and Appreciation of Our Good Moments Are at the Heart of Healing

CHRISTOPHE   What strikes me a lot in listening to you, Matthieu, is that in the midst of anxiety—when it is actually happening—we need something like an act of faith to get out of it. If I were suffering a devastating bout of fear, I would have a hard time believing what the therapists say, what Matthieu and the Tibetan masters say! But it's necessary. I would have to go all out and give it a try. I would have to try taking their advice because it's a method that has been validated by science and experienced by these masters. The moment, the instant, in which the anxiety sufferer stops believing herself, stops thinking she's right about being in danger or about her children being in danger, or about believing totally and completely in some other fear—that tiny instant is the determining one. That could be the tipping point, the point at which she could say to herself, "Maybe I'm wrong. I'm lost, blind. I'm the slave of my fears. That simply can't go on. So it's worth it—I have to try to let go of my negative beliefs, take a leap into the void, and try to catch the hand the master or therapist is reaching out to me. I have to listen to their advice, apply their methods."

MATTHIEU   This is what distinguishes belief from trust. Ordinary belief consists in believing in something that is not validated by any proof. Blind belief is continuing to believe, even if it is proved that this belief is false. Belief can take myriad forms because it does not need to be based on reality. Trust, on the other hand, consists in having one's opinion be confirmed either by direct experience, by logical reasoning and valid inference, or by an authentic authority worthy of trust.

CHRISTOPHE   But that's also in some way an act of faith. In Latin, *fides* means both "trust" and "belief." And that's doubtless why many anxiety sufferers find it hard to take the leap unless a caregiver explains it to them and perhaps even guides them through it. Their whole mind is telling them "Noooooo! There's a danger here! Don't take the risk, don't go there!" Advice doesn't work unless it comes from someone they have confidence in.

MATTHIEU   For that to happen, we have to feel that the person we place our trust in has great compassion. We have to be able to say, as is the case in the presence of a spiritual master, "This person seems so wise and compassionate that, in the absence of proof to the contrary, I can place my trust in him."

CHRISTOPHE   But real masters are rare, and sometimes their teachings are not concrete and practical enough, at least in my opinion as a caregiver! This is where therapists come in. They are easier to find, less intimidating, and more grounded in the concrete and practical. I'm thinking of patients who are haunted by anxiety or sadness. As I see it, they are not looking in the right direction. They place much greater importance on their unhappy life experiences than on their happy ones. And they skip over the moments in their lives that might help to save them — for example, moments when they are taking a walk in a natural setting or when they are with friends — because they are not present at these moments. Their minds do not attend to them because their hearts are not open to them.

My role as a caregiver is to help them correct this small error. I say "small" because the effort that needs to be made is not a very big one, and it can bring about immense changes. There are moments when a patch of blue sky or a friendly word really can touch their hearts. It's of the greatest importance to open their eyes to that: "Doesn't the truth of your life lie in both these areas — the area of suffering but also the area of tranquility, love, affection, and admiration?" We try to balance these two types of life experience, to draw their attention to these little bits of tranquility, and to ask them if these moments don't also perhaps have something to say about the human condition. We have one foot in adversity and the other in bliss.

MATTHIEU   In response to that, the devil's advocate would say, "Yes, it's a magical moment, but what is that going to change? It's not going to last." That's doubtless true, but we can also make the effort to understand why we felt peace during these privileged moments. Why not try to pay more attention to the characteristics of this state, as you say, and cultivate them?

CHRISTOPHE   The problem our patients have is that they are not really present at these moments of beauty, friendship, and security. They are still involved, sometimes heavily, in their sadness, suffering, anxiety, and they have only one objective: to find lasting solutions, definitive answers. Of these good moments, they'll say, "It was nice, but that doesn't solve anything; it didn't keep me from falling right back into my anxiety afterward." And what we have to tell them, all that we have to get them to understand by themselves is: "As long as you keep seeing the good moments as antidotes for the bad moments, it's not going to work. The important thing is to give yourself over fully to these moments of friendship, admiration, being in nature, without attributing a purpose to them. If you make them serve your anxieties, if you continue applying this hierarchy in which anxiety, fear, sadness, and loneliness are regarded as intrinsically more significant and more real than the happy, peaceful moments, it's not going to work. Let the moments of serenity be as real as those of malaise. Dwell on the good moments the way you dwell on the bad ones. Set them on equal footing, and you'll stop limping!"

ALEXANDRE   Yes, we have to pay more heed to what lies within us and have the courage to disconnect from those things that constantly push us in the direction of hyperactivity. Plunging into the depths of our basic nature, the ground of grounds, already means starting to deprogram ourselves, starting to realize that no circumstance prohibits us from experiencing genuine joy.

A thousand times a day we have to persevere in our ascesis and dispel the adventitious clouds that prevent us from accessing our buddha nature.

Dropping the logic of consumption, connecting with something bigger than ourselves, and connecting with the environment, for example—that's the challenge! Nowadays, it seems, there are children who have never seen a cow in the flesh and who think a fish is something rectangular and breaded. But let's not play the moralists when the real task is to extricate ourselves from emotional addictions and to play deaf to the sirens of appearance.

Hooked on Anxiety?

ALEXANDRE   One question torments me: Is there a mechanism of self-destruction in the hearts of human beings? How does it come about that, being fully aware of the facts of a situation, we keep traveling on a road that heads right into a wall? Why at certain moments in our life do we persist in behavior that drags us down? What imperious forces turn us into addicts of the causes of our suffering?

CHRISTOPHE   Hooked on one's anxieties? I really don't like much accusing suffering persons of being in collusion with their symptoms. But in fact, there could exist in each of us a quite voluntary dependence on our suffering. Sometimes when we try reassuring someone with extreme anxiety, we get the feeling that this person is attached to their anxiety. And sometimes we get into a kind of argumentative tug-of-war where that person tries to convince you that she's right to feel anxiety, and you try, just as stupidly, to convince her that she ought to be less anxious. It's an impasse: your conviction against hers.

ALEXANDRE   Could it be that we prefer a painful, harmful habit over opening ourselves to the unknown, over opening to the void?

CHRISTOPHE   Exactly. That's why, even though I'm a therapist, I believe that in every cure, at some moment, there is an act of faith. We let go of our negative certainties and hurl ourselves out into the void in order to catch hold of the trapeze swung toward us by the spiritual master, the therapist, or a well-intentioned friend. We are hanging above the abyss, swinging in all directions. Nothing is under our control, and over there someone is shouting, "Let go of everything! Throw yourself into space and try to catch the solution I'm offering you!" It's normal to be afraid of launching yourself into space. Instead, you keep clutching the trapeze of your suffering, which—at least for the moment—is tangible and firmly in your grip.

MATTHIEU We could define *samsara*—that is, the ocean of existence conditioned by ignorance and suffering—as an addiction to the causes of suffering.

ALEXANDRE What are the mechanisms of that addiction? Where does it come from?

MATTHIEU From the distortion of reality characteristic of delusion. We head for the causes of suffering and turn our back on the causes of happiness. A Buddhist text also says that sometimes we treat happiness as though it were our worst enemy. So it's not a sense of collusion with the symptoms of suffering, but a lack of clear understanding.

ALEXANDRE But at times, to our great misfortune, it seems we are definitely avid to deceive ourselves, to let ourselves be deluded, to persist in illusion and ignorance.

MATTHIEU Stubborn persistence in replicating the causes of our suffering is without doubt a characteristic of mental delusion. One of my teachers, who teaches in France's Dordogne region, says this: "What people call happiness, we call suffering." This drastic assertion refers to our pursuit of goals that are incapable of bringing us real well-being. On the one hand we have a thirst for possessions, fame, power, and superficial pleasures, and on the other we fear unpleasantness, loss, failure, anonymity, and criticism.

ALEXANDRE How can we put the high aspirations that exist in our hearts to work in daily life? I know full well that generosity is a treasure, a key to human relationships, a gift from heaven. There's no question that nonfixation is a remedy for many ills, and yet it's hard for me to roll up my sleeves and persevere on this path, because the forces of inertia and habitual patterns turn out to be incredibly tough.

MATTHIEU   We lack role models in our contemporary world. Who do we really admire? And who merits being held up as a model for human life? We'd like to play chess like Bobby Fischer, one of the most brilliant geniuses in the history of chess, but who would want to be like him—a profoundly disturbed person, impossible to get along with? When we look around at our parents, teachers, the great people of this world, thinkers, and artists, we are a little disconcerted. There are admirable people, but also a lot of people whom we would certainly not want to be like as human beings, regardless of what special talent they might have. On other hand, when we do encounter a person full of real wisdom motivated by inexhaustible compassion we would like very much to possess the qualities of that person.

Toolbox for Working with Fear

MATTHIEU

Observe fear the way you observe a blazing fire, and let it dissolve gradually by itself under the eye of awareness that is not identified with the fear.

Get out of the narrowness of your anxiety-ridden mind by contemplating or imagining a vast landscape.

Use reason to reconnect with reality. Among our myriad fears, how many have really materialized as bad situations in reality?

Analyze fear in order to understand that it is nothing more than a mental fabrication and that there's no reason to give in to it.

ALEXANDRE

Employ the therapy of the real. For cases of afflictive emotions, inner chaos, and emotional mayhem, the Stoics advised us to return to the facts. What is actually happening before my eyes? What am I afraid of? What is putting me into a state like this?

Expand your field of consciousness. When your mind is fixated on your woes of the day, try having slightly more panoramic vision. Dare to look at what is going on around you, to connect with your sensations, to open yourself to the vastness of the world.

Practice the art of the detour. Realize that logic does not necessarily have an answer for everything, that rational arguments are not always successful at dismantling your irrational fears. When needed, practice the art of the detour by visualizing something that takes the focus off the fear.

Don't overestimate your strength. There are fights that leave us exhausted and drained. Don't stay alone with your burden. Dare to surround yourself with your friends in the good when you lose your footing.

CHRISTOPHE

Recognize how fear reduces freedom. The real problem of the fear in us is not the discomfort or pain it causes, which eventually passes, but the fact that it lastingly reduces our freedom. In order to not experience fear, we spend our time avoiding things that seem dangerous to us without really knowing whether these things are actually dangerous or not. Avoidance doesn't teach us anything, either about the dangers or our own capacities.

Disobey. Fear tells us to withdraw; we should advance to see what happens. Fear forces us to think about nothing but itself. We should open our field of attention and think about all the rest: our breath, our body, the world around us.

Train yourself to confront minor fears. Facing our greatest fears may be too difficult, so we should seek out the smaller ones that can be affected by our efforts. And we should repeatedly train in facing them, because once is not enough. The mechanisms of liberation remain the same, no matter what the fears are like. The efforts you make to free yourself from the small fears are the same ones that will serve you in facing the big ones.

Don't forget psychotherapy. Psychotherapy has some of its best results against fear and anxiety. I'm talking especially about behavioral and cognitive therapy, acceptance and commitment therapy (ACT), and therapies based on mindfulness.

4

Discouragement and Despair

In Brittany, I met a mother who experienced a moment of distress every afternoon at five o'clock. That was the time her son had died five or six years earlier on the way home from school. Her mourning had never ended.

I knew another mother who had found her son drowned in the family swimming pool. At the time it happened, she said to herself, "I have a choice in my life now. I can either live in this state of despair until the end of my days, or I can decide that I will live and honor my son's memory in another way."

It was a decisive moment when she chose to live her life fully and to dedicate to her son's memory the many charitable acts that she then began using her financial fortune to carry out. She had felt that it was a turning point and—whatever we may think of free will—at that moment, in those extreme conditions, she saw the possibility of going in either one direction or the other, and she said, "I choose life rather than despair."

—*Matthieu*

CHRISTOPHE   Discouragement appears to me like a kind of stool that stands on the three legs of being worn down: fatigue ("I'm discouraged because I've been trying for a long time"), an absence of results or at least satisfying results ("It's not working"), and loss of hope ("I'll never get there"). It's the stressed-out schoolboy doing math homework that he's just not getting, the irritated home handyman who keeps failing at repairing something, or the sad person who is becoming exhausted by helping a depressed friend.

The danger in discouragement is giving up, which is the concrete consequence of it. It also represents an insidious loss of freedom. I can fail without getting discouraged, and I can then keep hoping that a solution will appear later, but discouragement immures me in the certainty that there is no solution that I can bring about. If I feel profound discouragement, there isn't anyone or anything that can create a solution.

Let me point out that there are two kinds of giving up: giving up as a matter of choice and giving up that we submit to. In the first, one sees one's fatigue and momentary inability to deal with a problem. One accepts this, lets go, and allows oneself to take a break to think about the problem and ask for help. This form of giving up is a way of preventing discouragement. But the form of giving up that we helplessly submit to—the consequence of a big effort and then exhaustion—weakens us and diminishes our feeling of effectiveness and freedom.

Learned Optimism and Discouragement

MATTHIEU   One aspect of freedom is the availability of a large range of choices. Discouragement makes us give up on all these possibilities, which it rejects out of hand. We say to ourselves, "I'm not capable of doing this" or "This project is destined to fail."

We often say that optimists are naive and that pessimists are more realistic. It has been shown that this handed-down idea is false: pessimists greatly exaggerate the negative aspects of a situation, and if we suggest solutions to them, they don't try them out because they don't think they will work. Conversely, the degree of freedom of optimists is much greater: they try out dozens of solutions, one or another of which eventually succeeds. The pessimist is the victim of a kind of chronic discouragement.

CHRISTOPHE There are interesting studies on this subject in experimental psychology. Mice are put in a large vessel of water too deep for them to touch bottom. The experimenter measures the length of time they swim before letting themselves sink—in other words, before they become discouraged because they are exhausted and have concluded that they have no hope of surviving. Incidentally, this is also the way antidepressants were formerly tested: they were supposed to increase the swimming time of the mice, and only those substances that had that anti-discouragement effect were retained. But there's another way (nothing to do with medication) to prolong their swimming time—by familiarizing them beforehand with a successful outcome of their efforts. The mice are put in a tub where beneath the water is a raised surface that isn't visible but is within reach of their paws. At a certain point, they encounter the surface by chance and can then stop swimming and say to themselves—maybe, in their little mouse brains—that their efforts have been rewarded, that it was worth it to persevere, and that there's always a possible hopeful outcome of their efforts. This has the effect that if they are put in a tub with no raised surface under the water, they will continue to swim much longer than other mice, motivated by memory and hope. This is called the sense of "learned effectiveness."

The contrary result emerged from experiments with dogs. The dogs were put in a cage that had two parts separated by a small fence, easy to jump over. The wire-mesh floor of the cage could be electrified, and the dogs were subjected to small, unpleasant shocks. They would jump over to the other part of the cage to avoid the shocks. Then the conditions of the experiment were changed: they were subjected to the shocks but leashed so they could not jump. They were no longer able to take action to protect themselves. After that, it was observed that even if the dogs were no longer leashed, two-thirds of them had become resigned and no longer tried to avoid the shocks by jumping the fence. This was the opposite of what the experiment with the mice had shown. Psychologist Martin Seligman called this phenomenon "learned helplessness" or "learned desperation."

These experiments, which were adapted for human subjects (without shocks or forced swimming) illuminated certain behavior that we should not be too quick to judge. Individuals who are too frequently faced with situations in which they feel helpless often become completely resigned. In life situations in which they have been beaten by their parents, mocked by their peers, or treated as inferior by teachers—and if these various experiences of failure have accumulated—discouragement and giving up are their immediate reaction to any initial difficulty. These people suffer from constant and overwhelming doubt about their ability to deal with life. Their recurrent discouragement shuts them up in a cage like animals who have been held in captivity for a long time; even if you open the door to such animals' cages, their initial reaction is to stay and pace around and around inside. Similarly, some people have been shut inside of mental cages for a long time, and they have difficulty leaving, even if the external conditions of their lives have changed. They are the victims of all-consuming doubt as to their capacity for freedom and self-determination, because being free presupposes dealing with a lot of obstacles, and such people do not believe in themselves enough. They suffer constant doubt and recurrent discouragement.

Discouragement and Hope

ALEXANDRE   Doubt and a critical mind are tools for life, but they can quickly turn against you. They can spin their wheels meaninglessly and cause horrendous damage. Discouragement and despair can gnaw at the heart. However, the Zen tradition sees in doubt a tool for liberation. Realizing that ego is incapable of solving the problems of life—that it is really not built to bring us peace—it becomes a great step toward wisdom to learn to mistrust it, to cease taking it at its word. This has nothing to do with hesitation, the dithering about that continually puts off the moment of progress and mires us in a state of perplexity and advanced insecurity. To counteract that, the masters urge us to show determination and commit ourselves unconditionally to the path of the spiritual life with confidence that sooner or later we will attain enlightenment. It's like a river flowing down a mountainside. No matter the detours and obstacles it encounters, it inevitably ends up in the sea. But it's difficult to maintain this kind of faith, this conviction, in the midst of a storm of the conceptual mind. Nevertheless, here we are—on our way toward the good, no matter what the external decor and circumstances may be.

As for discouragement, as I see it, it perhaps has its origin in an absence of confidence. I wake up in the morning with no strength and no energy, completely beaten down by the weaknesses I have been trying to overcome for a very long time. I'm always being laid low by the same contradictions. If this keeps going on and I don't catch sight of some kind of solution soon, I'm going to tumble head over heels into a black pit of despair. This will surely happen if I don't find some meaning in this inner desert, in this total void that I find myself in some days and that, at the worst of times, leaves me open to the temptation of suicide.

On this path, what inspires me is all the men and women who are masters and sages, but also the many, many anonymous people who have gone through hell and managed to come out the other side. They relight the flame, give us faith in the goodness of life, help us stay the course. What leads to discouragement is immobility, the inability to change and make our life into a dynamic process. That leaves us feeling like we're standing in front of a wall.

Discouragement and despair come also from a feeling of helplessness, when no way out is visible. Suddenly there's nothing meaningful anywhere. But wisdom can make good use of whatever arises and can integrate failures, hassles, torments—and maybe even betrayal and pain—into a dynamic process.

Perhaps at this point it would be helpful to distinguish faith from hope. The latter seems to me restricted, limited, focused on a specific object: "I hope to win the lottery." I get up every morning with my eyes trained on this objective, and the rest of the world doesn't exist. Faith, on the other hand, is connected with an inner availability, an openness. This is what gave Etty Hillesum, who lived in Nazi concentration camps, the guts to say, "I will have the strength." Hope seeks security; faith immerses us in a sense of trust and letting go. Faith does not cling to some custom-made happiness; rather it nourishes the conviction that, no matter what, life always authorizes moments of joy and progress.

CHRISTOPHE True, in discouragement there is the sense that it might just be a transitory state. I am discouraged because I made efforts that didn't work, or it seems to me that they're not going to work. In despair, this becomes frozen into a certainty: no matter what I do, it won't work. Despair is frozen, crystallized, and entrenched discouragement. In the term *discouragement*, there is a movement from more courage to less courage. This courage is not an attitude in the face of danger, but something broader. In the ancient use of the word, there is the sense of a moral force or an energy for action. Discouragement is not related with the emotion of fear, but rather with the emotion of sadness—and with all the degrees of intensity, which go from listlessness, to discouragement, and then to despair.

What you were just saying, Alex, reminds me of an idea by André Comte-Sponville that's found in his impressive and inspiring book *Traité du Désespoir et de la Béatitude* (*Treatise on Despair and Beatitude*) and also in his very, very simplified adaptation of it, *Le Bonheur, Désespérément* (*Happiness, Desperately*). He says sometimes the best thing to do in our lives is to give up hope—in other words, give up waiting for something and give up being blindly bound hand and foot to goals. I agree with Comte-Sponville in theory, but nevertheless it's quite pleasant to have plans, hopes, and expectations!

MATTHIEU Determination, flexibility, lucidity, pragmatism, equanimity, and strength of spirit are the qualities that psychologists have associated with hope and that they have found in people who are optimistic in nature—people who do not abandon themselves easily to discouragement. These same psychologists define hope as the conviction that it is possible to accomplish the goals one has set oneself and to find the means necessary to do it. We know that hope improves students' results on exams as well as the performance of athletes, but we also know that it helps people tolerate painful illnesses and infirmities. One study showed that people inclined to be hopeful could stand having their hand immersed in ice water for twice as long as others (one way of measuring tolerance for pain).

The undeniably curative effects of placebos are based on the hope of healing that is associated with having chosen to follow a treatment that we think will work for us. The placebo effect changes one's attitude toward the illness or the remedy. It brings about a change in patients that engenders hope and then brings the conviction that such and such a medicine can cure them. Based on this, patients will refocus their attention and physical and mental resources on the cure that the medicine has made them hope for. The placebo effect revives the desire to survive. Doctors and nurses know that sick persons motivated by a fierce determination to survive have more resistance at times of crisis. Those who yield to discouragement and think they're goners sink into a passive resignation and die more quickly.

However, chronic overexcitement of our hopes and fears can also destabilize our minds. This dysfunction can be explained most of the time by a tendency to be excessively focused on oneself. In relating to life's events, a person is constantly asking, "Why me?" or "Why not me?" We know that excessive dwelling on the past and anxiety-ridden anticipation of the future is one of the signs that depression is coming. Thus, freeing ourselves from the push and pull of hope and fear brings us closer to inner freedom.

CHRISTOPHE Sometimes I have patients whose hopes are so strong that it makes me worry about them, and I constantly check to make sure they are taking an active approach to things. Hoping to win the lottery and thus not doing anything else in one's life is not at all the same thing as hoping to win the lottery while still continuing to work and enjoy the company of one's friends. I think a hope does not become toxic unless it is accompanied by some form of shrinking the focus of our life exclusively to the object of this hope and abandoning everything else. One might be very much in love with someone and hope that one day a relationship with that person might become a real thing. This does not become a pathological hope if in addition one continues to see friends, work, and take pleasure in all the other things in life. We don't panic if there are sources of suffering *and* sources of hope in our life, but we have to make sure that they are integrated into a relationship with the world that remains open, fluid, alive, and active.

MATTHIEU The problem begins when we superimpose our attachments on things and people. We have a tendency to think that certain things, certain situations, or certain people are intrinsically desirable or detestable, whereas these characteristics, like all things, are subject to change and are to a great extent the result of our mental projections.

Freeing Ourselves from Despair

CHRISTOPHE   What can we say to a person in despair? Even I as a therapist sometimes get distress signals regarding a person suffering from despair; I'm afraid that I won't be able to help them. At such times, I try to pass along to my patients words that I sometimes have to say myself:

"This is not necessarily an abnormal condition. You have the right to be discouraged. You have the right to feel despair. Maybe you didn't even make a mistake of any kind or do anything wrong. Could it be that what's making you feel despair today will disappear tomorrow? Even if you don't believe it at this moment, take a moment anyhow to breathe and repeat to yourself these words, without judging it or pushing it away. Any human being can be discouraged for good or bad reasons. You have nothing to reproach yourself for. This is just a part of human life.

"As best you can, do something—some little thing for yourself or for another person—even if it has nothing to do with the situation. Don't stay focused on this problem, tearing yourself up inside. If you are discouraged and in despair, it might quite simply be that the situation is really discouraging and desperate, and for the moment there is no simple solution. If there is a solution, it will present itself; if there isn't one, other things will happen. In either case, don't be overly concerned and don't stay shut up in the very small piece of your mind related to this problem. Go out, move, get around, run. Don't stay alone; talk to somebody, but not necessarily about your problem. Make a connection with somebody who likes you, who might change your way of thinking or advise you and console you.

"And then, later, when you have gotten through this period of discouragement and despair, it's important for you not to move on right away to something else. Take the time to look at what has taken place. Sit down, write, reflect, observe where you are today with regard to this despair. Try to understand why the despair isn't there anymore, how it disappeared—maybe it has just changed to sadness. Today you're no longer in a state of despair. Why was it possible for you to tumble into the abyss of despair? What kind of a state were you in? What were the steps in the process that led to your getting out of it? Remember your moments of 'despair over nothing'—or almost nothing—which you finally survived."

Just as we should remember our great moments of happiness, we should never forget the moments in which we have been self-intoxicated, completely hypnotized by our despair. It is essential for all of us to know how deeply we are capable of immersing ourselves in our errors and weaknesses. We must be very clear about this, not for the sake of judging ourselves but for the sake of being capable of compassion toward ourselves, being capable of good sense in relating to our next discouragements, today and tomorrow.

"Here, There Are No Failures"

MATTHIEU I'm reminded of my sister Ève. She was a speech therapist who worked for thirty years at Saint Anne Hospital with children from very underprivileged backgrounds. A few of the children sometimes refused to talk at all; they had great difficulty learning to read and write. One of them couldn't remember my sister's name and called her "Word Lady." A few of them told her they had always failed in the various institutions they had passed through. She replied, "Here, nothing is ever a failure." At the end of one re-education session, one of the children had written only a single sentence in his notebook: "Here, nothing is ever a failure." He explained to Ève that he was very happy to have been accepted just as he was.

In dealing with people suffering from despair, we must be very humble and not pretend to have an answer for everything. Sometimes just a kindly presence is the best thing we have to offer. If circumstances provide an opening, we can remind them that we always have the potential for change in us. If a person appears receptive to the idea, we can also suggest that there is always something in the deepest part of us that is not touched by despair, the pure awareness I have spoken of before. Clearly, distress and suffering are not going to evaporate all at once on the spot, but by recognizing the space of peace in our heart, we can encourage it to gradually grow. We can also suggest to people to recall whatever peaceful moments they have experienced in their life. Recalling these will help them to remember that such peace is a real possibility.

The important thing is not to let oneself be defined by one's mental state and not to identify with the despair. You don't go to the doctor and say, "Doctor, I'm the flu." Well, we are no more despair than we are the flu. It's an ailment that's afflicting us, and one that we can remedy.

ALEXANDRE In order not to identify totally with our mental states or with the hassles of the day, it might be a good idea for us to get rid of the voracious desire we have to solve our problems on the spot. Sometimes when I am swamped by my to-do list, I manage to persuade myself that to go faster, I should slow down. Dealing with things in a hyper-agitated state, I might easily get carried away and make mistakes. Why shouldn't I dare to try the no-hurry approach? And if I go to bed that night without having taken care of all my problems, is that necessarily a catastrophe?

Paradoxically, in order to learn patience, it's a good idea to do something, to get out of one's head and break out of the state of inaction. Not long ago, I was waiting to hear from a doctor about something, and it seemed like the phone would never ring. Panic started having a field day with me. At that point I recalled the Zen teaching that tells us to devote oneself heart and soul to action. I got hold of a broom, and I cleaned up my room. Then I meditated and dedicated my practice to all suffering people around the world.

Identify the psychological mechanisms before you get carried away by them: that's the challenge facing the practitioner! Often in Seoul, I used to pass through the prostitutes' quarter and see men standing by the doorways. It's a tragicomic spectacle to see individuals hesitating whether to go ahead with something or not. The spiritual life lives in these micro-choices, these fractions of a second in which we could still avoid painful regrets. How is it possible to have just a little bit of perspective in these crucial moments? There's nothing better for calming down the agitated mind than returning to the present, to terra firma, to "just do what you're doing." We know the words of the sage: "When you walk, walk. When you sit, sit. Above all, don't hesitate!" When everything is going wrong, when ego is tormenting us with its mad deliriums, let's have the courage to keep faith with daily life and continue taking our children to school, answering an email from a person who needs help, and daring to extricate or divert ourselves from our inner cinema.

Toolbox for Dealing with Discouragement

ALEXANDRE

Make your life into a dynamic process and concretely ask yourself what action you can take here and now in order not to get bogged down in failure. Perseverance, the art of staying on course, is a potent antidote to resignation and it takes place in the present.

Don't turn doubt on yourself by sinking into guilt and self-deprecation. Instead, use this instrument of life to strike a blow against ego and advance toward the genuine confidence that lies beyond the conceptual mind.

Dare to use the no-hurry approach. Slow down when everything is pushing you to rush to achieve solutions at all costs.

CHRISTOPHE

Question yourself. Discouragement might actually be legitimate; sometimes it's a signal that it would be better to halt your efforts. But how do you know? Maybe discouragement applies when it's a matter of free choice: "I could continue. I have the strength and the capacity to do so. But it seems to me I've tried hard enough already. And it also seems to me that there are other possibilities."

An anti-discouragement slogan can sometimes give us the energy to carry on and to keep discouragement at bay. One of the best known and enigmatic is from Samuel Beckett's novella *Worstward Ho*: "Ever tried. Ever failed. No matter. Try again. Fail again. Fail better."[1] And more on the academic side, there's the epilogue to Jean de La Fontaine's fable "The Wagoner Stuck in the Mud": "Heaven helps those who help themselves."[2]

Despair calls for two precautions, which are quite important. First, when you feel it coming on, don't stay by yourself. Next, while you're under its influence, don't make any important decisions.

MATTHIEU

Confidence. Discouragement can lead us to give up our efforts even though it's still possible to overcome the difficulties we are facing. It is therefore important to gather our energy reserves so we can transform the obstacle into an accomplishment.

Optimism. Optimists stay calmer than pessimists do. They yield less easily to discouragement and save their energy for real dangers.

Equanimity. If for one reason or another we fail, it is pointless to feel discouraged. Seeing reality as it is does not have anything discouraging about it. We're better off maintaining our equanimity and turning our efforts in a new direction.

5

Egocentricity

One day as I was splashing around happily in the municipal pool, I caught sight of the back of a child whose skin was completely crimson. He had gotten himself one incredible sunburn! For a moment my heart seized up. "Good heavens, my son Augustin has gotten his back roasted!" Then I completely relaxed, seeing that, fortunately, it was not my son.

It's crazy how indifferent I was to the health of this other little guy, who was in danger of getting sunstroke. What optical illusion, what incredible dysfunction, makes me indifferent to the fate of others? It is precisely the role of ascesis, practice, to correct this biased, navel-gazing, self-centered approach to the world. Why should we blind ourselves to the suffering of others? Why should I not have been equally touched by that other unknown child's hellish sunburn?

—Alexandre

MATTHIEU Many people think that by considering only themselves they enjoy the maximum possible freedom. Their approach is, "I'm not obliged to accommodate the will of others. I get to decide what I like, what I do, and how I live. I won't consider the welfare of others or what's good for the situation as a whole." But if we follow this approach, we will just become so many narcissists, whose principal preoccupation is how we feel. We lavish attention on the slightest reactions of our ego, which we can't pamper enough.

Egocentrism is a fundamental obstacle on the path to freedom. It narrows the world. If we live with an exaggerated sense of self-importance—if we see the whole fabric of our relationship with others and the world from the point of view of our ego—then we turn people into mere instruments. (Are they going to bring me some benefit, or are they a threat to my interests?) We become subject to the dictates of this little potentate whose whims and demands are without limit. The world begins to appear to us like a kind of catalog from which we can order whatever we want. And we are unhappy because the world is not set up to satisfy our endless demands. Egocentricity leads to frustration and self-torment. We end up being obsessed by our least pleasure or displeasure; we become the plaything of endless microclimates made up of our reactions of attraction and repulsion. And far from being free, we become extremely vulnerable.

CHRISTOPHE   In general, when the word *ego* appears in a conversation, it's not a good sign. Most often, it refers to an *excessive* attachment to self, to one's interests, to one's status. In the language of psychology, we have numerous terms to describe the relationship we form with ourselves. For example, there is *egotism,* a more technical term than an everyday colloquial term. According to philosopher Paul Valéry, egotism designates a development of consciousness for the purposes of knowledge. This means accepting the fact that the gaze we turn upon the world cannot originate from anywhere else but ourselves. It is a primal, spontaneous movement, and that is why the essence of our efforts in relationship to this "ego" should be to free ourselves from it rather than feeding it, and then to develop a lucid relationship with it rather than trying to get rid of it at all costs.

What we call *egocentricity* refers to a tendency to place ourselves at the center of things, to consider our own interests before those of others. For example, in a discussion, it might mean always being the first to speak rather than allowing others to speak or, at a meal, serving oneself before anyone else. Even if you don't finish the dish and you leave food for others, you still serve yourself first. Egocentricity is not necessarily accompanied by scorn, disregard, or a negative view of others; it is just prioritizing attention to oneself. It is a naive and incomplete vision of communal life that is found at one time or another in young children, and it is not particularly an organized philosophy of life.

With *egoism* we move up a level. Egoists couldn't care less that others exist; they care only about their own needs. The motto "After me, the flood" (*"Après moi, le déluge,"* said by Louis XIV) is characteristic of egoism: "Once my needs are satisfied, I don't care what happens to others in the future. I don't mean them any harm, but I don't make any effort on their behalf." This is the philosophy of life based on the idea of every man for himself.

And finally, there is *narcissism* in the sense in which we use it in psychology and psychiatry. It is a major egoism, an overvaluation of one's value (in other words, a superiority complex) that is accompanied by disregard for others, to whom one feels superior, and by the rights one accords oneself as a result. Narcissistic individuals do not feel obliged to respect the rules of social life because they think their rights are superior to those of others. They think they are entitled to talk more than others (because they say more intelligent things), to get in front of others in line (because their time is more precious), to drive faster (because they're better drivers), to disturb others without tolerating being disturbed by them. In narcissism, there is a combination of egoism, a feeling of superiority, and relative amorality. The American president, Donald Trump, is unfortunately a rather good example. The narcissistic philosophy of life is pathological and toxic for human groups: it causes them to regress wherever collaboration and respect for others are associated with progress of any kind.

MATTHIEU Narcissism is described in psychology as a tendency toward the grandiose, a need for admiration and a lack of empathy. The narcissist is an unconditional admirer of his own person—the only thing that interests him—and he works tirelessly to reinforce the flattering image he has of himself. He has little consideration for others because for him they are only possible instruments for enhancing his image. For a long time it was thought that, deep down, narcissists didn't like themselves and overestimated themselves in order to compensate for a feeling of insecurity. But research shows that, in fact, narcissistic people do indeed actually suffer from a sense of superiority. When the narcissist is finally confronted by reality, he generally gets angry at others or himself. Studies have shown that those who overestimate themselves present an above-average tendency toward aggression.

The psychologist Jean Twenge clearly demonstrated that North America has been suffering for about two decades from a veritable epidemic of narcissism. Over thirty years, the number of adolescents who agreed with the statement "I am someone important" rose from 12 to 80 percent. Today, again in the United States, one student in four can be qualified as narcissistic. According to the researchers, one of the causes for this egocentricity is participation in social media, which are largely devoted to self-promotion.

By way of contrast, all religions remind us of the virtues of humility. Christians emphasize "self-emptying" (*kenosis*). The Benedictine Rule describes the twelve stages of humility a monk must practice. As for Hinduism, the Bhagavad Gita tells us, "Humility, modesty, nonviolence, tolerance, simplicity, . . . self-control, . . . non-ego, . . . such, I affirm, is knowledge. The contrary of that is ignorance." Buddhism considers humility to be a cardinal virtue, resembling a vessel placed on the ground, ready to receive the rain of good qualities. Those who are humble are not remarkable people who strive to persuade themselves they're nobodies, but people who do not make a big deal about their ego. They open more easily toward others and are particularly aware of the interdependence of all beings and of belonging to the greater family of humanity. Researchers have also demonstrated the existence of a correlation between humility and the ability to forgive. Those who consider themselves superior judge the faults of others more harshly and consider them less worthy of forgiveness.

Suffering Can Make Us Egocentric

ALEXANDRE   Perhaps in the very depths of our personality, a mini-Trump is hiding, who isn't proclaiming "America First" but rather "Me First." Seven billion human beings live on our lovely planet. Why does this benighted mentality insist on raising itself above the entire multitude of men, women, and children in the world?

MATTHIEU   If we draw a line and put ourselves on one side and the seven billion other human beings on the other and persist in thinking that we are more important than these seven billion individuals, we're making a gross error in our arithmetic! That would be a perfect example of blind subservience to ego.

ALEXANDRE   What an aberration! How absurd to get stuck in that gross illusion: 1 (me) > 7 billion (the rest of the planet's population)! It's a dreadful error, which is not, however, entirely a matter of depravity. In the throes of suffering, something like a reflex turns us back on ourselves to the point of making us forget the whole rest of the world. I'm so afraid of being hurt that I cling to the persona I'm playing. *Why* am I striving night and day to protect, pamper, and save this little persona that I've ended up identifying with? Because we all want so much to save our skin at any price, so we are strongly inclined to neglect or disregard others. By doing this, we're shooting ourselves in the foot.

CHRISTOPHE   What you are describing, Alex, makes an impression on me as a doctor. We regularly regress toward egocentricity, but especially under the influence of suffering. Suffering captures our attentional resources and relentlessly places us at the center of everything, filling us with ourselves. When we are suffering a lot, even when we are listening to others, we are still thinking about ourselves. We look at the whole world thinking of ourselves. It's exhausting and very sterile.

Some very interesting scientific experiments have been carried out at the Hôpital de la Pitié-Salpêtrière in Paris by Philippe Fossati and his team. They have lists of words including negative words (*egoistic, cruel, cowardly, lying,* etc.) read to depressed persons as well as to people who are not depressed, and they observe the reactions in their brains by means of neuroimaging devices. With the depressed people they observed major activation in the areas of self-reference (like the ventromedial prefrontal cortex), especially when negative words were read (which corresponds with their tendency toward self-accusation and self-devaluation). They are very centered on themselves, but in contrast to narcissists, their self-centered attention is self-critical. On the other hand, the nondepressed people did not feel implicated by some of the negative words, at least not by all of them. They did not relate everything to their own person but only what made sense in their particular case.

We could say that depression is a case of self-toxic egocentricity — as well as self-aggravating: by centering on ourselves in this negative way when we are suffering, we aggravate our suffering further by focusing on that aspect of ourselves that is ailing and assimilating it to our entire person. In this way, we make ourselves less accessible to possible solutions and relief, which are not to be found within ourselves at that moment, but could come from any interest we take in the world around us. That is why depressed persons might seem egoistic; it's an involuntary egoism, because they have neither the energy nor the capacity to make the effort to divert their attention from themselves and direct it toward others.

To a lesser degree, this is what is happening in people who are uncomfortable in their skins and with their lives. They talk too much about themselves. In every conversation, they bring the discussion back to their own preoccupations. I am reminded of the cremation ceremony for a close friend. In the car on the way back to his family home for a farewell evening, we were speaking of his ashes, wondering what his last will had been with regard to them. Right away one of the passengers in the car interrupted the conversation to say that, as for her, she had asked that her ashes be scattered from the top of a mountain she had climbed several times. There was an uneasy silence in the car, until one of her friends drily put her in her place by reminding her that she was not the one who was dead.

To be completely honest, I have also observed this tendency in myself. When I'm not feeling well, I'm too full of myself and my sufferings, and if I don't watch myself, I have a tendency to let my ailing ego invade my thoughts (a problem for me) and my conversation (a problem for others). The worse I feel, the more I keep an eye on myself to make myself limit my time of egotistical talking: I talk about my worries for a while, if I'm asked to or feel the need to, then quickly switch the talk to the experiences of others. I know that will do me more good anyway.

It's also important to remember that egocentrism is a necessary stage in human psychological development. There is a period in the life of a child when an identity is emerging, during which the child is naturally and temporarily egocentric. The child begins by seeing and comprehending the world from the point of view of herself, with reference to herself, on her scale and according to her rules. The essential point of any educational process has to be to teach her to pass beyond this childish egotism and to teach her, by example and advice, to recognize the existence and importance of others. Any education that is too "narcissizing" will create child tyrants, intolerant of frustration, unfit for happiness and for good companionship with their peers. My friend the psychologist Didier Pleux has clearly shown in his works how "child kings" often become adult tyrants and narcissists. They are unhappy themselves and make others unhappy.

Ego Is Neither a Vice Nor a Solution

CHRISTOPHE   It is important not to be judgmental toward egoism. Quite obviously, it's not a good solution. It mainly has to do with an emotional error (when suffering is the source of it) or an intellectual one (when the calculation is that one can gain more by going it alone than working with others). Most often though, it's a lapse in intelligence rather than a moral deficiency. Even if we are not intending to benefit others and are interested only in achieving our own personal ends, I think we make a fundamental mistake by shutting ourselves up in the "bubble of ego," as you call it, Alexandre. To shut ourselves up in ego is to impoverish and weaken ourselves.

It is a profound oversight not to recognize how much good others can do us through their help, their advice, their views, their affection, their esteem. It's also a profound oversight not to recognize how much well-being we gain through exchanges with others: a significant part of what makes us happy comes from what we give and receive. Let's not ask egoists to become altruists, but let's understand this truth: by not engaging with others, egoists clip their own wings.

Egoists should be motivated not only by their material interests but also by the emotional consequences of opening to others. Many studies have reached a similar conclusion: the more egoistic and narcissistic we are, the less happiness there is in our lives. And it is in a state of happiness that we feel free, because happiness is a state that brings us energy, motivation, and opening. Our freedom is acquired through good relations with others, even if that takes some effort on our part to begin with. Not being concerned with the interests of others might initially seem to leave us freer (a little less effort, a little less pressure), but in the end we will be the losers. The quest for freedom also takes effort!

MATTHIEU In physics, in chemistry, and in mathematics, the expression "degree of freedom" indicates the potential of a system to develop without limit in a particular direction. When the system cannot change its state, that is considered the minimum degree of freedom. A low degree of freedom allows us to move from state A to state B. If there is a very high degree of freedom, many states and configurations of the system are possible.

In life, egocentricity is an impoverishment because relating everything back to one's little prison is a self-limitation of one's potential: the world is centered on oneself, even though one is only a single individual among an infinite number of others. Thus, one limits one's degree of creativity, of freedom, of potential for action. The possibilities of life are truncated, and one's room to maneuver is reduced.

ALEXANDRE By way of getting rid of ego, let's finally stop playing the federal-prosecutor game. Let's stop considering ego a sin, a vice, when in fact it's a deadweight. Why should we feel guilty about having to lug this burden around? Egocentrics, whose ranks I often personally swell, are more like convalescents, more like burn victims than perverts.

Never forget Spinoza's lesson: look at our defects, our sad passions, as though they were curves, volumes, or lines; try to understand them, to address the problem nonjudgmentally in the manner of Chögyam Trungpa's body-shop repairman. It's no use condemning the lousy driver who had the misfortune to crash our car into a wall when the real job at hand is hammering out the dents and getting the vehicle back on the road. The job of doing away with egoism has nothing to do with self-flagellation. Instead, let's start without delay treading the joyous path devoid of exaggerated gravity and psychodrama and give up our treasure hunt for mistakes and blunders. Egocentricity, in fact, derives from a sense of poverty, from destitution, as you have indicated. It means limiting our field of vision, forcing our consciousness to dwell solely on our own interests. Suffocating in itself, it places us in a situation of disability, cut off from the infinite, one might say, from the world, from others.

One step further, and we would be caught up in the narcissism of the soulless dummy who cherishes and adores his own image. At that stage, without a doubt, we suffer a double punishment and a double restriction: first of all, we shrink back into ourselves, and then we reduce ourselves to the album photo we carry of an ego perceived as an impervious, autarchic entity. The Buddha's diagnosis becomes a vivid fact: fixation of any kind brings suffering. From this we can see that the narcissist never knows an end to his torment. By reducing the world to his categories, he amputates his connection to things as they are. Fascinated by an image that cuts him off from reality, he wanders in total illusion.

In dealing with these various forms of pathological navel-gazing, there's no use in putting ourselves down as presumed sickos when what is urgently needed is to detect and identify our optical illusions. We're still dealing here with the tough and spiny problem of akrasia. Even if I know perfectly well that I'm headed straight for the abyss, where do I find the courage to change course?

People involved in the culinary arts use flavor enhancers, special condiments that improve the taste of dishes. Could ego also have its "flavor enhancers"? Blows of fate, trials, suffering, self-loathing, lack of confidence, the self-preservation instinct, fear of death, comparisons, wounds—all of these conspire to help this little ego further entrench itself, to turn back on itself more. What would Buddhism say of these elements that enhance the sense of this much talked-about ego of ours?

MATTHIEU   It is said that the Buddha should be perceived as a skillful physician. His teaching is like a prescription and our practice like the medicine. Therefore we should consider ourselves ill instead of blaming ourselves. You spoke of the survival instinct. The Buddhist premise is that every sentient being wants not to suffer and to stay alive. The most fundamental aspiration is to move in the direction of liberation from suffering and, as a consequence, to live one's life fully. If we are to do away with suffering and its causes, wisdom and knowledge are necessary. In tribal societies — in the Amazon, for example — one of the reasons that old people are very much respected is that they have succeeded in surviving into old age, which is a considerable feat in conditions that are often very difficult. So what is respected is the teachings the elders have drawn from their experience of life, which have allowed them to survive in difficult circumstances. Insight, experience, and wisdom are thus key values that allow us to identify the causes of suffering and free ourselves from bondage to them. Though this process may start with oneself, it in no way presumes neglecting others.

How to Combat the Flavor Enhancers of Ego

CHRISTOPHE   Yes, we must make an effort to reason and act in both dimensions at once. It's not "me *or* others," it's "me *and* others" — whether we're dealing with happiness or unhappiness. It's not *my* happiness versus that of others; I have to learn to rejoice in the happiness of others, initially as a matter of principle, through logic. Their happiness does not take anything away from mine, and if it has any effect it is a positive one, because if the people around me are happy they will be better able to help me, to listen to me, to love me.

At the same time, we have to watch out for the toxic competition that takes the form of "Which one of us is the unhappiest?" Sometimes people who are suffering have a tendency toward excessive comparison, whether it's for the sake of reassuring themselves ("some people are worse off than I am") or to be able to complain even more ("my suffering is the worst"). It's preferable to turn away from these kinds of comparisons as best we can and to respect all suffering, that of others and our own, without hierarchizing.

As a complement to what Alex was saying on the fact that egocentricity is not a vice, it's important for us doctors to remind people, "Don't accuse yourself, don't blame yourself; just notice the moments in which you are overly self-centered and ask yourself what they are a symptom of. Where is the problem behind 'me me me, me me me'? Where does the suffering lie?"

When I realize that I have an excessive urge—once again, there *are* legitimate urges—to talk about myself, to complain, I could ask myself what I actually need. More attention, understanding, affection, love? And I should see if I could obtain them by other means than by forcing all the attention on myself—by expressing these needs directly, for example.

What makes this task more difficult is that our egocentric tendencies are regularly reactivated by the society we live in, which pushes us to attribute considerable importance to ourselves. Consumer society as a whole abuses the "flavor enhancers of ego," to use Alexandre's expression. And not for our good, not with no ulterior motives to improve our morale or boost our self-esteem, but rather for the benefit of the shareholders in companies that have wares to sell. The flatteries of our little egos that the commercials use—"You're fantastic. You deserve better, right now, without delay. Go for it!"—obviously have the objective of selling us something. I'm waiting for the day when a commercial will say, "You're terrific just the way you are; don't buy anything. You have everything you need!" I think I might be waiting a long time. Whenever we're flattered that way, there is an ego enhancer involved with the objective of deregulating our appetites: eat more over-sweet, over-salty, or over-processed foods, for the actual food flavor enhancers, or buy useless but social status–conferring goods, for flavor enhancers of ego.

Thanks to the La Fontaine fable "The Crow and the Fox," we know that "flatterers thrive on fools' credulity."[1] But after just a few seconds, we forget and begin to believe in contrived commercial flatteries. So these commercial disrupters push us to consume in order to increase our happiness (that new couch, that new car), our beauty (those new clothes), and our youthfulness (those new cosmetics), but also our freedom. The ads constantly tell us, "Look out for number one." "Listen to yourself." "To hell with constraints and limitations; give in to your temptations!" This vision of freedom is a dead end. We rapidly collide with reality—the reality of our bank account, the reality of the real needs of those around us.

MATTHIEU   In New York, the stores of a chain of pharmacies put up signs across their windows, saying, "How do you look? How do you feel? What do you need, *now?*' I have the urge to write underneath them, "I don't care how I look. I feel quite well, thank you. And I don't need a thing."

ALEXANDRE   Let's immediately do away with the horrible misunderstanding that makes us believe that altruism requires sacrifice. How can we throttle that little misleading voice in our heads: "Up till now, I have devoted myself to others. I have given, but what did I get in return?" Generosity, compassion, giving of oneself cannot be a matter for your accountant; you don't keep books on it or look for a return on your investment. What a calamity it is to reproach your kids for ingratitude by saying, "After all I've done for you!" Altruism rises above any sense of investment. It makes no sense to expect a quid pro quo.

CHRISTOPHE   "Nice guys finish last," people sometimes say. To begin with, is that true? You can also be stupid and finish last due to egoism or stinginess. Finishing last is not reserved for nice guys. The question seems to be about the disappointment that threatens people who give with the expectation of being loved for it, of having it recognized, of some reciprocity. Basically, there's nothing abnormal about feeling good when someone thanks us. It makes us feel good, and it's a supplementary source of motivation to continue. But expecting this is something we have to go beyond; we can't remain prisoners of this expectation. It's okay to expect something in return, but we have to accept that it won't be there sometimes. Let's take an example: You invite friends to your house a few times in a row, and they never return your invitation. Often the reflex response is to say, "Since they don't invite me, I won't invite them either" instead of saying, "Don't we have a good time together?" And then we must ask ourselves the real question, "What am I looking for, a fair audit or some fun?"

MATTHIEU   I have personally heard the Dalai Lama say: "If you have an altruistic attitude, it's not a sure thing that others will like it. But either way, you're the 100 percent winner because it's a state of mind that is eminently satisfying in itself." Raphaële, one of my close friends, who works on construction of schools and clinics in Tibet, has experienced moments of discouragement and has been hurt through encounters with the machismo of people who treat her harshly and unfairly. She went to one of our masters seeking advice, and he told her, "Your job is not to make everyone perfect along the way—that's the job of Buddha—but to build schools and clinics." We can't expect people to behave nicely simply because we are helping them. When engaging in humanitarian projects, it is important to recognize that the objective is to provide care and to educate, even though in the process you might run into people who are ungrateful, crooked, or even malevolent. Moral judgment is one thing, compassion another. Compassion's aim is to relieve people's sufferings, whatever they are, wherever they are, and whatever their causes are.

CHRISTOPHE What you say is of the essence, Matthieu. In the end, altruism is a felicitous solution for egotism. But there may well be more than one way of getting there, and several stages in the process.

There are people who are naturally altruistic—it's a matter of genes, education, and their path in life. It's great that these people exist. Their altruism is right out there, as plain as day, and they practice it with the same simplicity as just breathing. They are a source of inspiration. For the rest of us though, and I am one of those, altruism requires regular effort. We often begin with an altruism with expectations. Like all beginners, we need to be rewarded and guided. There's nothing wrong with this as long as it's a stage—but watch out for disappointment! I have to regularly remind myself that if I'm disappointed, it's my problem rather than the other person's.

Then there's altruism with no expectations, which is the direction we're working toward. Depending on the context and on where one is at that moment in one's life, it's possible to get there—to behave like a bodhisattva, as described by Matthieu. To put it simply, in Buddhism, bodhisattvas are people who work to help others to progress on the spiritual path while they themselves are also traveling the path. (The idea is don't leave anyone behind.) The bodhisattva is attempting to attain enlightenment while at the same time helping others to attain enlightenment.

Quite obviously, working in this way all the time is difficult for most of us. Sometimes we have a toothache, a backache, and various worries of our own, and we just simply can't get there. But when we succeed in working on this level—living this way, thinking this way, feeling and acting this way—this experience leaves us with a feeling of wanting to get back to it. The people Alexandre was talking about who regressed to egocentricity from altruism with expectations, on account of disappointments or exhaustion, are perhaps people who haven't tasted the benefits of altruism with no expectations. Because there we really experience inner freedom—the lightness of being altruistic without expectation of anything in return. To expect something is to be less free.

When one is a doctor, sometimes one has patients who moan and groan all the time and thus are not satisfying to work with. Some days it gets heavy. I tell myself that my role is not to have nice patients, but to provide care. And I treat them as though they were nice. I make the effort not to let my attitude get caught up in theirs. In general as a human being, but still more as a doctor, I strive for this. There is too much at stake in the caregiving relationship for me to allow myself to get caught up in the need for reciprocity. Moreover, it's not a completely equal and symmetrical relationship: because of their suffering and their expectations, my patients are in a vulnerable position in relation to me. But this is true anytime we are dealing with someone who is suffering.

In any case, I think it's necessary to be in a good state oneself in order to be capable of this attitude. And that's why it's important to take care of oneself.

MATTHIEU   In being altruistic we have to stay within our limits in order to avoid burnout. We have to preserve our faculties in order to remain capable of helping others. If we go beyond these limits, we will accomplish less than we could have otherwise.

CHRISTOPHE   Once again, the egocentricity stage is not to be eliminated but rather transcended. It's a starting point and sometimes a necessary and justified fallback position.

I'm quite fond of the example of the oxygen mask. When airplane crews give security instructions to passengers, they explain that in case of depressurization of the cabin, the oxygen masks will fall down in front of us. And they tell parents, "Put a mask on your own face first, before putting one on your child's face." You begin by helping yourself in order to better be able to help others later. That's not egoism at that point; it's pragmatism.

I take a five-minute break between patients in order to recuperate emotionally, breathe mindfully, relax, and get recentered. That's time I devote to myself rather than to them, but I do it without compunction because I also know that I'm going to be able to listen to them better after doing that.

MATTHIEU There are two types of expectation we can transcend: expectation of recognition and of success at all costs. Obviously, when you commit yourself to some cause, you expect it to bear fruit. But it's also necessary to be able to let go if the job you have undertaken is not successful for one reason or another. Being devastated by failure is in part an expression of egocentricity. Wanting a project to succeed at all costs comes from a kind of arrogance. When a project fails, it's better to tell yourself that you've done your best, that you have nothing to blame yourself for (if that's really the case!), and to move on to something else with a sense of equanimity.

ALEXANDRE Rousseau distinguishes self-love (protecting oneself from illness, bad weather, taking care of ourselves psychologically) from vanity, by exposing vanity as the desire to dominate, to outshine others, to set oneself apart. In sum, vanity applies to narcissism or, even worse, the will to power or the most unbridled egoism.

Toolbox for Working with Egocentricity

ALEXANDRE

Identify the flavor enhancers of ego. Fear, trauma, impossible expectations. In this way, rediscover the taste, the savor of life.

Don't self-flagellate. Instead, adopt the attitude of an auto-body repairman and identify the main work you need to do on yourself. Why should I be riveted to what others think of me? What do I ultimately expect from life? Who am I in my basic nature, my ground of grounds?

Abandon the accountant attitude in relationships. If relationships with other people are frequently exhausting, it's perhaps because they are mixed up with a great load of expectations that are bound to be disappointments. If that's the case, gradually abandon the attitude of an accountant in your relationships with others. This means parting ways with the logic of self-interest and ceasing to bet on your relationships. Instead, invest in them, and meet the other person in pure love.

CHRISTOPHE

Pay attention to small details. In your speech, for example, hunt down the *I*'s and *my*s so that they don't begin sentences too often. When you have conversations with your friends and acquaintances, don't talk about yourself too much. Ask instead for the other person's news.

Be aware. When we have been self-centered—and that can happen—we should ask ourselves, what was it that was "off" in me during that time? What was I afraid of? What did I need? Was it fear that others wouldn't take a spontaneous interest in me? Was it needing to be liked? Could I have gone about things in some way other than by focusing everything on myself?

Act. Initially try self-treating egocentricity through benevolent or charitable activities in the service of others, rather than going right away to a psychotherapist. Or consider both if your case is serious.

Go on a digital diet. Beware of social media, which often push us into self-promotion.

MATTHIEU

The best tools are those that permit us to understand how to bring about the welfare of both ourselves and others.

With egoism, everybody loses. We make life miserable for everybody around us as well as ourselves.

With altruism, everybody wins. We contribute to the welfare of others, and this is also the best way to flourish in our own lives.

Egoism shrinks our universe. Altruism opens our universe to all sentient beings.

6

Delusion

An Indian friend told me the following story:

A fisherman is sitting in the shade of a tree at the edge of a lake. He is playing with his children.

A person from the city comes along, observes the scene, and starts a conversation. "Hello there. What do you do in life, my good sir?"

"I'm a fisherman. My boat is over there on the shore. I was fishing all morning."

"Why don't you fish in the afternoon?"

"I have enough fish to feed my family for the next two days."

"But if you fished in the afternoon, you could also sell some fish."

"So?"

"So you would have enough money to pay a helper. You could catch more fish and augment your income."

"What would I do with it?"

"Well, you could buy a second boat and become more prosperous!"

"And after all that?"

"You could stop working and enjoy yourself by relaxing and playing with your children."

"But that's exactly what I'm doing right now!"

—Matthieu

CHRISTOPHE   Straying into delusion is losing one's way; it's wandering off the path of what is good for us, what is important for our lives. We somehow get lost because we aren't careful to pay attention to what counts, to staying on the right path. This already tells us quite clearly what kind of continual efforts we have to make in order not to be deluded too long or too often.

We can become deluded in three ways: because we have not defined the path and have gone off at random, without an objective; because we have not defined the right goal; or because we have not gone about pursuing the goal in the right way. In all these cases we become disoriented, mixed up, troubled. We wander off; we go astray.

Looking at delusion in daily life with its three possible sources, we can take the example of child education. If we do not set ourselves the goal of educating our children — hoping, for example, that life will take care of it — we stray into delusion by not having a goal. If the goal is only to make children obedient and learned, we delude ourselves by not choosing an appropriate goal. If we set an accessible goal (that children should develop fully and be autonomous and happy), but we go about accomplishing it in the wrong way (by being too lax or not living up to our educational message ourselves and being stressed out and uptight), we are equally deluded.

The same thing goes for the pursuit of happiness. We delude ourselves if we expect happiness to fall from the sky; by seeking it alone by ourselves in a corner in an egoistic manner; or by trying to find happiness through materialistic means alone — by accumulating money, possessions, the buyable pleasures. Our mutual friend Christian Bobin remarked one day, "It's because of distraction that we fail to enter Paradise during our lifetime, simply because of distraction." Distraction and scatteredness bring delusion; they turn us away from the essential—smoothly, hardly noticeably, as though it were hardly happening at all.

In psychology and psychotherapy, we put great emphasis on the obstacles to our happiness, represented by ill-regulated emotions and a poorly digested past, but perhaps not enough emphasis on the idea of delusion. This is doubtless because it would require reflecting on our existential choices (what are my life's goals?), which is something not often dealt with in psychiatry, where we work more on clearing the path from accumulated sufferings than envisaging more distant horizons.

MATTHIEU   Being deluded, or disoriented, is not having any idea where to go, what choices to make, what direction to give one's life. A first form of delusion comes from our not being in possession of the criteria or the knowledge for finding the right path, especially in complex situations. We have good intentions, but we are lost, like someone walking alone in a big forest who is incapable of finding their way. For this type of delusion, the solution is to consult sources of valid knowledge beforehand: for instance, refer to an experienced guide or get a detailed map before setting off at random. In dealing with the choices and challenges of life, the source could be a person with a great deal of experience or, in the ideal case, a sage or spiritual master.

A second form of delusion comes from a lack of judgment and lucidity. For example, we want to be happy, and we think for that we have to be rich, powerful, and famous. We learn one day that some people who have succeeded in acquiring all those conditions of life are actually depressed, addicts, or have committed suicide. We say to ourselves, "That's weird. In my case, if I had all that, I would definitely be happy." But if we had taken the trouble to reflect, we would have realized that this false path does not lead to profound satisfaction. We have thus shown an absence of clear judgment and have turned our back on values like friendship, equanimity, inner peace, and emotional balance, which really can bring about lasting and full development. Being deluded is going against one's own aspirations—being happy, being a good person—in one's choices and actions. This was well understood by the fisherman in the story at the beginning of this chapter.

Sometimes we are stubborn in pursuing this false route. Neither reason nor logic seems to have any effect on this kind of stubbornness. We disregard the advice of wise people who alert us to the fact that we are turning our back on well-being. Sometimes this advice even reinforces our stubbornness. We act like someone keeping their hand in the fire, hoping not to get burned.

Buddhism speaks of a third form of delusion: a false perception of reality. For example, we become attached to things thinking they are permanent when, in fact, they are by nature impermanent. Sooner or later, we will lose all the things and people around us. And if we don't lose them, they will lose us! That is one source of suffering. Many unhappy consequences come from this error, this distortion of reality.

To take another example of delusion, in the early days of a relationship, one finds that a person is 100 percent likable, and one doesn't perceive any of their defects. Then come the arguments and the misunderstandings, and one comes to regard the person as 100 percent hateful, whereas give or take a few changes, the person is still the same. In both cases, there is a distortion of reality. Like everybody else, the people involved are a mixture of good qualities and defects. We are prisoners of our mental fabrications, bound by an inaccurate vision of reality, passing from unconditional attraction to pure hate. Enslaved by delusion, we react in an excessive and inappropriate manner.

CHRISTOPHE You describe delusion as a refusal or inability to see the world as it is. We often tell each other stories that are either reassuring and idealize reality or are alarming and depict reality as overly dark. In both cases we are off the mark; we lose our lucidity and freedom because we are in partially virtual worlds that correspond to our expectations. Sooner or later, we collide with reality again.

The only freedom that is worth anything over the long run is the freedom that is found in the midst of reality. And delusion means departing from reality or sometimes only perceiving a small bit of it—the part that confirms our expectations, the part that is reassuring to us for better or for worse.

MATTHIEU Yes, the ability to see things as they are liberates us. Any false vision of reality lays a yoke on us that will inevitably cause us pain.

There are all kinds of ways to be a prisoner of false visions, but only one way to be free: seeing reality as it is. For that, we have to understand that reality is impermanent and interdependent, that the characteristics we attribute to things and beings are to a great extent our mental projections.

The Wounds of Exile

ALEXANDRE Certain Sufis compare the spiritual journey to a caravan traveling through the desert. Let us move from oasis to oasis, stage by stage, in such a way that we can travel without getting exhausted, knowing where the wells are, the places where we can quench our thirst and rest. Listening to our fears, dancing obediently to the tune of our fantasies, we tumble into a distressed state. In order to extricate ourselves from these psychodramas, ascesis urges us to gain a firm footing in reality. In exile from our ground of grounds, we continually have to return home, dare to go deep, leave behind the superficial "I," say goodbye to our constantly agitated ego. A kind of inner exile makes us strangers to the world, shuts us up in our own bubble. A thousand times a day, the caravan traveler must get regrounded, leave behind fears and mirages, and open his eyes so he can stay on course using whatever means are available.

The Buddhist tradition also provides us with a precious tool: naked awareness. Make yourself available to experience; live the everyday without rejecting or grasping, without labeling reality as good/evil, pleasant/unpleasant.

The spiritual exercise at this point consists in gaily unraveling our egocentricity. The moment I start straying into delusion and try to hotfoot it away from reality or put on a mask, I should have the courage to be naked, without any protective padding. Vulnerability can't kill, but playing a role all day long can exhaust us and distort our interactions.

What is the first step? Catch a glimpse of the immense carnival—the distractions of ego, the fears, the whims of conceptual mind—in short, everything that misdirects the mind, distracts us, leads us astray. The ancient philosophers spoke of false goodness, meaning whatever is not capable of satisfying us in the long term: repute, honor, vainglory, excessive pleasures, wealth. It's impossible to find freedom in that direction. You were speaking a little while ago, Matthieu, of artificial goodness. How can we eradicate all these hankerings in ourselves, this inner cinema, all the smoke and mirrors?

We can initiate the process of gradually going back home and returning from exile by means of a question: What is my true inner homeland, the center of my life? Starting with that, at any moment I can attempt a retreat or a deep-down search of who I really am—especially when during the day, the dictatorship of "they" and the sirens of the false good somehow manage to trap me.

Traveling toward freedom means crossing lots of stony ground, bumping into walls, collapsing from exhaustion, and getting back up again and continuing the journey. A host of factors pushes us toward exile: listlessness, ennui, crushing banality, the call of faraway places and things. The psychologists call "hedonic habituation" the singular process that causes pleasures and joys to pale and go dull, and that renders us blasé and hungry for strong sensations, for novelty. In the desert—in our journey toward happiness—how can we avoid these thousands of side roads, these perilous detours, these dead ends?

It is dangerous to be exiled from our ground of grounds, but it takes a certain amount of courage to get off the freeways so conveniently laid out by ego.

Chögyam Trungpa helps us in our journeys deep in the desert. When you bring the repairman your dented fenders, your shattered windshield, your buckled car doors, he doesn't bother with judgment. He sees what is there and then, without further ado, goes about repairing the damage. In the same way, without superfluous drama, we should observe our singular faculty for self-deception. Why do we sometimes prefer to crash and burn rather than admit we're wrong? What strange forces bind us to our point of view, our habits?

How to Find Your Way Back to the Path

CHRISTOPHE   It's normal to stray into delusion. We have all experienced periods of delusion, at least momentarily. Like periods of adversity, they can be rich in lessons. They allow us to understand that we have betrayed ourselves.

For example, I understood at one point in my life that I was getting out of touch with my inner compass by working too much. I had replicated the goal orientation of my parents: don't end up in poverty; safeguard the material security of your children. This was not a bad objective, but it had taken over too much. I was sacrificing too much. At one point I asked myself, if I die tomorrow, what will I regret? Not having worked enough? Or not having benefited enough from life and from my close relationships? It's too obvious, almost idiotic, to be asking those questions, but what a lot of years I spent in that state of delusion.

And yet we can do otherwise. These false directions in life are often revealed to us by emotional signals; it's rare that being on the wrong track feels comfortable. For my part, every time I strayed into delusion, I was lucky enough to feel painful emotions that brought me back to my senses. I slept badly. I was sick all the time, irritated by what I normally enjoyed, and altogether, I was not happy. Our emotions are an intelligent system; they're made to help us. Pleasant emotions give a signal that we are getting near something that is good for us. And the unpleasant ones tell us we are getting farther away. We can decide not to heed them, no matter how much squeaking and rattling there is, but I have observed that in the long run you can't be deluded and comfortable at the same time.

ALEXANDRE Does life give us clues when we're on the brink of delusion, when we're about to bang into a wall? Taking refuge in secretiveness, trying to hide some behavior from the people close to you, telling tall tales—all these are signs that should tip us off. Why should we try to hide an action, a habit pattern? A prerequisite for freeing ourselves from it is approaching some caring friends and daring to be transparent with them about it. We should not give credence to those little voices that are trying to dupe us. We should perk up and watch out the moment we hear ourselves saying things like, "It's just for a little while," "Enjoy yourself a little bit," "After all, you only live once." Those little voices are just so much bull, proof that there's a struggle on. Some gear is seizing up and screeching.

I have described elsewhere the sad passion that bound me to a young man and the unorthodox means that saved me from this fierce addiction.

In my efforts to get out of it, I took part in a group of people with emotional and sexual dependencies, and I found masters of transparency in it, people who could act as resources and guides at the same time as they were going through extreme hells of their own.

CHRISTOPHE Yes, it's very important not to feel alone and not to be extremely critical of ourselves, but simply to recognize our delusion even if we don't see any immediate way of getting out of it. But that absence of self-criticism doesn't exempt us from having to get to work on the problem right away. There's a stage in which many people are trapped and have trouble getting on with the work of freeing themselves because they have convinced themselves that they have no choice. For example, if they were overworking, they would say that they couldn't do otherwise. These people were deluded, unhappy, but also stubborn! Letting go of something solid that already exists, whether it is a relationship, a profession, or a situation, is frightening—even if it's our mistakes we are letting go of.

ALEXANDRE Nietzsche, Freud, Marx, and many others teach us to ferret out all forms of illusion, of lying. The exercise here is to identify the fear that binds us to our judgments, our beliefs, our credos. Why don't we go right ahead and make an enjoyable pastime out of examining our personal mythology, the convictions that we hang on to tooth and nail? The immense challenge we face is dethroning our idols, tossing overboard the cargo of preconceptions that prevent us from living nakedly.

MATTHIEU Many people have said to me, "It must have been really hard for you to give up everything—the Pasteur Institute, your Parisian lifestyle, your career—and leave for the Himalayas." But in my case, it was such a no-brainer that I made the transition joyfully, very smoothly. It was like discovering a beautiful valley when you reach the top of a mountain pass. When the direction to be taken is clear, you take it without hesitation. Today, I congratulate myself every moment for having made the choice that best corresponded with my aspirations early enough in my life.

CHRISTOPHE Sometimes delusion is just staying on the rails, accepting daily life conditions in which we are not thriving, but which have the merit of already existing. We prefer having a path to follow, even if it is flawed, to having no path at all. Our delusions become habits, and what is more difficult than freeing ourselves from our habits?

ALEXANDRE In the Nicomachean Ethics, Aristotle says that the happy medium, or the mean, partakes of the quality of perfection. Confronted with unhappiness and dissatisfaction, the temptation is strong to do a 180-degree about-face. But isn't that just fooling ourselves in the same way? By either stubbornly keeping to the same course or constantly changing course without dealing with the root of the evil, don't we delude ourselves equally? Here again, we have to pay close attention to our inner compass so we can respond in the best way to the demands of reality, to the call of life.

Toolbox for Working with Delusion

ALEXANDRE

Drop the hunt for labels. In order to keep Mental FM at bay, Zen recommends a powerful exercise: drop concepts — the series of labels, prejudgments, and hidden agendas that we lay over the world and people — and return to perceptions, to sensation, to what is happening here and now. In concrete terms, when I meet a person, I have to refrain from imprisoning them in my mental categories and from reducing them to their past, and instead I have to ask myself, "Who am I looking at? What is the fundamental nature of this person, in their ground of grounds?"

Return to your fundamental nature. Go home to the heart of your inner nature. Like travelers in a caravan who cross the desert stage by stage, find the oases and that which makes for lasting change.

Never confuse the spiritual stages and mental states, the mystics tell us. We can be torn apart inside, be wandering in the darkest night, and still be growing, progressing, advancing by leaps and bounds.

CHRISTOPHE

There are a lot of ways to stray into delusion. Not having goals (living haphazardly under the influence of external factors or our past), having too many goals (we are unable to prioritize what counts most for us and our lives), and being too attached to our goals (sometimes delusion is continuing on the same path at a moment when it's necessary to change).

Our emotions are an alarm signal—worry and discontentment, especially. We have to learn how to listen to them and trace them back to their source.

It's normal to stray into delusion regularly. Life is treacherous and complicated. Any time we become aware of having gone astray is the right time to have a talk with ourselves or a meeting with a few friends to figure out what new goals and balances we should set ourselves.

MATTHIEU

Find your way back to the path. After having reflected thoughtfully and sincerely, identify the external conditions and mental states that are conducive to happiness—conceived as an optimal way of being—and distinguish them from the conditions and states that undermine your well-being and that of others.

Analyze the nature of reality as best you can in order to understand that it is, by nature, impermanent and that the characteristics you have attributed to things and beings are, to a great extent, projections of your mind. They are not as solid as you would like to think.

Learn to manage your thoughts and emotions and to liberate afflictive mental states as they arise in your mind. That is, let them pass by like birds flying across the sky without leaving a trace.

Part II

the ecology
of freedom

ALEXANDRE   Ecology could mean the art of living together happily. All of us are co-tenants of this beautiful blue planet. Why, then, should we turn on each other and compete with each other as rivals? How can we really become collaborating members of the same team and take a shot at this adventure together?

The ecological challenge cannot be lived on the purely abstract level. It implies a host of concrete questions that ultimately shape our everyday life. What is our relationship with nature? Is nature a store, a self-service restaurant, a toolbox where we can consume trees and animals or use them and throw them away? Why regard the whole universe as a big supermarket? Do we really have to stuff our faces in total indifference to the deluge we unleash? If we want to approach our world wisely, we might need to revisit the way we inhabit it and take another look at the relationships we have with the men and women we have the good fortune to meet.

Nature continually reminds us, quite fortunately, that we are not the center of the universe. Surely there's something greater than us. Its power and majesty politely dislodges us from the "me/my" attitude—from the consumer slumbering inside us—and defeats our false sense of omnipotence. On top of a mountain, at the foot of a tree, or in the company of another human being, how is it possible not to experience the grandeur of the cosmos, infinitely vast beyond the fragile and narrow borders of our individuality? Ecology calls out to us: change your ways, grow spiritually, escape from the dungeon of conceptual mind so as to offer yourself to the world.

Can we maintain contact with nature in the midst of all this concrete? Even here in the city, as in all places, we need to respect the super-potent miracle of life. In order for all of us to cohabitate in this gigantic house, Planet Earth, we urgently need to rehabilitate our relationship to ourselves, to others, to the whole. This is one of the main challenges of ecology: to live together without leaving anyone behind.

For the ancient philosopher Plotinus, the soul becomes whatever it contemplates. What are we looking at all day long? What are we feeding on? Does this spectacle of malice, competitiveness, mad speed, and struggle for life leave us unscathed? Returning to nature, taking up the challenge, would already stop all this avidity, or at least slow it down or pause it for a while. In short, it would begin to make the switch from "I" to "we."

CHRISTOPHE In changing ourselves and changing the world, our personal efforts count, but our environments also play a fundamentally important role. The three dimensions of ecology that influence us greatly are the natural, relational, and cultural dimensions. They are the medium in which we evolve from day to day without realizing it, and they infuse us with their vices and virtues. They hinder us, and they help us.

From my point of view as a doctor, I see that our environments can contribute to our health or damage it. This is what is called "environmental medicine." One can't be in good health in a sick environment or in a human ecosystem that is polluted, whether we're talking about physical pollutants (pollution of the air, water, food), relational pollutants (constantly being in a state of competition or comparing oneself with others), or cultural pollutants (living in an egoistic and materialistic society). Conversely, a favorable environment benefits both our health and well-being. Having regular contact with nature, having friends and relatives who love us and are ready to help us, and belonging to a culture that promotes the values of solidarity and respect and brings them to life in us—all that is good for our little person, even without any effort on our part.

Ecological thinking is thus not only about protecting nature but also about protecting the best aspects of human relationships and human societies. It is also about being suspicious or taking preventive action with regard to our worst human aspects.

All that counts a lot, even if sometimes we are not aware of it. A favorable environment liberates my mind by bringing about pleasant emotions, by giving me a feeling of personal security, and thus by permitting me to have an open and serene relationship with the world. It gives me the feeling of living in a predictable, just, and coherent universe. Conversely, a toxic environment puts me under stress, makes me unhappy, and forces me to be distrustful and stay on alert in order to protect myself from it. These are so many fetters and restrictions to my inner freedom. What I like about this notion of ecology is that it reminds us that we are not immaterial beings who grow without soil. Wherever we put down roots—in our culture, in our physical environment, in our relationships with our peers—we find nourishment. A tree in town does not grow the same way as a tree in the woods. That is why it might be valuable for us to think about an ecology of our inner freedom and to define the external conditions that might be favorable or unfavorable to it.

MATTHIEU From the point of view of the search for inner freedom, our physical environment and the people we keep company with—at least for the beginners that we are—have a considerable influence on our inner state, on our feeling of freedom or servitude.

7

The Physical Environment Acts on Our Mental State

One day when I was in New York with Rabjam Rinpoche, the abbot of Shechen Monastery, we were in the middle of Times Square, a place famous worldwide for its concentration of theaters, movie houses, and big stores. The facades of the skyscrapers are covered with immense advertisements in lights, announcing shows that are playing as well as touting various drinks and things to eat.

Rabjam Rinpoche contemplated the hundreds of multicolored signs flashing on and off around us, and with a thoughtful air he said to me, "They're trying to steal my mind!" Quite clearly, this was not a place conducive to inner freedom.

In the Himalayas, instead of huge signs like "Drink Coca-Cola" on every street corner, we see mantras on the mountainside, like the Buddha's compassion mantra, formed out of lines of innumerable white stones. The hills are covered with flags with prayers printed on them, "May all beings be happy," which the winds blow in all directions.

—Matthieu

MATTHIEU   Places have characteristics that influence our mental states and, by extension, our search for freedom. Though seasoned meditators know how to preserve their inner freedom under any circumstances—from congested cities to the foothills of the Himalayas—we novices are better off not taking any chances and choosing a place conducive to contemplation. Our state of mind will not be the same in a chaotic, noisy, dirty, or seedy place as it will in a harmonious spot where all we see and hear favors inner peace. In the beginning we are too weak and vulnerable to be able to make something constructive out of unfavorable external conditions. Therefore it's necessary to take the time to cultivate our psychological strength in an environment that facilitates this kind of training rather than making it more difficult.

Propitious Places for Our Inner Life

MATTHIEU   The Tibetan teachings describe the characteristics of places favorable for spiritual practice as well as those that hinder it. Certain locations and psychological environments reinforce our mental poisons: aggression, lust, pride, and other emotions that trouble our minds and obscure our judgment. It's a good idea to avoid such places, and that includes avoiding social and familial situations that are marked by tension and conflict. We should also make sure that the elements necessary for survival (water, food, shelter) are easily available. It's better to avoid places where we are constantly preoccupied by potential dangers or anything else that might interrupt our practice, especially armed gangs, bandits, dangerous animals, floods, and landslides. The point is certainly not that we should seek out coziness and comfort, but rather that we should avoid external difficulties that might hinder our efforts.

These teachings also describe the characteristics of places that are favorable for particular practices. When the aim of practice is inner peace, *shamatha*, we should look for forests or other sheltered and secluded spots where soft, subdued light rests the mind and calms one's troubles. In such a place the air is filled with soothing scents.

If we wish to cultivate vast and penetrating vision, *vipashyana*, and meditate on pure awareness and the nature of our mind—a practice centered on clarity and the luminous aspect of mind—we will choose elevated places, where the air is fresh, that look out over spacious landscapes and have a clear view of the sky. The luminosity of snowbound landscapes is favorable to this state of mind.

On the banks of rivers with swift currents and loud rapids, mental fabrications are reduced to silence. If we are training to gain mastery over our strong emotions, we will look for places with lots of ups and downs, such as gorges and ravines, which intensify our mental states. If we are trying to cut ego at its root, cultivate detachment with regard to worldly preoccupations, and meditate on impermanence and death, practitioners in Tibet would go to "sky burial grounds," which are places in the mountains where corpses are left to be eaten by vultures.

We will avoid polluted places where the atmosphere is heavy and unhealthy; places that foster greed, lust, anger, and jealousy; and places where conflicts arise easily, where we are constantly preoccupied with promoting our interests and outdoing rivals, and where we give ourselves over to nonstop activity. To the extent that we can keep away from such places, mental disturbances diminish. The mind becomes clear, serene, and self-controlled—confident in the appropriateness of the lifestyle that has been chosen.

The Tibetan texts also describe in precise terms places that are suitable for the establishment of a monastery or a contemplative retreat center. The ideal spot faces south, is completely open toward the east—toward the rising sun—as well as to the south. There should be a slight elevation to the west and a higher mountain to the north—that is, behind the monastery. It is good to have a river flowing from east to west in the valley and for this valley to contain scattered low hills, like heaps of jewels. It is undesirable, on the other hand, to have a chain of mountains to the front, with a peak rising above them like a menacing tooth. Thus, we should choose the place for our spiritual practice with discernment.

In more prosaic terms in the modern world, if you happen to have an alcohol dependency, it's best to choose a spot where there's nothing to remind you of the bottle. If you are obsessed by women or men, you will avoid beaches populated by Venuses in bikinis or well-muscled Adonises. Protected environments will give you the space to cultivate more resilience in dealing with your dependency; they will not compromise your still-fragile training by confronting you constantly with whatever triggers your desire. These "guiles of war," as my father wrote, "obey a common principle: flee those situations in which reawakening the beast is inevitable."

ALEXANDRE   During my Korean escapade, I tried to swap a hyperactive life for a slightly more contemplative existence using the means at hand. I tried orienting my daily life in a more practical direction. Quite early on, I noticed that the external setup did not have such a big impact on my quality of presence, on my inner availability. It seems that no matter what place we flee to, we lug our pots and pans and our traumas and wounds along with us. It's very rare for our inner phantasms to leave us in peace.

Right in the middle of Seoul, in the midst of the skyscrapers and markets, there is a Buddhist temple called Jogyesa. All day long women and men come there to recite prayers, to practice in the middle of the tumult of the big city. Their wisdom, devotion, and compassion convinced me I should transform any place and any moment into a mini inner retreat. Meister Eckhart urges us to open ourselves to God in all things and to see Him continually in our minds, in our intentions, whether we are in a church or a monastic cell. At Jogyesa, I enjoyed contemplating the lotuses and water lilies that usually grow in the brackish waters of certain swamps. Nothing, no circumstances whatsoever, can prevent us from thriving.

In the Korean forest, where I did a retreat, I got a full dose of solitude and privation. Doubtless there are rats in the fields and rats in town. Some prefer the desert for communing with their fundamental nature; others find the road to peace in interactions with others. In short, cut off from the telephone, without internet, in the midst of the trees and raccoons, I found that the inner life follows its own cycles; it progresses in a way that has nothing to do with hurrying and pushing. The danger is to try to force-deliver peace with a forceps, to constrain ourselves, to dream of ideal conditions when in the end we can meditate anywhere, even at the foot of a skyscraper.

CHRISTOPHE   Yes, we can meditate anywhere, especially if we are experienced, but it's more difficult when you are a beginner. In any case, being able to meditate from time to time for a prolonged period in a peaceful and inspiring environment can certainly deepen one's practice. It's easier to practice, in any case, and that's the advantage of "good" environments. They are no substitute for effort and skill, but they do make life easier and help us to go further. For me personally, it has been during prolonged periods of meditation, immersed in nature, where I have most often experienced profound peace, existential fulfillment, or clarity of mind.

It seems to me that what we could call a favorable physical environment has three characteristics: beauty combined with harmony, calm, and at least a minimal dose of nature. This dose of nature seems vital to me. I remember one day attending a cremation ceremony for a friend. We were all seated in a big hall with no religious symbols, a simple and sober room, devoid of charm. Suddenly the wall we were facing lifted away to reveal a very large picture window that looked onto a small garden, a pond, and the vast blue sky above. I still remember the feeling of peace and solace I felt deep within me when these natural elements appeared. It was as though my grief was eased by this connection with nature. I remember saying to myself, "All that was there before we were and will be there after we're gone. Being born, living, and dying is simply the order of things." I felt at that moment that I needed the message this connection with nature offered; no mere architectural environment, no matter how good, no matter how harmonious, would ever have this effect on me.

Conversely, an unfavorable physical environment deprives us of these three elements. It is ugly and crude; it is noisy and artificial. Many urban environments, unfortunately, are that way. They are an assault; they are hard on us. So then we immediately withdraw into ourselves (many city-dwellers take refuge in their earbuds and screens) and we are stressed, obliged to stay on the alert, on our guard. We have to watch out not to bump into anyone on the sidewalk and not to get run over crossing the street. All the energy we expend in this kind of environment is self-centered. It is turned inward for the sake of protecting ourselves, not directed outward toward opening and discovery. We are on the defensive; we lose the lightness, freedom, and well-being that we get from beautiful, secure, and nourishing environments.

But what should we do if we are city dwellers—if we are condemned, so to speak, to submit to these kinds of environments most of the time?

Many city people dream of being able to go off and live closer to nature, and some do. But most make do with going to more natural places as often as possible, and that's why we have huge migrations on weekends and times of vacation! Taking part in these migrations is legitimate because the benefits of being exposed to nature last far beyond the actual time we are able to spend in nature.

The Proven Benefits of Contact with Nature

MATTHIEU We are attracted to natural places, and it has been proven that they are favorable for our physical and mental health. Caring for all living things and appreciation of natural places with a rich diversity of forms and colors has been called *biophilia,* a concept developed by the biologist E. O. Wilson. Researchers have shown photographs of various landscapes to inhabitants of the five continents. The photos they all most appreciated were those that depicted vast, lush savannas with lakes scattered here and there and small wooded hills. This preference was even held by Inuit peoples, who perhaps had never seen such landscapes. Lush plains and lakes evoke a sense of abundance and provide conditions conducive to survival. Contemplation of such landscapes brings most of us a sense of harmony and security.

Another study demonstrated that after a surgical procedure, patients recuperated better and faster if their hospital room had a view of a natural landscape (parks, ponds) rather than of buildings. Patients who had a natural view left the hospital a day sooner on the average than those with a view of buildings. They had less need of painkillers and were calmer and more composed.

In a town, our perception of our own human scale is reduced. Our evolution formatted us to compare ourselves to the size of trees, rocks, and other elements of the natural landscape. In another study, researchers monitored the physiology of city dwellers, using bracelets that constantly transmitted data and by questioning them. The scientists observed that as passersby were walking in front of a long facade made of concrete or frosted glass they felt less emotion and tended to become somewhat sullen.

They quickened their step in order to hurry up and get out of this dead zone. By contrast, they were much more animated and alert when walking down a street lined with commercial booths, restaurants, and stores. When they walked through green zones—for example, an avenue lined with trees or that bordered a park—their emotions and moods became much more positive. The most appreciated towns were those that made people feel good rather than those in which people were just in a hurry to get through.

Several disturbing studies show that growing up in a city doubles the probability of children developing schizophrenia as adults and increases the risk of other mental problems, particularly chronic depression and anxiety disorder. In children, the thickness of the gray matter in certain areas of the brain is reduced. So it is important to renew our contact with natural environments, to increase or preserve green areas in cities, and to develop architecture that is more human in scale.

CHRISTOPHE　On the whole, if we want to follow the recommendations of the many scientific studies you just mentioned, Matthieu, what we have to do is design our cities like groupings of small villages or small neighborhoods, making sure that each one provides people who live there or who pass through them with the "nutrients" that our brains and bodies require: shops and small businesses for a human presence, areas that are calm and green and have benches where people can relax and interact with each other, sidewalks that are wide enough so that we don't have to be constantly on guard (especially older people) and can be at ease walking on.

The other problem in cities is the interference or destruction of the place's human quality by international companies. Take, for example, the big-brand firms that do home delivery rather than opening stores because it's more profitable. These companies sell goods at lower prices than in brick-and-mortar stores, often by avoiding the sales tax. By causing shops to disappear little by little, these companies cause city centers to lose a whole network of places where people can socialize. Another example, as perverse as the first one, are the chain stores that do indeed provide convivial meeting places but use them for their profit. Commercial malls are pleasant places where there are bits of nature in the form of green plants, spots where you can sit or walk without worrying about your children being run over by a car, and social areas where you can meet with friends and chat. But as soon as you enter the mall, you are pushed to consume and spend. And without extreme vigilance, we are certainly tempted to do so.

A study done in poor, outlying areas of cities in the United States showed that fast-food restaurants were the only convenient places for socializing outside the home. They are heated in winter and air-conditioned in summer, so they are somewhat pleasant and comfortable. However, the food people are given to eat there makes them diabetic and obese, which leads the authors of the study to conclude that the epidemic of obesity in the poorer social classes is not so much their weakness of will as the fault of social locations that provide them with comfort and poison at the same time.

This is certainly ecology we are talking about here—the ecology of toxic environments that push us, without our realizing it, in the wrong direction. If all these people could benefit from public gardens and communal vegetable gardens instead of fast-food emporiums, no doubt the epidemic of obesity and type 2 diabetes (which is connected with excessive weight) would not be as big as it is.

MATTHIEU   Another study shows that twenty minutes of walking per day does not bring the same benefits in a city as it does in the country. People are no doubt going to call us back-to-nature freaks or tree huggers nostalgic for some golden age. But whatever they say, it's definitely true that there are environments that stress and destabilize us, whereas others are conducive to calmness and equanimity.

CHRISTOPHE   These studies are very interesting because they put us on the track of the mechanisms that explain the benefits of natural environments. Why is walking, which is a beneficial activity, *more* beneficial in a natural setting, given that the physical effort involved is the same? Because in nature there are no billboards, no aggressive sounds, no incessant attention interruptions. Our mind can live its life quietly. It is free to reflect, wander, imagine, and so on, with tranquil continuity. In an artificial or urban environment, there are devices expressly conceived to capture our attention, either to protect us (car horns, light or sound signals at pedestrian crossings) or to trap us (ever-more omnipresent advertisements). We are no longer comfortably enjoying our inner life. We are in a state of reactivity, no longer enjoying freedom but in servitude, paying attention to what we are being shown rather than choosing what we would like to look at.

ALEXANDRE Nietzsche, who was burdened by illness throughout his career, taught that the question of the climate and place we choose to live is an essential one for our "greater health." Moreover, the philosopher warns against "having lead in our asses," a veritable sin against the Holy Spirit that, according to him, inclines us toward having prejudices. I get a kick out of his telling us to sit as little as possible, to nourish our ideas in the great outdoors, to keep life moving. In his eyes, the choice of food, climate, the place we live, and the means we choose for recreation are crucial. Although we always carry our unhappiness with us, there are perhaps terrains that are more conducive to dispelling it.

We are also a body, a physiology: muscles, nerves, passions, desires. Believing ourselves to be independent of the environment — thinking that we can skip out on nature — is surely shooting ourselves in the foot. Listening to you, my dear Christophe, I'm amazed to note that up until today, I have paid little attention to sources of stress. If you're pedaling with your head down, not looking where you're going, how can you *not* go over a cliff? How do we find the courage to slow down and identify the causes of our agitation and the places where we can rest? In the spiritual life, the danger of exhaustion is always lurking. That's why it's vital to know where the oases are, the places where we can relax and revive. In short, we have to open ourselves to the environment.

MATTHIEU We know that intensification of direct contact with nature has a major impact on the cognitive and emotional development of children. Observing nature close up, seeing the play of interdependence in the biosphere, observing how plants and animals survive, relating with each other, cooperating or competing, evolving, regenerating, and meeting often complex challenges is also a valuable form of learning, a valuable way to find solutions to many problems that we encounter in life. Children don't have this opportunity in the frozen universe of urban buildings. If today's children don't even know the names of plants, birds, animals, and fish, why will they appreciate them and desire to save them?

In *Last Child in the Woods*, Richard Louv asserts that children who live mostly inside are more subject to obesity and attention deficits because of the fact that they do not profit from the spiritual, emotional, and psychological advantages of being exposed to the marvels of nature, which promotes stress reduction, cognitive development, and cooperative play. A study from California reports that children who benefit from classes outdoors in nature have better scholastic results, greater competence in problem-solving, critical thinking, and decision-making. Time spent in a natural environment also stimulates creativity in children.

CHRISTOPHE Yes, data concerning the impact of regular exposure to nature on the brain are certainly not lacking! Looking at images of nature brings about increased activity in the anterior cingulate cortex and insular cortex (cerebral zones associated with emotional stability, altruism, and empathy), whereas the contemplation of urban views augment the activity of the amygdala (a zone that responds to emotionally aversive stimuli). Various studies show that contact with nature facilitates psychological recuperation after complex tasks; improves subsequent performance; reinforces vigilance, attention, and memory; and so on.

The mechanisms that produce these benefits are found in a variety of factors—for example, that our brain is sensitive to biodiversity, without our being aware of it. The sense of increased well-being we feel in nature is proportional to the multiplicity of plant species and bird songs. There again, this is logical. We have preserved an ancestral and unconscious memory of what is beneficial for us in terms of resources, in terms of both abundance and variety. The bird populations in our rural areas are in full collapse (60 percent fewer tree sparrows in the last ten years, a third of skylarks gone over the last fifteen years), not to mention all the other population losses, especially insects. This is obviously not good news—for the birds or us!

MATTHIEU When the three of us take walks, we never get tired of looking at nature. It's a constant, soothing source of wonder. The great

Buddhist masters all have praised wild places as being propitious for spiritual practice. The eighth-century monk Shantideva, in particular, writes that forests, animal, birds, and trees are ideal friends who never gossip or engage in malicious talk. He spoke of getting himself established, mind free from all distraction, in a hermitage in a cave or at the foot of a tree, having for his sole concern to gain mastery of his mind and let it rest in its original nature. In the great open spaces of Tibet, by the side of a lake, by the ocean, on a mountain from where your view is almost infinite, meditation practice feels just as good on the outside as inside. And we do not have the feeling that in meditating we are swimming against the current because of an environment that is hostile to concentration and inner peace. We can open ourselves entirely to the surrounding milieu instead of trying to protect ourselves against it, as would be the case in a noisy city or an apartment situated on a major thoroughfare, where you have to unplug the phone, the television set, even close the windows, if you want to enjoy a moment of tranquility. When we are caught in a vortex of chaotic activity, we end up losing control of our inner vehicle.

In nature, everything around us inspires us to meditate rather than discouraging us. Tranquil places provide continuity and regularity that are favorable to spiritual practice. Personally, at the beginning of a retreat I find it quite positive to know that I have a certain number of days, weeks, or months—even years—ahead of me that are going to be dedicated to spiritual practice, and that I will not be subject to interruptions all the time.

Toolbox for Creating a Favorable Environment
MATTHIEU

Find your oases. If you live in a city and you have to stretch your neck to get a glimpse of a bit of blue sky from your window, how do you find an oasis in your life, in space, in time, and in the midst of other people? It would be a pity to give up your aspirations for serenity and calm because you are not so fortunate as to live in a hermitage in the bosom of nature.

That oasis could simply be your home. Without offending or disturbing your family, stay somewhere in your home by yourself for twenty minutes.

You can also go to a park. Sit down on a bench, and collect yourself for a moment.

On public transport, instead of reading a magazine, you can close your eyes (the other passengers will think you're dozing) or gaze into an undefined space with your eyes half-closed. This is the way to take advantage of moments considered to be lost time to compose yourself or meditate. In this case, you can almost say that your body is a hermitage and your mind the hermit.

Create an awareness practice. If you have to walk in the street for fifteen minutes every day, try to maintain awareness of the space you're passing through instead of letting your mind drift elsewhere.

At work there are always short breaks. Instead of cultivating constant interaction, you can take a moment to collect yourself. At the Pasteur Institute, I had a small office, five meters square. After lunch, I would close the door and sit quietly for fifteen minutes. We have to appreciate the value of such moments.

CHRISTOPHE

I'm careful to remind myself regularly of the necessity of the "invisible nourishment" that comes to us from natural environments: pure air, gentle and regular sounds, gradual changes, calm, slowness, continuity. We should offer this nourishment to our brain and body as often as possible.

Take time to immerse yourself in nature if you live far from the city (contemplative walks or outdoor meditation sessions) or in the nature bubbles of our urban parks if you are a city dweller. Try this at lunch hour, for example, several times a week. It's better to take the time to walk in the park than to shut yourself up in a crammed and noisy restaurant. (You can always mindfully eat a brown bag lunch sitting on a bench.)

During work breaks, above all, no screens. To clear your head, just get up, stretch, walk over to the window, take a few deep breaths, and watch the sky and the clouds.

Even when it's only every now and then, immersion in nature is always beneficial. Studies show that, for example, a two-hour walk in the woods continues to benefit our immune system for more than a week (compared to no walk at all or a walk in the city). So no weekends without an excursion in a natural setting, in the woods, the countryside, the mountains, or along the shore!

Be an activist. *Ecology* is not merely a matter of profiting from the benefits of natural environments; it also means acting to protect them in order to preserve our ecosystem of living beings. Whether this is in our garden or on our balcony, it means no insecticides, no weed killer. On our excursions, we shouldn't litter, and we should pick up anything that inconsiderate people have thrown on the ground (always carry a small plastic bag with you). We should put pressure on those we elect to public office to protect the natural spaces near where we live and also to create new ones. Or we could get elected ourselves in order to carry out such programs!

Pay attention. We should take the time to observe what state the exposure to natural spaces puts us in, to breathe, and to notice how natural spaces change the state of our body, thoughts, and emotions. The more attentive we are to these benefits, the more motivated we will be to make them thrive and to let them help us thrive.

ALEXANDRE

Let us dare to cohabit in solidarity without closing the doors on anyone. Let us gratefully explore every nook and cranny of our great house; let us watch over our natural habitat with respect and compassion! Because without altruism, without generosity, this little shanty of ours could easily end up resembling—to paraphrase philosopher Arthur Schopenhauer—a tavern full of drunkards, an asylum full of lunatics, a den of thieves. Ecology requires a gentle subversion: you have to do whatever is necessary for solidarity to triumph and truly to leave no one behind.

A quick glance at the place we live in can prove immensely fruitful. What is cluttering up my house? What in it is useful to me? What is a saving grace for me? What genuinely nourishes me? What's the point of piling up stuff if I don't know how to enjoy what every day brings me?

Without falling into obsessiveness and spiritual materialism, devote yourself to the physical and mental gymnastics that your being requires.

Take care of the mechanical side; lend an ear to the needs of the body, this wonderful instrument that serves us day after day—but don't over-load it. Take care of your mind so it is not polluted all day long with resentment, hate, and the sad passions. In short, take action so that there is lots of circulation in your life. And why not, for example, disconnect yourself for a while from the social media and instead form some real relationships with your actual physical neighbors, with passersby, with some real flesh-and-blood people?

8

An Ecology of Relationship

I suppose, my friends, that you have gotten very nice mail from readers, accompanied by totally anonymous little gifts (a book, a paperweight, a jar of honey, etc.) without even a return address that would allow you to send thanks. Sometimes maybe it's an oversight, but more often, in my opinion, it's a simple wish to express gratitude for our work accompanied by a desire not to burden us by obliging us to reply or by asking to meet us. I'm always very moved by this approach.

And among human beings, there are many such people. For example, there are "do-gooders," people who do good for others anonymously, such as employees in a company who help colleagues in trouble, boost morale, and take care of everybody. People who in the anonymity of big cities smile at people they don't know, talk to beggars, stop spontaneously to offer help to people who look like they have lost their way. The omnipresence of these do-gooders, who are much more numerous than we think but are so discreet that we forget about their existence, is a major part of what makes life in society possible and makes life more beautiful. These human beings do good for us without directly addressing us, just like pure air does, the blue sky, nature, flowers, the laughter of children, the beautiful things."

—*Christophe*

MATTHIEU   It's true, some people reassure us by their presence. They make us feel calm and good by a kind of positive osmosis. Even if they don't seem like anyone special, it is good to be with such people, who are real exemplars. With them, we feel neither domination nor constraint. We are at ease with them. And, in fact, this ease is very close to a kind of freedom.

By contrast, other people make us feel uptight and uncomfortable through their attitude, their posture, their behavior, and their actions — even without saying anything. They constantly give us the feeling of being on the brink of conflict. Being around them forces a tenseness of mind on us. This state of permanent semi-alertness wears out our composure and shrinks our freedom of being.

The same thing is true for social environments. In businesses or offices, the atmosphere can sometimes be tense, tainted by the irritability or arrogance of some people and the forced submission of others. It's an unhealthy environment. By contrast, in a monastery or a retreat center, the members of the community are careful not to create disturbances, to reduce frictions, and to respect the peace of all. Everyone is aware of the fact that each person needs space, time, and comfort. Thus a community, by its very presence and qualities, can hinder or promote our inner freedom.

How Others Facilitate or Hinder Our Freedom

CHRISTOPHE   It is indeed amazing to see how the mere proximity of certain people is enough to influence us without their speaking to or interacting with us. It seems to me that in the ecology of social relations, there are three levels: the level where relations manifest in the form of interactions; the level where mere presence is enough, even without interaction or speech; and the level where relations exercise an effect on us even from a distance.

This last one — influence from a distance — is what happens to me when I spend time by myself, far from Paris, in order to meditate or to write. I might not see a soul for days and days, but I know that my family and friends and my readers are there, at a distance — that I am thinking of them and they are thinking of me. That reassures me and makes me feel good.

This level also accounts for the joy we sometimes feel at knowing there are people on this earth who are doing great things, carrying out just actions. That makes us feel good (influences our emotions) and inspires us (influences our motivations), even though we've never met these people. The fact that they exist and belong to our human ecosystem is enough! On the other hand, for victims of violence this is painful. Knowing that the perpetrators are out there and at ease, even at a distance—and especially if they have not been named, exposed, or punished—is a source of suffering, instability, and obsession, and therefore a limitation of inner freedom.

However, there is no doubt that the influence of physical presence is still greater. We all have people in our environment who nourish us and others who stress us out. Even if we don't speak to these people, we observe them, listen to them, see them living, and we feel saturated by what they embody: lightness and freedom when they embody joie de vivre, altruism, attentive listening, flexibility (anything that feels meaningful, positive, and inspiring to us) or cramped and limited if these people convey egoism, a tendency to contradict others, or talk without listening.

In my work with my colleagues, for example, even if I'm not directly involved I am sensitive to positive people—people who always go in the direction of "yes," who find solutions, who simplify things. Others, however, put a damper on things, especially those who find fault, argue, or start off by saying "no" or "It's impossible." Even if these pain-in-the-neck people are sometimes basically right, their way of going at things is a drag, sterile. They activate unpleasant emotions in us that consume energy we would rather devote to finding solutions and moving forward. Instead, we work our butts off disengaging the mental emergency brake of people around us!

But it's important not to judge. These people have not chosen to be pains in the neck. What if we began with empathic listening, rather than doing a "reframing" job on them and reminding them of our needs and views? By trying to be more tolerant with them, we can also remind ourselves that if biodiversity is good for our health, a certain amount of psycho-diversity is too. Learning to be with people different from us—whose opinions are sometimes the opposite of ours—is a good exercise in mental flexibility and openness of mind. Just as adversity causes us to make more progress in working on ourselves than success does, we often achieve more personal growth by accepting, listening to, and examining the arguments of those who contradict us than by only talking to friends who agree with us.

MATTHIEU   It's not that difficult for me to relate to people who have a worldview or a lifestyle very different from mine, especially if I know that we are only going to be together for a short time—in a work relationship or on a trip. I don't want to infringe on their way of being and am ready to talk about our differences if they're interested.

On the other hand, if people insist as a mark of friendship, respect, or trust that I perceive things the way they do and react to people and situations the way they do, *that* becomes very difficult for me. This happens, for example, with pessimists who are offended if I don't share their vision; with people who feel I'm not supporting them, especially in public; or if I don't evaluate others and situations or react the same way they do. It's quite a strain to keep these sorts of people satisfied. It would mean constantly having to be different from who I am. Such people exhaust our resiliency resources because they force us to keep doing things reluctantly.

CHRISTOPHE   It's the question of the expectations others might have of us. People who can't tolerate contradiction or who require continual signs of attention or affection do indeed limit our freedom and our spontaneity. It's up to us to see how much we can give them. It's normal to take into account the fragilities and expectations of our family and friends—and even acquaintances or anyone else we're talking to—and make an effort not to cause them too much suffering. But at some point this becomes too burdensome, for us as well as for them, and these accommodations only sustain them in their foibles.

MATTHIEU   Some people also show us by their behavior what extreme approaches we should *not* follow. People, for example, who think only about signs of external success and prosperity, about their image and reputation, who are obsessed by how they feel and also by their physical appearance. The extent of the inner disaster they put on display makes them very instructive negative models.

CHRISTOPHE   That's a constructive way of looking at that! When people irritate you by their way of being, tell yourself to take them as negative models! Human beings need real-life models in order to learn and make progress. Inspiring models are people who embody and further the values we hold dear by their way of being. And the inspiring negative models are people who walk all over these values or uphold others that seem toxic to us. In dealing with them, let's do our best to put Spinoza's famous teaching into practice: "I have striven not to laugh at human actions, not to weep at them, nor to hate them, but to understand them."[1] As best we can, while limiting our negative thoughts and emotions, we should understand and learn in contact with these negatively inspiring people. And let's not be too smart about it! I like La Rochefoucauld's maxim: "Unless we have no faults, we should not take such pleasure in discovering them in others."[2] I've often observed this in myself. When I'm working to be more generous, I more easily notice the stinginess in others; if I'm working in the area "be more optimistic and enthusiastic," I more easily notice the pessimism of others.

MATTHIEU   You can also consider the negative models as unintentionally benevolent people who show us the path to freedom when their behavior is the very illustration of what we ourselves should refrain from or do away with in ourselves. These negative examples provide us with the tools we need to progress and with the encouragement to eliminate our own faults, including impatience. It's quite nice of them! We can also wholeheartedly wish for them to be liberated from their foibles and superficial views.

Friends in the Good

ALEXANDRE   In the Platform Sutra, Hui-neng refers to "friends in the good," a brilliant formulation that reminds us that we cannot achieve liberation all alone in a corner, that we actually have to open to each other, give of ourselves to each other, encourage each other, support each other, offer each other a helping hand. This spiritual relationship, this inner companionship, has two major characteristics, as I see it. First, it requires unconditional love that does not judge and unfailingly and tirelessly supports the person bearing the load as far as its own strengths permit. At the same time, far from being indulgent, it invites friends to surpass themselves, to go beyond themselves, to tear themselves loose from the thousand and one fatalisms that could bar the route. Hui-neng, like Aristotle, sees in friendship a complicity that makes the other better. Unfortunately, as Seneca said, the relationship to the other is often only a transactional matter, which ends when it ceases to bring profit or advantage.

As you remind us, Matthieu, even the coldest and most uncouth person can serve to set us on the path to freedom. But how do we tolerate the frictions and misunderstandings that come along without letting ourselves be wiped out or used up by them? As a good Stoic, Epictetus provides a path for us by urging us to prepare for the pains of life: he advises a person who is going to the public bath in ancient Greece not to lose sight of the fact that he is likely to be splashed and taunted and, in short, is bound to experience a good dose of stress. The exercise is simple: try to keep your composure and inner freedom intact in the midst of these inevitable vexations, and understand that they are part of the decor. If your relationship with others is distorted by selfish interests and calculation, spoiled by a thousand expectations, it is hardly surprising that you wind up in the end with disappointment and bitterness.

Rather than collecting and accumulating friends in the good, we can ask ourselves—without playing the hero—who we can really help in our life. The big question of the hour is this: Whom can I help and support today?

MATTHIEU There are all kinds of friends in the good. Some of them are our traveling companions on the spiritual path. Within the framework of a spiritual process, they play a crucial role. For example, in a *sangha,* a term which literally means "virtuous community," every member can have a constructive influence on the others. So if you are tempted to behave in a way that contradicts your ideals, your traveling companions will help you stay on the right course. It's a little like mountain climbers on a rope together: when one climber slips or stumbles, the others help him, but without reproaching him. Each in his place provides the others a helping hand so they can get back up and continue with the climb.

I used to sail in my youth, and my experience was that there's nothing worse on a boat than people who don't get along with each other because you are stuck with them for the rest of the voyage. On the other hand, if you all share the same values, the chances are good that the expedition will arrive safely at its destination and your memories will be good.

Other friends in the good are the anonymous heroes of compassion: the millions of benevolent folks in national and international nongovernmental organizations (NGOs), in neighborhood groups, and caregivers of whatever stripe—with the proviso that their only goal is alleviation of other people's suffering, not status or medical acclaim.

In short, friends in the good are those who share the same values; who are open, patient, flexible, and enterprising; who are considerate of the feelings and opinions of others; who are competent without being arrogant.

This is true on the spiritual path as well as in life in general. Keeping company with friends in the good will help us develop our good human qualities. But if we associate with people who behave in an unethical manner, there is every likelihood that their toxic attitudes will rub off on us.

When Others Make Us Suffer

ALEXANDRE   A thousand questions come up here. Why do relationships with others so often make us suffer? How can we get ourselves out of the mess of projections, misunderstandings, and disappointments that arise? Can we protect ourselves against these things? In short, is it possible to have harmonious relationships without the torments, without the conflicts that make a heart heavy?

If Aristotle was right, if we are eminently political creatures who attain happiness communally, then we are obliged to conclude that our relationships do not automatically fall in with this scheme. Sigmund Freud, in his book *Civilization and Its Discontents*, paints a picture that could make shivers run up and down a person's spine. He identifies three major causes of our suffering. First, there are the forces of nature, which can unleash earthquakes, tsunamis, natural catastrophes; they all conspire to condemn us to quasi-permanent uncertainty and insecurity. Then there is the frailty of our body, whose decline advances inexorably day by day in the direction of our inevitable death. And, finally, the father of psychoanalysis tells us that the inadequacy of the institutions that govern human relationships causes profound suffering. Everything seems to be in league to spoil our lives. This is why it is vitally necessary for us to work toward harmony. We must make ourselves the artisans of peace and eliminate all the mental poisons that transform communal life into a veritable ordeal.

Philosopher and playwright Jean-Paul Sartre reminds us of the hardness of other people's looks, the weight of their judgment, the danger of reification and labeling. Is it destined to be, as he said, "Hell is—other people!"?[3]

MATTHIEU Personally, I think hell is egoism, being shut up in oneself, and indifference toward others.

CHRISTOPHE When a relationship with another person is making us suffer, the questions we have to ask ourselves go in two directions. First, in this suffering, how much is due to me? As you were saying, Alex, are some of my expectations and projections excessive? If I expect from someone more than he or she can or wants to give me, I am the one manufacturing my suffering.

Second direction, second question: What is coming from the other? For a long time when dealing with relationship difficulties, therapists always turned patients back on themselves and their own problems: "If the other person is making you suffer, it's because that's what you're looking for or what you're letting happen, and maybe you even like it!" (Entirely unconsciously, of course! Because the unconscious cannot say, "No, no, definitely not!" it's the ideal guilty party.)

But we have come to recognize that there's also such a thing as toxic people, toxic "others." I'm not even talking about deviants or people with other kinds of psychological profiles who intentionally want to hurt us or exploit us or who get a kick out of getting the better of us. Rather, some toxic people who make us suffer actually suffer themselves from personality problems recognized by psychiatry. We speak of personality problems when psychological suffering expresses itself as disturbed relational attitudes: a narcissist's pathological egoism, a paranoiac's pathological distrust, the abandonment anxieties of a dependent, a sadist's enjoyment of other people's suffering. The incidence of such people in adult populations is reckoned at about 10 percent. Generally speaking, such people complicate everything rather than simplifying, cause stress rather than pacifying, take rather than give. As a result, they necessitate major efforts of adaptation on our part. There are three possibilities: either we avoid them whenever possible; we "reframe" their approach to us (in other words, we don't try to change their personality—that's the job of the therapists—but we try to change their behavior toward us); or we put up with them (in the long term, that takes its emotional toll).

ALEXANDRE   Thanks to you, dear Christophe, I understand that in a relationship, we can be completely off the mark on both sides without there necessarily being an executioner and victim. Often two clueless losers embark on an adventure that is completely beyond them.

One day I opened up to you, Matthieu, about my emotional dependency, and you gave me a fantastic image that was oh so liberating: in the company of certain persons, we end up being like nails or scraps of metal that when placed near a magnet have no choice but to undergo an almighty, irresistible attraction. There are two solutions: Try to transform inwardly so as to cease being influenced by, Scotch-taped to, or bolted to the object of attraction, thus putting an end to the infernal magnetism. Or in the meantime, practice the art of the detour, keep your distance, or even leave the scene altogether.

In my case, the addiction began that famous day I've spoken to you about, on which a friend who had called me on Skype opened the door of his bathroom. This revealed a silhouette—legs, arms—in short, a being who seemed to have a certain effortless capacity for life. I was immediately magnetized by this body that was revealed to me in the nude. It was the embodiment of my dream, a body unimpaired by any handicap. Fascinated, I wanted to become this fellow who was so solidly made, so at ease in relation to life. For months at a time, I remained glued to this magnet. Every day at 3:00 p.m. sharp, I saw my idol again. I was sinking deeper and deeper into a kind of hell. The unconditional love of those close to me—my family, my friends in the good—as well as a few rather unorthodox measures, finally yanked me out of the abyss. The monopoly of this lethally toxic relationship had to be busted. So with a sense of death in my soul, I visited a few webcams, dared a few encounters. Today, I recognize the mechanism: scorn toward one's body, traumas, wounds—they all conspire to project our deficiencies, our neuroses, our wounds onto the other.

CHRISTOPHE The logic that allowed you to liberate yourself from this obsession is the same logic that makes it possible to surmount our fears. We have to say to ourselves: "Stop retreating. Stop submitting to your chains. Go forward and go into the fear to find out if the dangers that it seems to threaten you with are virtual or real." This is the only way to make contact with what is real and to free yourself from what is only virtual.

MATTHIEU Your problem was idealization of the body; we've talked about it. The body is what it is. If I visualize myself for years in the form of Mickey Mouse rather than Matthieu, it won't do me much good. In Tibetan Buddhism, we take a different approach. Because we have buddha nature within us, in order to facilitate recognition of this nature, we visualize ourselves in the form of an archetype—the Buddha of compassion, for example. The point here is neither to superimpose on reality an idealized and artificial vision nor to manipulate one's image as with Photoshop in order to look more beautiful, younger, and wrinkle free, but rather to enter into contact with our fundamental nature and visualize ourselves in a form that is in harmony with this nature.

ALEXANDRE Along with meditation, it was your happy distinction, as I said, that got me out of hell. Thank you, Matthieu. Let's say it again: The zones of the brain connected with pleasure are fickle, transient; they run after every new novelty. By contrast, the mechanisms responsible for desire are more hard core, more tenacious, really tough as leather. Of course, those Skypes left me with no joy. And once I had this tragicomic episode behind me, I was able to get closer to a kind of detachment and freedom.

Without a doubt, you have to go through a lot of twists and turns to actually reach freedom! Chögyam Trungpa, after the fact, clarifies my journey for me: "[T]he ultimate meaning of passion is communication, making a link, relationship. So there is a kind of open space, the possibility of communication."[4] Opening to the other without anybody getting their hooks into anybody, loving without hating oneself—that is the challenge!

The Power of Relationships and Their Maintenance

CHRISTOPHE The benefit of relationships with others is not only the subjective side, not just a matter of emotional well-being—even though that's already a lot. A number of studies have tried to evaluate the concrete results of relationship. On the biological level, for example, when a person is subjected in a laboratory to a stressful situation (improvising a speech in front of an audience made up of people with disapproving expressions on their faces), their level of salivary cortisol (a stress indicator) is lower if just one of their good friends is also in the room. But relationships also change our vision of the world and of the difficulties we have to deal with. An amusing study shows that when volunteers are asked to estimate the height of a mountain, the mountain appears less high and its slope less steep if a good friend is with them. If they are alone, the mountain looks higher to them and the slope steeper.

MATTHIEU This reminds me of something that happened in Nepal, where my hermitage is. Two years ago a tigress with two cubs was sighted nearby several times. One evening, I heard her growling about a hundred meters from me. I was returning to my hermitage after having paid a visit to a lama about five minutes away. My blood froze in my veins. A few days later, I was going along the same path, also around nightfall, with another person. Although even two of us would have been no match for a tigress, we felt completely safe.

CHRISTOPHE Other people are a very precious resource for us! When I meet my patients for the first time, I always take stock of their resources. When we speak of "a person with no resources," we usually think of material resources. That is, of course, important; money doesn't necessarily bring happiness, but in our society it is a good stress reducer that makes it possible not to worry too much about daily material concerns. But there are also the resources represented by relationships. These are essential! Isolation—that is, solitude that one is subjected to rather than solitude one has chosen—is a big risk factor for people's health, both mental and physical. Not having people one is close to, not having a network of friends and acquaintances one can count on, makes one fragile when problems come up. That is why as a young psychiatrist I was very interested in socially phobic patients who, in addition to the anxieties they felt relating with others, were people "with no relational resources," whose condition, as a result, often became dire quite quickly. Conversely, having a large and varied social network (family, friends, acquaintances) is a source of resilience and well-being confirmed by all the studies.

MATTHIEU Studies have shown that a having a set of quality social relationships is good for our health, increases longevity, and diminishes depression and the risk of dementia, as well as consumption of addictive substances. This means having good relations with people we can count on, from whom we can ask advice, or who have the ability to comfort us; but it also means manifesting friendship and concern toward others. A poll carried out by the Organization for Economic Cooperation and Development (OECD) showed that, among ten factors contributing to well-being, the quality of human relationships was the most important. (Monetary income came in sixth.)

ALEXANDRE No doubt the preconception that human beings are *causa sui,* self-made men and women, is very tenacious. But between the extremes of being fully self-reliant and merely being used, we move back and forth quite a bit. One thing that definitely ruins relationships is self-interest, calculation. We run to others in the hope of gratification, reciprocation, solace. If that's the case, how can relationships counter our self-centeredness, enlarge us, liberate us? In *The Prisoner,* Marcel Proust says: "The only real journey, the only Fountain of Youth, would be to travel not toward new landscapes, but with other eyes, to see the universe through the eyes of another."[5] But it's just wacko to think that relationships free us from attachment or that they remove our blinkers and open us to the world.

CHRISTOPHE That's another thing it's important to remember. There can be frictions and discord of all kinds in social relationships. The mark of a functional human relationship is the capacity to mend itself, not being in a permanent state of agreement. We have to be able to express differing views and even disagree. This is also the difference between a living relationship and a dead one. Something alive is something that can heal itself, scar over. That's why the capacity for reconciliation, or sometimes forgiveness, is so important. It's not a question of principle—that peace is better than war—it's a question of survival. If we're not capable of tolerating disagreements or outright conflicts, and then of repairing the relationship afterward, we are impoverished. Contradiction is like food that might be bitter but is often very rich in nutrients; it provides ideas and points of view that our minds could not produce on their own.

That's why attention to maintaining our relationships is very important. I recommend this strongly to my patients, even though I'm not necessarily a great example myself.

It's important to take into account the notion of relational appetite to adjust our personal user's manual to our own optimal level of social bonding. For example, I am an introvert. (So sorry to be talking about myself again, but I know that this will be reassuring for quite a few readers.) In psychology, introversion is defined as the need (and the pleasure) of being frequently alone and as intolerance toward an excess of social stimulation. Introverts are not necessarily misanthropes; they may appreciate other people but quickly tire of contact with them. They are quite happy loving others at a distance and don't feel the need to keep checking in with them to make sure they feel appreciated. Thus, we could define introverts as sociable loners: people who like both contact and solitude but in a ratio of 20 percent social time and 80 percent solitude. The needs of extroverts are the opposite ratio: 20 percent solitude and 80 percent social time. It's up to each of us to evaluate our needs in this matter and to adjust our relational ecology to these needs.

The Power of Example

MATTHIEU The Tibetan texts speak of certain qualities or "powers" of a spiritual master. Here the notion of power is not synonymous with authority or constraint but rather refers to a manifestation of enlightened compassion that allows the master to guide the disciple in the best possible manner. To be able to teach, masters must be capable of identifying the various aspirations of their disciples. Especially they must know if disciples aspire to enlightenment in order to acquire the ability to bring about the benefit of others or if they are concerned only with their own personal liberation. Qualified masters can discern the faculties and mental dispositions of disciples, especially the preponderance in their mind of certain negative emotions, as well as their predisposition to a life of contemplation and compassion. Thanks to their experience and their inner realization, such masters can also gauge the progress of disciples and see the obstacles they are facing.

In order to truly benefit others, these sages must have cultivated the boundless compassion that allows them to accept unconditionally all individuals just as they are, with their lights and shadows, with the sole motivation of helping them to extricate themselves from suffering and its causes. In essence, a qualified master — man or woman — must have mastered the teachings of the spiritual tradition they embody, attained profound inner realization, and be filled with compassion toward all beings without exception.

For all these reasons, it is crucial not to trust yourself to a master until you have minutely examined him or her — first from a distance, by getting information from sources who know the teacher, and then from close up, by verifying that the opinion you have formed conforms with reality. It is even recommended to wait several years and to follow the master's teachings before giving him or her your entire trust. Putting yourself in the hands of an unqualified master is like taking poison.

All the same, not everyone who causes us to advance in the realm of inner freedom is considered to be a sage or spiritual master; some people give us lessons in life through the power of their example. These are people who have behaved in an admirable manner or have shown great strength of mind. Anne-Dauphine Julliand, for example, whom we met during a session of Les Journées Émergences in Brussels.[6] She lost two marvelous little girls, who died from a genetic disease. Her courage and strength of mind in dealing with this trauma make her a very inspiring example. We have so much to learn from such a person.

Closer to me, I also see such an example in my sister Éve. Stricken very young (at the age of forty-three) with Parkinson's disease, she teaches us courage with simplicity, constancy, and dignity by confronting this trying disease, from which she knows she will not recover, and maintaining an exemplary attitude toward her affliction: "I know I have a disease, but nevertheless I am not this disease, and I never will be. I let go of what is letting go of me." There are times where she doesn't feel well enough and tells us that it's not the best day for a visit, but she never acts or speaks with ill humor, even when she's exhausted.

Such examples illustrate the connection between wisdom and freedom. Wisdom consists in knowing what we can change and what we cannot have any effect on, and in placing obstacles and tragedies in a greater perspective that takes into account the potential existing in human life. Freedom is the courage not to be floored by adversity and to find in ourselves the resources that permit us to live a rich and constructive life. We are thus liberated not only from events themselves but also from the destructive impact that they can have on our zest for life and the joy we find in it.

CHRISTOPHE Role models are figures of wisdom. They are not necessarily masters with a teaching, but they are humans who manifest extraordinary qualities in certain areas or at certain times. This phenomenon is much more frequent than we imagine. To draw nourishment from their example and their concretely expressed teachings requires that we awaken our capacity for admiration. Being able to admire is good for us. Admiration of noble human behavior helps us feel what researchers call a "sense of upliftedness." Psychologist Jonathan Haidt studied this phenomenon in his laboratory. He showed that when admiration is directed toward moral acts (deeds of altruism or tenderness) and not toward performances (athletic, artistic, or intellectual), it stimulates our parasympathetic nervous system (which relaxes and soothes us) and provokes secretion of oxytocin, a neurotransmitter that increases our sociability and our capacity for friendship and affection for others. Admiration inspires us, makes us feel good, and makes us more sociable.

MATTHIEU Celebrating the good qualities of others and taking pleasure in their accomplishments is also an excellent way to grow and develop ourselves. Taking pleasure in others' accomplishments is an antidote for jealousy.

With a spiritual master, we move a level higher. Sages inspire us not only through a particular aspect of their being, but also through the totality of their intellectual and spiritual human qualities, their knowledge, and their way of being. They are a perfect reference point for wisdom, altruism, ethics, consistency, and inner freedom. Moreover, an authentic sage will manifest these qualities at all times and in all circumstances, in private as well as in public. My two main spiritual masters, Kangyur Rinpoche and Dilgo Khyentse Rinpoche, behaved in the same way toward a humble farmer as they would with a king. The same is true of the Dalai Lama, who treats hotel service staff members and heads of state in the same humane way. Finally, in the case of a spiritual master, these good qualities must prove themselves in the long term. "Do what I say, not what I do" is simply not applicable. The perfect consistency of a sage imparts unshakable confidence in his or her integrity. In short, this is not a case of a charming facade tainted by shabby behavior behind the scenes.

In a number of Himalayan Buddhist cultures, the sages are still at the heart of society. People don't respect them as they would a potentate, but they show them admiration and devotion. People are attracted to them naturally, like bees to flowers, even though the sages don't seek to attract them or keep them as retainers. A spiritual master is one who confers inner freedom, not a tyrant who tries to control our existence for personal profit. The spiritual master has nothing to lose or gain but everything to give.

CHRISTOPHE   The question is, why are these "sages" no longer at the heart of our societies? Given all the benefits they offer us, it is regrettable that regular contact with persons wiser than ourselves is not more often presented as something beneficial and desirable. The sages bring together competence and compassion, and this cocktail is a helpful one. People who have mastered an area and are also compassionate are not afraid of being replaced. They have only one aspiration: for people to be happy and advance on the path, even surpassing them.

ALEXANDRE   Where are our guides, our reference points? Who governs us? Is it the dictatorship of "they," the belief in or the law of the market, blind egoism, unbridled individualism? Just asking this question is already taking a big step in the direction of freedom. Always there is the call to become what we are deep down, to stop being fascinated by illusory models, by idols, so we can humbly turn away from the state of self-alienation.

In daily life we continually encounter masters of humanity. Caught up in panic, I like to contemplate these privileged beings, these super-beings, who live beyond anxiety. Apart from the philosophers who nourish and sustain me, there are my friends in the good—witnesses who everywhere and always attest to the goodness of life. Opening oneself to social connections means going back to school and allowing oneself to learn, to be touched. Every day brings its lessons. A smile in the subway, an attentive ear, a hand offered—all these are teachings and occasions to unlearn our defense mechanisms and advance nakedly into interaction.

Roman emperor Marcus Aurelius began his *Meditations* by recording what he received from people close to him, his parents, from the gods. Why shouldn't we in our turn engage in this exercise in gratitude so that we can see how others create us, nourish us, dwell in us?

Toolbox for an Ecology of Relationship

CHRISTOPHE

For this toolbox I'd like to put forward a little bit of theory about how we are supported by relationships—that is, to offer an overall look at what we receive from our relationships with others.

The five benefits of relationship. Studies show that social support can be broken down into several families of benefits:

1. *Material support*: Others can help us in concrete ways. If I've broken my leg, I will be glad if somebody will do my shopping for me. If I have to move, I will be happy to have my friends help me transport the boxes.

2. *Informational support*: Others can advise us, give us useful information, and play the role of human search engines—as intelligent
as Google but alive and compassionate—and they won't resell our
personal information afterward.

3. *Emotional support*: Others are the source of positive emotions;
they give us affection, love, friendship, trust, admiration.

4. *The support of esteem*. Others can remind us of our value and good
qualities, tell us what they like about us, and sustain our self-esteem
at moments of uncertainty.

5. *The inspiration of their example*: This is more difficult to evaluate
scientifically, but it's quite real, as we have indicated.

The four varieties of relationships. Another important point is that it
is helpful to cultivate varied social relationships, just as it is important to
have a varied diet. There are four families of relationships, distributed in
four concentric circles:

1. *Our intimates*: the people we live with, whom we touch and
embrace practically every day. This means mostly our family and
best friends.

2. *Our close relations:* our friends and colleagues, people with whom
we regularly have close and regular exchanges.

3. *Our acquaintances:* the whole network of people with whom we
have a connection, even occasional, and who we keep track of and
who keep track of us.

4. *Unknowns:* those who we might also have relationships with, depending on our character. This includes people we might speak to on the
street, on public transport, in stores. They can also be sources of help or
information for us, as we can for them.

Specialists in social relations remind us that it is important to draw support from these four circles—not only from our intimate and close
relations—and to sustain our connections with these four relational
spheres by giving and receiving help, information, support, eye contact,
advice, and smiles. Because the idea is not only to receive but also to

give, by speaking to unknowns and maintaining warm relations with our acquaintances, neighbors, and shopkeepers, we do ourselves good. And we embellish the world, improve it, and make it more human!

MATTHIEU

The importance of social connection. We should choose to live in an environment where people are warm, altruistic, and compassionate. If this isn't the case in all areas of our living space, we should progressively try to establish these values or, if it's possible, we should leave the toxic environment.

In this connection, I like to cite the case of a community on the Japanese island of Okinawa, which claims to have one of the world's highest concentrations of people aged a hundred or over. It appears that the main factor in this exceptional longevity is not the climate or the food, but the power of this community, where people maintain particularly rich social relationships. From cradle to grave, they relate very closely with one another. The elderly people in particular get together several times a week to sing, dance, and have a good time. Almost every day they go to schools to greet the children (whether they have familial links with them or not) at the end of the school day. The elders take the children in their arms and give them treats.

Draw inspiration from the righteous, from people who, in our eyes, embody the values of impartiality, tolerance, compassion, love, and kindness. In these times of the migratory crisis, I think of all those who have taken great risks, and I remember those who protected Jewish people during the Nazi persecutions of World War II, particularly those who hid Jews in their homes. These people have since come to be called "The Righteous." The only common point that emerges from their many accounts is a view of others based on recognition of their common humanity. All human beings deserved to be treated with kindness. Where we see a stranger, they saw a human being.

Meditate on altruistic love. Studies in psychology have shown that meditating on altruistic love increases people's feelings of belonging to a community; it enhances the quality of social connections and compassionate attitudes toward unknown people, while at the same reducing discrimination toward particular groups, like people of color, homeless people, and immigrants.

Draw inspiration from friends in the good and spiritual masters. I recommend that everyone see a historical documentary made in India by Arnaud Desjardins at the end of the 1960s, in which we are shown the most respected of the Tibetan masters who took refuge on the Indian slopes of the Himalayas following the Chinese invasion of their country. The film is called *The Message of the Tibetans*.

ALEXANDRE

The audacity to live. Existing, opening oneself to the other, is running a risk. It means dropping one's armor, one's protective coverings, and opening one's eyes and daring to give oneself to the other and to the entire world. There's no way you can invest in a relationship, so throw out your logic of profit and loss! What if we were to embark on our day without any idea of gain or of using our fellow human beings? What if we stayed attentive to all the women and men it is given to us to encounter on that day, looking to find among them masters in being human?

Identify our profound aspirations. Helping others can often amount to imposing a view of the world on them without really paying any attention to what they really want in their hearts. A man bought an elephant without giving any thought in advance to how he was going to feed it. At a loss, he was obliged to turn for help to those around him, and what he got from them was, "You never should have bought such a big animal!" What does it mean to help others? Does it mean committing completely to being there for them? Does it mean going all the way with them?

Authentic compassion. A will to power might enter into our movement toward the other—a thirst for recognition, a twisted attempt to redeem ourselves. Daring a true encounter means quitting the sphere of your neurosis and walking the path of freedom together. There's no more "me," no more "you," but a coalescent "us," a primordial solidarity.

Coming out of the bunker. As a result of having been burned in our relationship with another, the temptation is great to put on armor, to completely shut ourselves up in a bunkerlike fortress, even to the point of suffocation. Don't our passions, our griefs, our loves, and the fierceness of our desire remind us that we are essentially turned toward the other, in perpetual communication? Is there a way to live the thousand and one contacts of daily life without our ego appropriating them?

9

The Impact of Our Cultural Environment

Coming out of retreat, a friend of mine drove his car gleefully onto the freeway. It was a beautiful day. The sky was magnificent. Life seemed to be his apple. He was far from the heaviness of mental poisons, unburdened by the machinations of ego.

He paused briefly at a service station, and as he was filling his car with gas, a voice blared from behind him: "Hurry up, asshole!" In a fraction of a second, he was smacked by aggression and violence.

Within the pungent medium of everyday life, with all its ups and downs, is where we have to learn to stay joyful, lighthearted, and loving. What a contrast between the kindly, calm universe of retreat and daily life, which is often like a jungle! This is where work on oneself takes place. Are the vexations of daily life a gift from heaven? Could they constitute the royal road on which ego bites the dust, where our stupefaction ends, where we cease to be caught up in some idealized world, in remote concepts?

—Alexandre

MATTHIEU There are many definitions of "culture," but specialists in evolution conceive of it as a body of information that affects the behavior of individuals belonging to a particular culture. This information includes ideas, beliefs, values, attitudes, knowledge, and skills. Instinctive imitation, for better or for worse, contributes considerably to the evolution of cultures. Conformity to norms is encouraged by communities, whereas nonconformity brings disapproval and various forms of sanction that are potentially disastrous for those who are the object of them. Certain values and beliefs confer greater chances of survival as well as greater chances of elevated social status. When different cultural groups enter into competition with each other, some flourish and others decline.

Culture Shock

MATTHIEU People don't act the same way in a monastery as they do in a casino, a department store, or a football stadium packed to the gills with overexcited fans. Studies have shown, for example, that people vote differently on ethical questions depending on whether the polls are set up in a church or in a school, without really being conscious of the influence exercised by the place they are in. Voters were assigned by lottery to one place or the other. The persons assigned to vote in the church were more likely to support a conservative candidate and voted for a smaller budget for reimbursement of the cost of contraceptives. Those who were assigned to vote in a school voted in larger numbers for an increase in education funds.

CHRISTOPHE Yes, and what's interesting is that these influences often work on us without our realizing it. We aren't aware of them or we pay no attention to them. They often manifest in unobtrusive or subtle ways. All cultures make use of three kinds of influence: *direct influence* (through education in schools, political propaganda, advertising); *indirect influence* (through the behavior of the people around us, for example, or through objects or images); *deliberately concealed influence* (through manipulations such as lobbying the media or aiming internet data at users of social media designed to get them to change their votes or their purchases).

These three families of influence have the quality of being able to impact our thoughts, our motivations, and our decisions. Thus, it is essential to know about them so you can learn to defend yourself against them. Information and education play a crucial role here.

The Factors That Alienate Us

CHRISTOPHE   Personally, I'm struck by studies on what is called "priming" in experimental psychology. They show how the arrangement of small, apparently harmless details in our environment can change our behavior. This process can be used for good purposes, as in the case of what are called "nudges." You know the famous example of the Amsterdam airport, where they arranged false flies at the bottom of the urinals so that users would make the effort to aim carefully. This improved the cleanliness of the restrooms and reduced how often they had to be cleaned. Another example: in the self-service snack area in a business, they diminished the risk of freeloading by putting the photo of a face giving you a direct look above the box where you're supposed to put your money.

But that can also work in a less desirable way—for example, with money, whose presence modifies our behaviors in a number of ways without our being conscious of it. There are a lot of studies on this subject. In one of them, volunteers are separated into two groups. The first group is subjected to a technique that activates the subconscious of the subjects on the theme of money. In concrete terms, the subjects are asked to perform a series of small exercises on a computer. The content of the exercises is not important, but they are intercut with images of banknotes on the bottom of the screen. In the second group, the subjects do exactly the same exercises, but the images of bills are replaced by flowers, tables, or other neutral images. The subjects of the second group are asked to sort pieces of paper in accordance with their size or the number that appears on them. But for the first group, the pieces of paper are replaced by banknotes that have to be grouped according to their value.

During the second phase of the study, the participants from both groups are gathered together in a room and are asked to solve some more or less difficult problems, with the added instruction that if they need help, they can ask for help from the other participants. The subjects who were exposed to the money images end up asking for less help from others, and when their own help is asked for, they give less advice and spend less time on it. When the examiner, seated in an easy chair, asks them after the test, "Come, sit down beside me. Bring your chair over next to mine, so we can talk a bit," the volunteers influenced by the money brought their chair less close to the examiner's than the members of the control group. Thus, the simple fact of being exposed to images depicting money makes us have less sense of solidarity with others and makes us more distant from them. And this lasts for some time after the experiment.

One of my patients, who works with taxes, had become hooked on comparative-shopping websites. Every time he wanted to buy something — a plane ticket, a pair of shoes — he compared the prices of the product online. He spent two hours a day on this. His mind was contaminated by the idea that he might get ripped off. Personally, I prefer getting ripped off to spending an hour searching for the best price, but I'm fortunate enough to be in a profession that doesn't force me to think about money questions all day, unlike my poor patient.

Another study on the problematic influence of excessive exposure to money showed that business-school students were significantly more narcissistic than psychology students in the same age group; they were also much more materialistic and attached to money. There's no point passing judgment on them: it's simply probable that the cultural values of a business school fosters this kind of attachment more than those of a university institute of psychology.

MATTHIEU The simple presence of a weapon sets off psychological processes that increase aggression. A psychologist gave volunteers the opportunity to get vengeance for insults made to them by someone (part of the experimenting team) by giving the insulter electric shocks (not real ones). In half the cases the experimenter also placed a revolver on the table, saying that it was going to be used in another experiment. The subjects in the presence of this weapon administered more electric shocks than the others.

CHRISTOPHE   Yes, a simple object can be all it takes to call up a certain number of attitudes associated with that object's cultural universe and with the meanings and values it carries. The same kind of study was carried out with mobile phones. Placing one on the table between two people was enough for their dialogue to be spoiled (perception of less empathy on the part of the interlocutor or a tendency to bring up subjects that were less intimate and engaging).

And then, beyond objects, there is the direct influence of advertising that targets our behavior. During the last few years, we have seen the proliferation of websites that promote adultery. It's amazing! On your bike, in your car, on the subway, you are exposed to all kind of inducements to deceive your spouse discreetly and with impunity! You go to a site, meet other married people who want to try out having an affair without getting caught, and, *bang*, it's all set up. These are urges that anyone might have, and it's not that that bothers me, but it's the commercial exploitation of it and the fact of encouraging it despite the obvious consequences and human tragedies that might result.

MATTHIEU   Advertisements touch people's weak points, arouse a temptation, and amplify it considerably.

ALEXANDRE   What can reason and will do against these hooks and sirens confronting us all over the place? How can we avoid falling into these traps when our environment urges us to consume, when our mailbox is crammed with ads for junk food? Roman philosopher Lucretius saw this clearly, even in his era when this plague of ingenious ads that excel in the art of seducing customers did not exist yet. He wrote: "The trouble is that, so long as the object of desire is wanting, it seems more important than anything else. But later, when it is ours, we covet some other thing, and so an insatiable thirst for life keeps us always openmouthed."[1]

CHRISTOPHE   Quite often, ads function because they insinuate themselves into the area of our authentic psychological needs, which they then burglarize. We aspire to happiness, and the ads promise happiness if we buy this couch (you see happy friends laughing on the couch) or this car (you see a happy family leaving on vacation in it), for example. However, we do not acquire happiness by buying these things, but rather a pleasure that is quickly gotten and quickly gone. The American researcher Robert Lustig, MD, tells us that these pleasures, linked with rapid consumption (video games, sweet foods, paid sex, shopping, social media, etc.) stimulate the secretion of dopamine, a neurotransmitter of pleasure, and lead rapidly to addiction. This is the supreme loss of freedom and the best way to turn your back on happiness, yet it is sought after. The same goes with ads for easy credit without conditions: "Buy today, pay tomorrow." We know that, in the end, these ads push the most vulnerable and impulsive people into debt. They make them buy goods or services that will lead them later to become more involved in commercialized pleasures instead of building their happiness tranquilly, as far as possible from the realm of commercial inducements. This is an enormous problem for social ecology.

What Are Our Cultural Reference Points?

ALEXANDRE   In order to develop ourselves and to help each other develop, we need role models more than reference points, beacons, and sources of inspiration. I was saved by books—the philosophers and writers—but also by a thousand and one encounters with people.

What do we devote our days to? What really nourishes our inner life? I turn on the television or surf the internet, and I end up with a flood of cynicism. And what can we say about the characters on YouTube, whose fishy magnetism takes possession of our brains for hours at a time? They make a singular contrast with the countenances of sages or the smiles of monks, with the prayer flags dancing in the wind that I saw in Nepal when I visited you there, Matthieu! Everywhere I looked, I perceived a gentle summons to inwardness—nothing to do with the advertising hooks or the half-dressed bodies and invitations to adultery you were talking about a while ago, Christophe. Nevertheless, I remain convinced that freedom can be gleaned in the midst of the tumult of this daily life we have.

MATTHIEU   The admitted goal of advertising and marketing, according to their founders in the 1930s, was to make us *desire and buy what* *we don't need* or to *create needs* to buy. You can get drawn into a state of compassion sitting in a department store, watching the customers magnetized by consumer items like children by sweets or moths by flames. Rather than looking down on them, we should arouse compassion toward them and wish sincerely that they will be able to free themselves from these illusory attractions.

ALEXANDRE   Society, the media, and social networks can convey very demanding standards that in the long term leave us drained, unsatisfied. How can we find our place without having to play Superman or Superwoman? Why do we have to be exceptional? Is it for fear of being rejected? Is it in order to be loved? What are the norms that hang over our lives? Do we absolutely have to distinguish ourselves from others, throw ourselves into the unbridled quest for performance? What do we place value on today? Devoting our whole life to others? Social success?

Here also, the call to wisdom has something subversive about it. Stop reifying the other, considering your relationship like a vulgar delivery of services, a quid pro quo, a transaction based on win-win. How can we learn to heed our inner compass, descend into ourselves, keep an ear out for some other voice than that of individualism?

The philosopher John Rawls proposed a thought experiment that could surely deliver us from parochial outlooks and blow away the myriad prejudices, favoritisms, and partisanships that keep us from thinking freely. And there's no need to adopt Rawls's values in order to try it. In *A Theory of Justice*, Rawls speculates how it might be possible to create a perfectly just social organization. He hypothesizes that legislators could make laws as though they hadn't a clue what conditions they themselves might have to live under in the future: "Tomorrow I might lose my job, get sick, have an accident." Burdened by certain baggage we carry, we instinctively think and vote to defend our personal interests. The philosopher encourages us to put aside our prejudices and interpretive biases, drop all rigid outlooks, and try to envisage other points of view. It is a highly liberating exercise to put ourselves in the place of others and visualize the walls that the most helpless among us are continually running into.

This is an ingenious invitation to take off our blinders and expand our view of the world, to do a grand-scale housecleaning and toss out the pile of labels that we judge everything by — other people, life, ourselves. Every society creates its outcasts and pushes people to the fringes. And there are many tyrannies that keep a lid on us: the dictatorship of norms, the despotism of ego, the weight of "what will they say?", conformism, and, in certain cases, anti-conformism. What we must urgently do is truly reconnect with ourselves and with others. We should disconnect ourselves a little from the turbulence and agitation that rages on the surface of things and dare some real relationships, devoid of quid pro quo and calculation.

MATTHIEU   It has rightly been pointed out that the hyperconnectivity of the social media can engender a kind of loneliness. What does it mean to have fifteen hundred "friends" on Facebook? This is certainly not what we usually understand by friendship. A sociologist commented that the media, bizarrely called "social," cause the individual finally to end up alone while being connected to a lot of other people. I remember a cartoon in a newspaper that depicted a high-rise building at night. Through hundreds of lit-up windows, you saw one person sitting alone in front of his computer "communicating" with someone else. It was a young man of sixteen, probably a big texter, who was commenting wistfully, "Some day, but certainly not now, I would like to learn how to have a conversation." We have gone from conversation to connection. Electronic exchanges are terse, fast, and sometimes quite blunt. Human conversations, face to face, are much more nuanced and subtle; you take the other person's facial expressions into account, their tone of voice, their bodily posture, along with many other factors that are conducive to empathy, with sharing of emotions.

It's undeniable that the social media provide citizens of the world with unprecedented potential to gather, to stay in touch with their friends, to escape the control of dictatorial regimes, or to unite their efforts for a noble cause. But these networks also become a display window for narcissism that permits everyone to draw the maximum amount of attention to themselves. The motto of YouTube is "Broadcast yourself." In the United States, some Facebook pages begin with the logo "I ♥ ME."

CHRISTOPHE   Unfortunately, all available data show that intensive use of social media is strongly correlated with emotional suffering, dissatisfaction with life, and symptoms of anxiety and depression, at least in cases of addictive, uncontrolled, high-dose use. The problem is that screens and social media also, quite obviously, have good sides to them.

Another subject of concern is that, in addition to compromising our inner freedom through the dependencies they bring about, the social media are a threat to our external freedom because of the collection and exploitation of personal data they enable. The revelation of the use of information drawn from social media for the purpose of influencing American voters at the time of the election of Donald Trump in 2016 is something we should remember. Every day the shopping behavior of tens of millions of consumers throughout the world is manipulated in the same way. It is important to expose and control these practices and, better yet, to get rid of them. Unnecessary consumption is more than mere accumulation of objects: it means devoting too great a share of our attention, of our mental energy and our values, to unworthy things. It means losing our freedom—materialism drives us to more materialism, consumerism to more consumerism—and thus, over time, losing our happiness.

ALEXANDRE   The thousand and one influences that remote-control us scramble our identity. Who am I? A docile consumer, a puppet, a marionette, a piece of straw carried away by the flood of the laws of the market, a beggar seeking affection? By way of breaking free from the tyranny of consumerism, one question comes up: To whom have I handed the remote control for my life? Who is holding the strings? As Renaissance philosopher Michel de Montaigne saw it, "The greatest thing in the world is to know how to belong to oneself."[2] This is the basis of a joyous ascesis, which makes it possible to free ourselves from our fetters, from roles, from masks.

Serene Simplicity

MATTHIEU   For some of us, the notion of simplicity suggests asceticism, an impoverishment of our lives. However, experience shows that voluntary simplicity is a source of profound satisfaction. Is it more enjoyable to spend a day at home with your children or friends, or to spend a day running from store to store or channel-surfing on your TV? Simplicity does not mean depriving yourself of what makes you happy—that wouldn't make any sense. Rather, it means letting go of the things that take you away from happiness.

Voluntary simplicity means a life that is outwardly simple and inwardly rich. A poll carried out in Norway showed that three-quarters of the people surveyed preferred a more simple life, focused on what is essential and necessary, over a luxurious life with many material advantages acquired at the price of an elevated stress level. Agro-ecologist Pierre Rabhi is of the view that a "happy sobriety" that moderates our need for useless things enables us to cease being suckers for the false attractions of consumer society and to once again make humanity our central concern.

The effects of consumerism have been studied by psychosociologists Richard Ryan and Tim Kasser. Their studies, covering two decades, have shown that the people who are most inclined toward consumption and who prioritize wealth, their image and social status, and various other materialistic values are less satisfied with their lives than those who emphasize the fundamental values of life like friendship, contentment, quality of experience, caring for others, and a sense of belonging and responsibility in relation to society and the environment.

CHRISTOPHE But it's hard to resist! We who are already old-timers and weren't born in this world of multiple stimuli can protect ourselves somewhat better. And yet how easy and enjoyable it is to buy tons of stuff on the internet, to yield to the "click" sirens by using your credit card. And if we find it difficult to resist, how much harder still is it for the younger generations!

MATTHIEU I'm thinking of a study conducted by the well-known psychologist Martin Seligman. It consisted in giving students a certain sum of money, then telling half of them to spend it on themselves for their pleasure—going to a restaurant, to the movies, having some ice cream, doing some shopping, for example. The other half were told to use it to participate in some philanthropic activity, such as helping old people, working at a soup kitchen, visiting sick children in the hospital. The results were conclusive: The students who did philanthropic things reported at the end of the day that they were happier, more enthusiastic, attentive, better liked, and more appreciated by others. Their degree of satisfaction was far greater than that of the students who had spent their time in the pursuit of hedonistic personal pleasures. Again, it is important to provide the kind of illustrative material that gets people to think.

Time Pressure and the Bystander Effect

CHRISTOPHE Among all the social influences that can modify our behavior and way of thinking and that can cause us to lose our freedom to act in accordance with our values and views is the pressure of time.

One experimental study, which is old by now but has become a classic, shows how time pressure can lead us to act in a way that is counter to our aspirations. This study involved theology students. They were asked to prepare a homily on the story of the Good Samaritan from the New Testament. This parable tells of a traveler who was attacked by bandits. He was beaten, robbed, and then left for dead on the side of the road. A first traveler passes by, then a second: neither stops. Only the third one, the Good Samaritan, takes the time to stop and help the traveler lying on the ground. The students were given the following assignment: "Study this text carefully and prepare a sermon, which you will then record at a studio a few blocks away." When they had written up their texts, half the students were told, "Hurry up, you're late! Get to the studio fast. Otherwise you'll lose your turn and won't be able to record!" On the route to the studio, the students passed a research assistant, who had been given the job of lying on the ground in a doorway and groaning like the mugged traveler in the parable. Two-thirds of the students who had not been put under any time pressure stopped to help the person. (I suppose the third that didn't stop must have been stressed by the prospect of having to record.) By contrast, only 10 percent of those in the group that was under an imposed time pressure stopped. One out of ten! And these were students of theology who had just been working on a parable about altruism!

MATTHIEU   In addition to the influence exercised by the pressure of time, a reduction in the tendency to provide help has also been observed when a great number of other people are present. When a person needs help or is in danger, the more people are there, the more one tends to say to oneself, "Why should it be me rather than somebody else who comes out of the crowd to help?" One hesitates to take the initiative and stand out from the others by offering help in front of everybody. A study showed that half the people who were confronted alone by an urgent situation (simulated in a realistic manner) stepped in to help, whereas this proportion fell to about 25 percent when two witnesses were present. This reaction is even more pronounced when there are numerous people present. This dilution of responsibility is also called the "onlooker effect" or the "bystander effect."

ALEXANDRE   Some authors try to explain the indifference, disinterest, and finally the absence of respect that lurk in us. In this regard, they talk about Bad Samaritan Syndrome. The Bad Samaritan, in contrast to his generous compatriot, does not stop when he sees a severely roughed-up guy on the side of the road. He continues on his way, doubtless having bigger fish to fry than lending a hand or providing support and help. It seems, as you said, Matthieu, that the group effect increases this coldness. The individual, absolving himself of the need for any effort, imagines that some charitable soul will step up and get the poor guy out of the mess he's in. It all happens as though in a group, in a community, our own responsibility is completely dissolved.

Recently a friend told me that, in his youth, he was shocked when he saw a person experiencing homelessness on the street. Nowadays, he is not surprised to see whole families sleeping on the sidewalk. How do we remain available and not delegate our commitment and responsibility to others?

CHRISTOPHE   Humans are a social species, but under the influence of overpopulation and time pressure, they may regress to a herd mentality. They are in close proximity to others but indifferent to them. This indifference is not a matter of freedom of choice or independence but rather profound regression and impoverishment.

How Social Environment Can Be Conducive to Freedom

CHRISTOPHE   What kind of social environment would facilitate inner freedom? Well, without a doubt it would be a milieu that strictly controlled all forms of incitement and manipulation. We realized that it was necessary to make laws limiting ads linked with alcohol or gambling, but we shouldn't stop there. The way advertising is astutely crafted to insinuate itself into the inner workings of our brains, called "neuromarketing," is clearly a problem for our inner freedom (we should be able to buy only what we need and not everything that's waved in front of our eyes and egos) and for our authentic well-being (the pursuit of happiness and non-addiction to pleasures).

Meanwhile, until these manipulations are prohibited or vigilantly restricted, all citizens should be educated on how to defend themselves. Some time ago, I participated in an experiment in high schools intended to protect the self-esteem of adolescents from the thinness craze and the unbridled pressure to have a physical appearance conforming with fashionable norms. We came up with an entire program to teach students how to read ads and understand their underlying intentions and lies. Along these lines, Radio France regularly encourages high school students to question information and its sources and to discern what is "fake news." More widespread programs of intellectual self-defense in the schools would doubtless help significantly to limit the dangers of the manipulation we are exposed to daily.

True, the task seems immense, but in view of the fact that people are spending more time in front of their screens than they are in nature, we can't help being wary of how much damage could occur if nothing is done.

ALEXANDRE   It's amazing what a terrific tool that could be: spotting the neuromarketing and having fun progressively deprogramming ourselves of the thousand and one conditionings that drive us to function in automatic-pilot mode.

Fundamentally, freedom requires constantly slaloming between the tyranny of "I" and the dictatorship of "they" — between the reign of whim or blind submission to "what will they say," to social pressure. It means becoming ourselves, joyfully and without forcing anything, while already knowing that we are men and women who are subject to influences. We are not born free; we become so. The critical mind, the capacity for empathy, and the ability to let go of one's convictions do not fall from the sky. I dream of a school that teaches tolerance and solidarity, that undermines stupidity and encourages dialogue, mutual aid, and respect. And believe me, friends, there's a lot of work to do there.

How do we break free from the determinisms of a society that is resolved to judge things according to appearances and, in so doing, consigns many people to the fringes? Why are there still so many ghettos, ridiculed handicapped persons, isolated old people, foreigners set apart, marginalized people being mocked? Working to make it possible for everyone to thrive and live happily is more than just a pious wish. It means fighting in a concrete way against discrimination, ceasing to bury people under a ton of labels, and daring to take a broader view of differences. Mental FM broadcasts fake news all day long; it dupes and bamboozles us. That's why it's necessary to develop tools for becoming oneself, for becoming one again with our true nature, which eludes all domination and remains infinitely free.

MATTHIEU   We can regain our freedom by simplifying our actions, our speech, and our thoughts and by avoiding letting ourselves be overwhelmed by time-consuming and distracting activities that bring us only minimal satisfaction. We should prioritize action—or non-action—that allows mindfulness of the present moment to stand above the current of time. Finally, we should take the time to renew our contact with nature in places where meditation happens outside as well as inside and where we do not have the feeling of having to swim against the current.

The Virtues of Humility

CHRISTOPHE   There is another risk that weighs on our inner freedom, that of misdirecting our spiritual aspirations. In psychiatry, we observe that many of our vulnerable patients find reassurance in the doctrines of sects that offer them promises of a simpatico environment here below and wonderful tomorrows in the beyond.

MATTHIEU   Nowadays, many people are tempted by à la carte religions that partly owe their success to their willingness to accommodate, even flatter, the ego instead of unmasking it. Particularly in the United States, celebrity evangelist preachers, far from encouraging humility, stir up people's narcissistic propensities. They sell T-shirts that say things like "Jesus loves ME." A well-known evangelist proclaimed, "God wants you to be rich." He himself provides an excellent example of this!

ALEXANDRE   Always in the air is the risk of taking ourselves to be the center of the universe and making the Most High into a tool, transforming it with our ego into a servant we can put to work however we like.

Speaking of "in the air," not too long ago, in a totally crammed airplane, a couple of believers cranked up their fervor and cried out to heaven: "O Lord, bless this flight and grant us a safe landing in Geneva!" A good precaution. But there was nothing in it at all about the millions of other people traveling throughout the world, zero concern for all those suffering on the surface of the planet. Why not include in our prayers all of humanity and all the planes in the world? Why not give our aspirations a universal perspective? We urgently need to leave our parochialism behind and relate to humanity as a whole.

Can we really practice religion for ourselves alone, retreat into our own corner without a care for how things are going for other people? Why the devil would religion turn in on itself? The great mystics forewarn us against any attempt to own our relationship with God, because it is very tempting to hang out in a kind of self-enclosed pseudo-security. God is not a milk cow or an insurance agent. You approach God with a pure absence of self-interest, with no idea of a quid pro quo.

In this connection, Saint Paul, in the Epistle to the Philippians, speaks of kenosis. For the believer following the example of Christ this means dropping the self—literally emptying oneself of narcissism, of egocentric desires, of all the roles we play ceaselessly from morning till night. In the Sermon on the Mount, Jesus proclaims loud and clear that the meek will inherit the earth. And what a magnificent example Saint Francis of Assisi is, never ceasing to preach and embody love and the giving of oneself without the least self-interest!

Without reducing it to a crude caricature, there's plenty of room for the faith that sets us free, that helps us get rid of our little "I," and that helps us to forget ourselves altogether and give ourselves completely to our fellow humans.

MATTHIEU Westerners are usually surprised to hear great scholars and contemplatives from the East saying, "I'm nothing special, and I don't know very much." They take these statements to be false modesty.

In the West, humility is sometimes considered to be a weakness and is even looked on with disdain. The American novelist and philosopher Ayn Rand, apostle of selfishness, didn't hesitate to enjoin us, "Discard the protective rags of that vice which you call a virtue: humility."[3] However, pride, the narcissistic exacerbation of the ego, closes the door on all personal progress, because in order to learn, you first have to admit you don't know. Humility allows us to recognize how much of the road remains to be traveled and keeps us from blowing out of proportion the few good qualities we have already attained. Humility is a forgotten value in today's world. We are encouraged instead to affirm ourselves, to put ourselves forward, to look good, to appear rather than to be.

ALEXANDRE We are not talking here about a sickly view of humility. This virtue has nothing to do with self-flagellation or the kind of self-loathing that sends us psychologically straight down into the third sub-basement. I like the fact that the etymology of this word—*humilis, humus*—is connected with the earth, with the direction down, with what is close to the ground. Being humble is thus looking reality in the face, keeping two feet on the ground, without undervaluing or overvaluing what is. We can safely say that this force opens up a genuine love of self, far from narcissism and the manic cult of the self. It helps us to integrate ourselves—our resources, our good qualities, but also our frailties and vulnerabilities—with what is. The paradox of spiritual life is enormous, because it requires us to take care of ourselves without making too big a deal of ourselves. It's a path along a narrow ridge road where at every step we might break our necks pitching down the slope of despair or perpetual self-disparagement or tumbling into the abyss of megalomania.

MATTHIEU   Free from hope and fear, humble people remain in a natural state of equanimity and don't worry about their own "image." Humility is thus a quality that is inevitably found in the sage. Traveling with the Dalai Lama, I have often seen the humility tinged with kindness with which he treats everybody. He is also present and attentive to everyone, both the humble and the great of this world. Once we were visiting the European parliament in Strasbourg and took part in an official luncheon that had been organized for about twenty delegation leaders of the European countries. When we entered the hall, the Dalai Lama spotted two or three cooks who were peering through the partly open kitchen door. Letting the representatives of the nations wait, he headed straight for the kitchens and spent a couple of minutes with the people working there. Then he returned to the long table where everyone was standing and waiting, and he exclaimed, "It smells great!"

CHRISTOPHE   Humility is also interesting because it is a form of freedom. It makes us aware of our limits and inadequacies, and thus we cease wanting to keep hiding them from others. Humility frees us from posturing and from obsession with social judgment because we are no longer trying to conceal our limits or make a point of them (as in false modesty). Our friend André Comte-Sponville has personally provided me the following definition: "The humble man does not regard himself as inferior to others, but he has stopped thinking he is superior." Through humility we withdraw from the self-promotion and race of the egos. We are quite aware that there are more things we are ignorant of than things we know, and we are much more interested in what remains for us to learn and discover than what we know already. Humility brings freedom from the ego in relation to social judgment and freedom of the mind—turning it toward the discovery of what it does not yet know rather than toward putting forward what it already knows.

And then humility has its significance in relation to materialism. Materialism wants to make us believe that we are perfect ("You're fantastic!" "Just be yourself!"), that there's an answer for everything and an easy solution for everything, without our having to make much effort. ("You have an urge to buy something? Just buy it and put it on your credit card." "You have an urge to eat lots of sweets, but you're diabetic? Well, just take some medicine that lowers your glycemia and eat all the sweets you want. They're so yummy!") If we listen to these siren voices that urge us to believe that we're free because we do whatever we want—when in reality, we're doing what *makes* us want—we will quite soon find ourselves in chains. Humility can also help us in this fight: We can say, "No, I'm not wonderful or exceptional; I'm normal, fragile, and manipulable, like everybody else. And I need to keep my eyes wide open in the face of flattery, especially when it comes from ads and addiction mongers."

ALEXANDRE The big challenge is to step beyond the cramped bounds of conceptual mind and one's inner cinema, which veils everything under a thick fog. Individualism, by its very nature, involves borders, enclosure, solitude—or to say it all in one word, *mega-isolation*. How could one not feel squeezed inside of that? How could I know real peace if I put up a big barrier between myself and others?

Here again, to get the bubble to burst, it's useless to stew in guilt, shame, and self-rejection. It's better to identify our persistent need for rewards, our inferiority complexes, and all the paraphernalia of our defense mechanisms. On that ground, humility would consist perhaps in offering a total welcome to all that I am. Doesn't Swami Prajnanpad advise the person on the path to accept that within us there is the worst of the worst and the best of the best?

Toolbox for a Cultural Ecology

CHRISTOPHE

Be vigilant. Let's never forget that we are developing within an ultra-materialistic society. As soon as we leave the woods and get into the city, as soon as we put down our pencil and turn to our screens, we become the targets of a host of multinational firms whose sole object is to make us buy or consume something. In this, we will never find happiness or meaning in our lives. And in this, we lose our freedom. On the street or on the internet, we are in polluted territory. Watch out!

Be aware. We should count the number of hours in our day that we spend in front of screens and then the number of hours we spend with nature—walking in it, looking at it, dreaming about it. Where are we with this? How can we regain balance here?

Safeguard our precious moments. We should never, never, never let mobile phones get between us and the good things in our life. When we take our meals, when we walk in nature, when we talk to those close to us, when we are with children, when we meditate we should put these devices aside or turn them off!

Do all kinds of fasting. From time to time, we should lighten up on tobacco, alcohol, sugar, and screens—or stop using them altogether. When the short time of feeling deprived is over, let's see what we get out of that, what it frees us from or how it makes us feel lighter.

Take back control. Let's turn off the alarm sounds on our devices. No beeps or red flags to signal a new text or email or any other new kind of message that hasn't come out yet that I don't know the name of right now. Let's take back our freedom. It's up to us when it's time to check our messages—at most two or three times a day.

Take an antidote. If we can't avoid being exposed to ads on the street, at movies, and so on that are unpleasant to us, we should repeat to ourselves mentally, "This ad is an attack. I will never buy this product." We should never swallow a dose of advertising without immediately taking the antidote.

ALEXANDRE

Guard against the effects of technology. Buying a mobile phone changes our whole relationship with others. What if we were to dare to disconnect for a while in order to reconnect with what makes us fully human: in-the-flesh engagements, culture, solidarity, inner progress?

Between relationships that nourish us and emotional dependency there can be an enormous space of freedom. We have not chosen to live on a desert island, so interdependence is the very tissue of our existence. That being the case, why try to armor ourselves against others when what saves us is unconditional love and radical openness?

Practice "happy sobriety." Epicurus teaches us the pleasure of living in order to dispel discontent and turn us away from the fantastical notion that would make us believe that racing ahead or accumulating brings complete happiness. He distinguishes natural and necessary desires (drinking, eating, philosophizing, seeking shelter); natural but unnecessary desires (sexual desire, eating refined food); and the desires that are neither natural nor necessary (the thirst for fame and glory, the need for power, the pursuit of wealth). This Greek Philosopher of the Garden was by no means the killjoy type, dishing out petty scoldings, or a heavy-handed moralizer. On the contrary, he was an authentic liberator who early on invited us to practice what Pierre Rabhi calls "happy sobriety." This marvelous expression opens the gate to a kind of freedom that perhaps constitutes the very height of subversion today.

Praise for humility, detours, and joy. There are a thousand paths that lead to detachment, freedom, and the abandonment of ego, and these paths may take many detours. Let us be wary of rigidity and all forms of uptightness. True ascesis is joy, lightness, relaxation, generosity, and tranquil descent into one's ground of grounds. Humility, that precious antidote, prevents pride from appropriating our desire for spiritual progress and shutting us up in sterile perfectionism.

MATTHIEU

Be content with what's necessary. Instead of running after what is superfluous, prioritize genuine friendship over friendship based on gain, the magic of freedom over symbols of "success."

Mute the complaints of ego, which says, "Why not me?" when it feels deprived and "Why me?" when it's irritated.

Understand that pride makes us vulnerable to the least failures and criticisms, whereas humility is fundamentally liberating from fear and the "What will people say?" attitude.

Don't place all your hopes and fears on external conditions. That way we risk continual disappointment.

Foster the inner conditions of happiness. They open up a horizon of possibilities for development and contentment.

Part III

efforts toward liberation

MATTHIEU Once we have a sense of the importance of inner freedom and have identified favorable conditions as well as obstacles, the time has come to make effort. We have to prepare ourselves as best we can. Then the important thing will be steadfast perseverance. The tempting promises of a secret of instant happiness are just smoke and mirrors. There is no secret: you have to spend time on it, and even then it's not easy. But it's definitely worth the effort!

CHRISTOPHE For many of us, there is something paradoxical in the association of the two words *effort* and *freedom*. We would be more likely to pair *freedom* and *spontaneity*, or *freedom* and *ease*. Defining the journey to freedom in terms of effort seems like a counterintuitive detour. It's like being on a hike and turning in the opposite direction of the one indicated by the compass because the only existing road requires you to make this detour.

MATTHIEU   Imagine an innocent person imprisoned by a dictator. To escape he needs intelligence, discipline, and perseverance. If he is resigned to just sitting there, he could rot in prison. Freedom is gained by the sweat of our brow. If we see this struggle as a laborious chore, we will end up getting tired of it. This effort must be accompanied by joy—a joy born of the certainty that we are heading in the right direction. This is where motivation comes in. Where are we going? Why? For whom? The answer to all these questions turns out to be our wish to become better human beings, to develop our strength of mind, our resilience, our compassion, for ourselves and for all beings. This is the motivation that permits us to persevere amid the ups and downs of our path to freedom.

10

The Horizon of Effort

One of my friends at Radio France, who is also a teacher at a school of journalism, told me one day that among her students, she preferred the "workers," the "drudges." When I asked her why, she explained that, as she saw it, this was the guarantee that later on they would become better professionals. The habit of working hard would make them more careful and patient than their more gifted peers, who might be more easily tempted by ease and speed. "My goal," she said, "is to train good journalists, committed to the truth, not brilliant editorializers inclined to aim for effect."

—Christophe

Why Effort?

CHRISTOPHE   If there's effort, it's because there's difficulty! If there's no difficulty, there's no need for effort. An effort is therefore a body of acts or thoughts that we set in motion in order to surmount, get through, or resolve difficulties, whether they are external (obstacles, adversity) or internal (laziness, negligence, pessimism, paralyzing worries).

To make efforts, we have to have good motivation upstream. And to maintain these efforts, it is necessary for them to be rewarded—that is, for them to produce results downstream—and for them to advance us in the direction of a horizon that we consider important.

MATTHIEU A goal, certainly, but one that we have to examine with care. We can have the ambition to become rich, powerful, and famous, and then be very disappointed twenty years later—all of our efforts having brought us not the least feeling of fulfillment. In fact, if we dash off without reflection, we risk becoming the prisoner of objectives that are scarcely worthy of our efforts. "The result derives from the motivation's intent," Buddhism tells us. We must ask ourselves, "Am I making these efforts for myself alone in a totally egoistic way? With others? For others? At the expense of others? Are all these efforts worthwhile? Will they bring me profound satisfaction? If I bring about the welfare of others, is it just for a few or for the greatest number? Long term or short term? Our intention determines the direction and magnitude of our enthusiasm.

ALEXANDRE Why do we decide to devote ourselves to practice? Is it a way to get away from the heaviness and pain of everyday life? Wouldn't trying to escape our condition be a vain effort? Do we really, truly desire to develop the immense potential that dwells in the human heart? Chögyam Trungpa warns us in no uncertain terms against the continual danger of using spirituality to try to provide ourselves with a life insurance policy. We have to stop being obsessed by the idea of obtaining some enlightenment or other, some gratification, something better. The point is to practice without any sense of quid pro quo, without any sense of investing in the future.

The essential point is to consecrate our effort and offer our practice to the greatest number, to others, for the common good. Attaining liberation is a process that goes beyond—far beyond—the limited framework of our personal projects. The ideal of becoming a bodhisattva, even if we're not always up to it, can illuminate our days and give some meaning to our relapses, to our journeys in the desert. I dedicate my joys and sorrows to the well-being of everyone. If I row hard, I do it also to provide support to all of my millions of fellow crew members who are in the same boat as I am.

CHRISTOPHE   Yes, all human life presupposes effort. And I sometimes encounter a snobbism of non-effort that gets on my nerves. Many people prefer to be considered gifted people rather than hard workers—even to the point of hiding their efforts—as though effort were opposed to talent, or as though talent made effort inapplicable. In fact, talent can be sterile or mere deception if it is not accompanied by effort.

We all know children or adolescents who are gifted at schoolwork and who, relying on their talents, don't do a lick of work and still pass from grade to grade until they reach the level of higher education. There, things usually don't go so well because they are confronted with material that requires some effort from them and by other gifted students who are more accustomed to making an effort. In addition, all creative people—artists, scientists, and the like—readily acknowledge that it's the combination of talent and effort that allows them to achieve success. This is what I like to call "fertile demand." Sometimes the need to make effort in the face of adversity, or simply in the face of difficulty, brings novel and delightful consequences that never would have come about through talent alone.

ALEXANDRE   In order not to get exhausted along the way, it's a good idea to lend an ear to Epictetus. He recommends that we should distinguish clearly between what depends on us and what doesn't. That's a piece of advice that should keep us from spinning our wheels meaninglessly and from risking running into a permanent obstacle.

Motivation

ALEXANDRE   On the sometimes slippery slope of the spiritual path, it might be a good idea to ask oneself: Who wants to practice? Who wants to make progress on the path, to attain liberation? Do we really leave the realm of ego when we devote ourselves, even with great sincerity, to practice? Isn't wanting to be a good meditator still the ambition of a state of mind turned back on itself? The Zen principle of "without goal or gaining idea" is truly an excellent guide for avoiding the lure of profit and gain, of the desire to be seen as exceptional, or to compensate for perceived inadequacies.

During a Jesuit retreat, a priest gave me very illuminating instructions summed up in some simple questions: What wholesome habits would you like to establish in your life? What habitual tendencies, what foibles in your everyday life would you like to get rid of? These words seemed like a call to identify the places in one's life where egoism, dependency, and akrasia rule— the thousand and one dead ends we stray into.

Where does our motivation come from? What drives us to jump into the swim? Is it a healthy, profound, and lively aspiration to embrace wisdom? Do the attraction of the carrot and the fear of the stick still hold sway in us? Finding out what drives us to develop and grow will surely allow us to steady our pace and envision the route in its full length.

MATTHIEU There is a balance to be found between tension and relaxation. The Buddha told the story of one of his disciples who was not able to mete out his efforts appropriately. "At times, I am absolutely not motivated, I'm completely relaxed, and nothing comes," he said. "And at other times I'm so tensed up that I'm not able to meditate." He was a player of the vina, a kind of sitar. "How do you tune your instrument to get the most beautiful sound out of it?" asked the Buddha. The musician replied, "I do it in such a way that the strings are neither too loose nor too tight." "It's the same with meditation," said the Buddha.

Being too loose can make the mind murky; excessive effort tires and agitates it. These two extremes are counterproductive.

Contemporary psychology speaks of a happy medium that is necessary in order to enter into a state of flow, defined by psychologist Mihaly Csikszentmihalyi as a profound absorption in action. Actions, movements, and thoughts follow one another in a fluid sequence; we forget the passage of time and fatigue, and self-consciousness disappears. To enter into flow, it is necessary for the task not to be too difficult; otherwise, tension arises. It also cannot be too easy; otherwise, boredom gets us. The fluidity of flow is felt as a very satisfying experience that gives the present moment its full value. One can also enter into flow without the support of an external activity. Contemplation of pure awareness—the nature of the mind, for example—is a profound and fruitful experience that is related to flow.

Here also the sense of self vanishes away, which is a source of inner peace and openness to others.

Thus, we have to find the right balance between effort and relaxation, which will allow us to make the best progress. Artists and artisans know well that a fevered super-effort risks ruining their work. "Patience leads to good, haste to nothing," says a proverb.

The Psychology of Effort

CHRISTOPHE Another important point about the psychology of effort is that its results can vary. In education, for example, the effort to teach our children this or that value (compassion, perseverance, honesty) can seem not to have any immediate results. The children continue to squabble, to give up when things get hard, to tell us fibs when it makes things easier for them. We then tell ourselves that our attempts at education are pretty useless, or that we are not going about it right, or we are not providing a good enough example. But quite often, the older the children get and the farther away they get from us, the more they surprise us by applying these good qualities and adopting these values in their lives, which they didn't do when we were on their backs, and maybe also because they simply weren't mature enough yet. We had a delayed effect! Even when we don't get immediate results, we have to make these educational efforts while they're children, without waiting till they're teenagers or adults.

What is sometimes painful is that we are not all equal with regard to effort. Some people lose their motivation because they have the feeling their efforts are futile and not sufficiently rewarded. They feel the speed of their progress is mediocre and everybody else is doing better. At that point, they might ask themselves if they have committed themselves to the right goals. Are they in the right field?

There are inferiorities that we do well to accept without a fuss, such as not running as fast as the others or not having as good a memory. Or if we do want to work in our chosen field, we should make sure we're not constantly comparing ourselves with others and that we're not stuck in the toxic states of envy or disappointment. Then we should stay concentrated on the progress we are making just in relation to ourselves.

MATTHIEU   Some people have more talent than others, but natural aptitude should not bring complacency. In the Tibetan world, teachers prefer a diligent student over a student who is gifted but nonchalant. But there's always room for change. Some people are very little inclined toward compassion to begin with, but in the course of life's ups and downs, they sometimes end up developing genuine human qualities. In the best cases, this transformation arises from a deliberate, considered, and wise intention. Experience has shown that, in the end, working hard on the spiritual path makes a considerable difference, even if people don't always start from the same point or end up at the same point. Training *always* bears fruit, simply because we have the capacity to change and because the brain has amazing plasticity.

It is vital to recognize this potential for change. Once again, training of any kind always produces results; it's in the nature of things. Having realized that, it's important to contemplate what the benefits of our efforts might be in order to decide what direction we want to orient them in. We should be clear: Do we want to learn to play tennis, play the piano, or cultivate inner peace and altruism? Choosing an inspiring goal generates enthusiasm. As we have pointed out, each step becomes joy in the form of effort.

CHRISTOPHE   There is something that has always struck me in observing the efforts accomplished by my patients, my family, or myself, which is that they are also a form of self-revelation. Learning to know oneself is not only a matter of introspection, but also of action and of everything that learning the results of our efforts is going to teach us.

Trying hard is rubbing oneself against reality and causing information to appear — information about ourselves, others, about whatever we're dealing with. This is particularly clear in the case of patients with phobias or avoidance behaviors. Out of fear, they carefully avoid confronting what they're afraid of. But in doing this, they are unable to comprehend that the danger is not that great — it is often even nonexistent — or that they have the resources to deal with it. Our actions transform reality and transform us at the same time.

In *The Journals of André Gide* there's a passage that I read and even copied down: "There is no more deadly doctrine than that of the least effort, the sort of ideal that invites things to come to us instead of our going to them."[1]

ALEXANDRE   In *The Care of the Self,* philosopher Michel Foucault calls on Seneca in showing the necessity of working on oneself: "He who wishes to come through life safe and sound must continue throughout his life to care for himself."[1] Humans do not come out of their mothers' wombs completely finished. True, there may be a narcissistic approach that gets us lost in vain introspection, but there also doubtless exists a means to free oneself from the sad passions and to drop automatic-pilot mode. In this area of effort, how do we arrive at the just balance between being fiercely strict and uncompromising and being totally lax and letting things slide altogether?

Effort and Letting Go

CHRISTOPHE   There's little doubt that some people commit the error of letting go before ever having gotten hold of anything in the first place.

Letting go, in fact, makes no sense unless it is an intelligent alternative to efforts that have turned out to be futile and fruitless, or in situations where the costs of the effort outweigh the benefits. After having worked in vain to solve a complex equation, there comes the moment when a scientist drops her work, takes a walk in the woods, and suddenly finds the solution. The same goes for the artist, schoolboy, or anybody!

An idealized image? Not entirely. Recent data on the functioning of the cerebral "default network," those parts of the brain that are activated and interact when we aren't doing anything, confirm that such moments of rest, when you let your brain idle, are especially important for our creativity. At these moments, our brain reprocesses all its data on what we have experienced and accomplished and interrelates them. But for the default network to have something to work on, we first have to have filled up our bank of experiences, ideas, emotions—and then we can let go. It's the alternation of periods of effort and periods of rest that proves most fertile.

MATTHIEU We know that IQ is very stable and that training this very specific type of intelligence hardly changes it at all. Some people's IQ is not very high; however, these people manifest extraordinary creativity or emotional intelligence and are quite successful in life. The American psychologist Scott Barry Kaufman was set apart in school because of his bad IQ results. Fortunately, he saw that he was very creative. By being very diligent, he became a neuroscientist, a specialist in the area of creative processes. His books *Ungifted: Intelligence Redefined* and *Wired to Create* explain that when one is creative, the zones activated in the brain during the process of creation are in competition with the zones concerned with focused attention. In other words, the creative state is one in which the brain is relaxed, loose, without fixation on one point or any predetermined subject. It's the state one might find oneself in the morning just after waking up or during a walk in the woods. This state is more conducive to the formation of new ideas than a highly concentrated state. Attention is present, but it is not focused.

In 2009, on the occasion of a Peace Summit in Vancouver, BC, I was participating in a roundtable discussion on creativity with the Dalai Lama, Sir Ken Robinson (a specialist in creative education), Eckhart Tolle, Pierre Omidyar (founder of eBay), and Murray Gell-Mann (Nobel Prize winner in physics). Eckhart Tolle mentioned a study showing that when kicking penalty kicks, soccer players who shot as soon as the referee blew the whistle scored less often than those who closed their eyes for ten seconds before shooting. They created a pause that allowed them to enter inside themselves and let inspiration come by itself—an elementary form of the creative process.

Robinson, with his British humor, chimed in, "I can visualize Eckart Tolle meditating for five years in front of the goal and missing the penalty kick." In other words, without thousands of hours of training, this creative letting-go would be in vain, whether it be in soccer or mathematics.

Murray Gell-Mann opined that in physics solving problems was neither the most difficult nor the most important thing. Real creativity consists in asking the right questions as well as in formulating new ones.

CHRISTOPHE That's what happens with the Nobel Prizes. If the prize is given for a discovery, and thus for problems solved, the committee of wise people declares every time that the discovery the award was given for "transformed its field" or "opened new and unexpected perspectives." That means that the discovery in question created new questions beyond the answers it achieved.

I remember an anecdote about Alan Hodgkin, a neurobiologist who won the Nobel Prize in 1963 for his research on the electric potential of nerve cells and his hypothesis on the existence of ionic canals, which was only proved ten years later. His students reported that every day he made the rounds of his laboratory and talked with the students and researchers. When he was shown the results of experiments of the previous day, if they corresponded with what was expected, he nodded his head and continued his round. The only way to get his attention was to present him with an unexpected result. In that case he would sit down, light his pipe, and think about what could be deduced from it. Like all good researchers, Hodgkin was much more attracted by efforts related to problems to be solved than by already-solved problems on their way to being confirmed.

Are We Headed Toward an Effortless World?

CHRISTOPHE At our ordinary, daily level, we have to ask ourselves some questions. We live at a time in which tools that free us from certain efforts are being multiplied. On the whole, that's a good thing. Not having to walk five miles to get potable water, having access to endless data on the internet, and not having to cross the city or the country to get to a university library—that's marvelous. But up to what point? Up to what point is what increases our comfort and economizes our effort really conducive to our happiness and freedom?

Take the example of having a GPS in our cars. If we use it all the time, we are no longer making the effort to memorize the places we pass through and the various possible routes. Does that increase our freedom? No—more likely it increases our servitude and dependence on this device. The day it goes on the blink, we're in a fix, less free than ever, very stressed, and very lost. Our freedom gain more by way of using our own brain rather than the brain of this device.

We have understood that we cannot totally do without physical effort and have therefore invented physical exercises that reinstate it in another form, this time more freely chosen. Doubtless it's going to go the same way with intellectual effort. The multiplicity of technological aids serving our culture, our attention, and our memory is not a tool of inner freedom unless the efforts they spare us are replaced by efforts of a higher order, not by mere leisure-time pursuits.

MATTHIEU Having things made easy can weaken our capacity for learning. Some readers were surprised when I mentioned that over five years I had done the research work myself for my book *Altruism,* which contains 1,600 footnotes. They presumed that I would have used some kind of research assistant. In fact, it was those efforts that allowed me to gain a good knowledge of all those studies and to discover the links and correspondences among the themes I dealt with. This effort was highly educational, and still today most of the ideas in these research works remain clearly present in my mind.

ALEXANDRE At a burial ceremony, I heard a priest say that in life we are not equipped with a GPS that indicates a route that is already all worked out, that gives us clear and precise instructions. But situated at the bottom of our hearts, we have a compass—a reliable one. He said that ascesis consisted precisely in lending an ear and listening to the voice that arises from our innermost being: the call to altruism, to freedom, to giving of oneself.

CHRISTOPHE I sometimes see that we have to make efforts without making any progress. For example, if we have physical, emotional, or motivational impairments—whether they are connected with our temperament or with illness—our efforts will be maintenance efforts, in order not to get worse. Brushing one's teeth does not make them whiter but prevents them from developing cavities. Insulin injections don't cure diabetes, but they prevent it from ravaging our bodies. Often in our lives, there is an ongoing frailty that requires ongoing effort just to maintain the status quo.

Where then is our freedom, when we have to exert so much effort just to stay alive? Aren't these "obligatory" efforts actually chains that bind us? The answer seems to me to be "no." They are like all efforts: preliminary work that helps us advance toward other freedoms. It's like rent that has to be paid so that afterward we can enjoy our habitation in peace.

ALEXANDRE Carrying around a physical impairment, facing the temporal inevitability of the development of an illness, dealing with a psychological problem or a wound that resists all healing efforts—all these without a doubt demand of us an art of living, and a robust one to be sure. What is perhaps of help to the *progrediente* is the idea of greater health. In *The Gay Science,* Nietzsche speaks of a knowledge, of an aptitude, that embraces the ups and downs of life. Sometimes when I am leaving the doctor's office and there is absolutely nothing to be done to make me any better, I say to myself that this is precisely where the challenge begins.

Good health leaves a lot of people on the sidelines. When we are confronted with helplessness, in order not to go under altogether it is vital to situate our life within a dynamic. What can I set in motion? What act can I perform here and now to keep illness from winning out, so that life will continue to pulsate with greater vigor? Every day, the first thought that comes to my mind is an overwhelming "I'm fed up." I've had my fill of this chronic fatigue, of these problems that are not necessarily going to work out for the better, of the mockery I am going to be the butt of. Maybe a breakthrough to freedom is possible even in the midst of this chaos? Maybe it would already be enough just not to add an extra layer, not to be fed up with being fed up, and thus to experience an art of living that enables me from moment to moment to carry on decently and to maintain myself in a state of joy.

Toolbox for the Horizon of Effort

ALEXANDRE

Embarking on the practice goes beyond the narrow framework of personal ambition. In some sense, all of humanity advances in us when we step beyond sourness, fatigue, egoism. Accomplishing such efforts is not speculating, not looking for a return on investment, but giving oneself entirely to life.

Put it on pause. A person who has been accustomed to scrapping and struggling against adversity perhaps has trouble savoring the blue sky or relaxing flat out on the beach. What does rest symbolize for me? A kind of death, being a zombie? Deep down in my ground of grounds, what regenerates me, recharges me, provides genuine recreation?

Find the intrinsic pleasure in ascesis. The ancient philosophers compared the *progrediente* to an athlete. We can imagine the drudgery represented by a marathon for a runner who doesn't like to run. Is there a simple joy in brushing one's teeth, meditating, getting up in the morning, or even toughing it out against an addiction?

The uptightness meter. A friend of mine sometimes reminds me that I could go through life without the extra additive of anxiety, ruminating, and perpetual agitation that does nothing to change the course of things, and that does not change the circumstances in which I am called upon to make progress. Since then, when panic strikes and amid the torment of hyperactivity, I try a practice: returning to my inner compass, a sort of inner uptightness meter that tells me when I am on the brink of overexertion and prevents me from falling into that trap. It's a healthy tool for not getting exhausted along the way and for traveling a little bit lighter.

MATTHIEU

Make regular and persistent efforts. Drop by drop, you end up filling a big jar.

Have a compassionate attitude toward yourself. Don't rebel against your limitations, don't reproach yourself for not having done more than was possible, and keep your courage up when a project doesn't succeed.

Don't underestimate your potential to transform your mind. Stay open to the multitude of alternatives. Change course with flexibility when it becomes necessary. Find equanimity in the deepest part of yourself when you fail. Nobody can deprive us of inner peace.

Cultivate altruistic love, which puts life's ups and downs back in perspective.

CHRISTOPHE

Effort is not shameful. If you're a person like me who needs to work at things rather than being highly gifted, don't be ashamed of the efforts you have to make compared with others who seem to get the same results by doing a lot less. That's what work is for — making up for inequalities. An inequality is not an inferiority. A person who can run faster than you is not your superior; they run faster, that's all. The same is true for people who are (or seem to you) more cultivated than you are.

An important rule. In terms of effort, don't compare yourselves to others but rather to yourself. Nothing is more tasty and satisfying than feeling the progress you've made from one year to the next and knowing that this progress is due to your efforts!

Sometimes ease and the absence of effort is a trap. Our freedom is nourished more by the results of our efforts than by the results of our talents. And psychological effort puts muscle on our brain just like physical efforts improve our body. One of the keys to successful aging is to remain an eternal apprentice in terms of curiosity and efforts to advance.

Results, yes, but not right away. Some efforts are disappointing: no immediate effect, no gratifying reward. There are efforts with delayed effect, like education or regulation of emotions, and there are efforts to stay in balance, like brushing your teeth or maintaining a healthy lifestyle along with chronic illness. These make more necessary a last kind of effort: the effort to be happy. Happiness is one of the major fuels in accomplishing all the efforts required in human life.

11

Difficult Effort, Joyous Effort

When I was a kid, I loved history courses. Our teachers would unfurl big wall posters illustrating a famous historical period or showing the life of a famous person. I remember an image that fascinated me. It depicted Jean-Baptiste Colbert, Louis XIV's minister, entering his office early in the morning and rubbing his hands with pleasure at the prospect of the work that awaited him. This sense of efforts to be made bringing a sense of joy surprised and attracted me at the same time. Perhaps I was having the intuition that this was one of the keys for becoming an adult happy with his or her lot?

Later, when I became a father, I remember doing my best to get my three daughters to enjoy studying. For example, every year I bought them notebooks entitled "Vacation Homework," and I was careful always to be joyful and in good humor when I was at their sides encouraging or helping them to fill those notebooks!

— Christophe

A Certain Discrediting of Effort

CHRISTOPHE It seems to me that we live in a time in which effort is discredited. In school, for example, there are many who think that students shouldn't be pushed, that good pedagogy should not demand effort from children; rather, we should *always* be playful and light. It's as though effort were tainted by two major sins: it makes us suffer (and our era dreams of eliminating all suffering), and it is suspected of being counterproductive (the way of pleasure is supposed to be faster). I'm wondering if the right approach to teaching is not alternating exercises that demand effort with more playful exercises. When students' parents grumble because their offspring are bored in class, what is the reality that lies behind that? Is this true for all the children in the class? Or is it that particular child who, even though intelligent, is incapable of making the effort to listen quietly or to think about something else and respect the rhythm of their classmates in relation to one thing or another, which might be different from their own rhythm? What would be the sense of an educational process in which we gave up on teaching efforts such as respecting other people or sustaining attention?

MATTHIEU Discrediting effort is the attitude of a spoiled child. I have heard the Dalai Lama say, "When we reach the state of a Buddha, then total rest! But until then, we have to make continual efforts." I later heard him add in a facetious tone at one of the retreats I attended in France: "Some practitioners would like the way to enlightenment to be easy, quick, and if possible, cheap."

Milarepa, the great Tibetan hermit of the twelfth century, practiced for twelve years in caves and other wild places. After that, he had many disciples. When his closest disciple, Gampopa, was taking leave of him, he asked for one last teaching. Milarepa stood up, turned around, lifted his long tunic, and showed him his bottom, which was covered with calluses, which were the result of sitting in meditation in caves. The lesson was simple: "Never relax your efforts."

CHRISTOPHE Effort has another virtue, in my view: it is pro-democratic; it is what compensates for inequality. Why are gifted people admired more than hardworking ones? Effort is what allows those who are less gifted by nature or by chance to make up part of the distance they are left behind.

I have developed a minor allergy to all messages that encourage minimal effort. For one thing, it's dangerous. It means that others will make the efforts in our place, and we will pay them for it one way or another, with money or ensnarement. (For instance, on the internet what you get for free is often paid for indirectly: you are super-exposed to ads, your data is collected, etc.) And for another thing, minimal effort is antidemocratic: though effort doesn't always guarantee that one can compensate for one's social, cultural, or medical handicaps, absence of effort does indeed guarantee that such compensation will never happen and that everyone will go their way purely on the basis of their good or bad luck.

I'm not speaking here of survival efforts—I know there are many miserable life circumstances in which every moment and every action is only an effort to survive hunger or poverty—but rather of efforts to develop and improve one's condition. How could we change, progress, and learn without effort?

MATTHIEU This tendency to make everything easy comes through pretty clearly in certain contemporary meditation instruction: "Enter within, quietly, gently." That's basically saying, "Above all, don't make any effort." That's rushing things just a bit. An Olympic skier said, after winning a race with amazing ease, "I felt just like a river." But before you get to that place, there's work to do!

ALEXANDRE Between a fierce discipline that makes us grit our teeth and total laxity, there is clearly a gulf, a gap into which with courage and perseverance we can introduce our freedom. How can we create an ascesis to our own measure? How, without falling into self-hatred, can we advance toward the goal? When I think of the beings I admire — the sages, the heroes of daily life — I see clearly that their joy, their peace, their immense wisdom did not fall from the sky. My spiritual masters Kangyur Rinpoche and Dilgo Khyentse Rinpoche each did thirty years of contemplative solitary retreats. And that was not because they weren't gifted. When you ask the Dalai Lama why people come in such great numbers to meet him and hear what he has to say, he often replies that it's perhaps because he has been meditating every day for sixty years. He meditates three or four hours before dawn every day on altruistic love and compassion. It goes without saying that, in our case, we shouldn't just rest on our laurels!

Difficult Beginnings

MATTHIEU   Effort cannot be avoided when you're beginning. Later, as you acquire some mastery, the practice becomes more natural. As Milarepa said, "At the beginning nothing comes, in the middle nothing stays, and at the end nothing goes." When you begin, you have the impression of not getting anywhere. So then you have to avoid becoming discouraged. In the middle, you do make progress, but it is unstable. So then you have to persevere. At the end, at the stage of mastery, everything happens without effort. At that point, the practice spontaneously pervades all our thinking, speech, and action.

ALEXANDRE   Nietzsche speaks of the "grand style," of the natural ease of the artist, the creative person. The dancer leaping on stage, executing graceful entrechats, shows no sign of her labors, her ascesis, her discouragements, the falls that gave birth to this lightness. Learning a musical instrument, perfecting a technique, and advancing toward mastery mean playing scales till your fingers are sore, experiencing failure and weariness.

How do we find joy right in the middle of the exercise, give ourselves the sense of working in a dynamic process? Nothing is more conducive to despair than immobility.

In the morning, if you see the possibility of some progress, the whole day is illuminated. But what do you do when you just see walls everywhere? If you want to learn to swim, you can read a whole library full of books on hydrodynamics and the art of flotation, but when the moment comes to dive in, you have to tame your fear and see that even if you don't do anything, you don't sink.

Aristotle speaks of the virtuous man, who finds his pleasure in the exercise of courage, temperance, justice, generosity, and so on. To reach this stage, you have to develop wholesome habit patterns. It always comes back to the need to practice. How fast our progress is doesn't matter; the essential point is never to cop out of the process.

CHRISTOPHE The philosopher Simone Weil is often adamant against certain kinds of effort, particularly the effort to be virtuous, which is something, according to her, that does not arise from true virtue. According to her, we should not have to choose between good and evil, between the effort to be good and to avoid being evil. One is truly virtuous the day one is no longer making an effort to be virtuous.

MATTHIEU True virtue is fully accomplished when it is an integral part of our being. Perhaps this is the sense of Simone Weil's words. When we cultivate compassion, for example, in the beginning it does not come easily. With practice, it becomes second nature and manifests spontaneously. Before reaching that point, though, we have to pass through a number of stages.

Effort is not unwelcome forced labor; rather, it is an essential ingredient in making ourselves into accomplished people.

Joy Leads to Freedom

ALEXANDRE Insisting on the necessity and the value of effort definitely does not amount to praising calamity, like the idea "No pain, no gain." This slogan can itself be disastrous. Why the devil do we have to suffer hardship in order to develop, grow, or achieve real sanity or wisdom? Spinoza clearly liberates me from this approach, and I never tire of citing what he says in his *Ethics:* "And, since human power in controlling the emotions consists solely in the understanding, it follows that no one rejoices in blessedness because he has controlled his lusts, but, contrariwise, his power of controlling his lusts arises from this blessedness itself."[1] The philosopher adds that this path is as arduous as it is rare, which is why perseverance is necessary. This is also the reason for Seneca's warning: nobody can heal if he changes his treatment and his remedies at every turn. So what then are the pillars of our ascesis, and how can we fully enjoy ourselves in the practice itself?

CHRISTOPHE   Yes, these two points are very important: First, effort is futile unless it is regular, constant, embedded in some logic, some overall vision; once again, it becomes a question of the goals we set ourselves. And second, there is the struggle we need to carry on against the erroneous idea that effort cannot be pleasant or enjoyable. We have all experienced efforts that are enjoyable, at least momentarily: in sports, studying, or practicing a musical instrument. When you're going on a mountain hike, you get up early, you take some trouble with your preparations, but if you have a goal—reaching a summit, seeing beautiful things—it's all extremely gratifying.

MATTHIEU   In Buddhism the perfection of diligence, one of the six transcendent perfections leading to enlightenment, is defined as a joyous effort toward virtue. We also speak of the enthusiastic joy of the bodhisattva, who works by all possible means to liberate beings from suffering. To this end, the aspirant on the path trains himself to arouse the wish first that a person close to him, then a neutral person, and finally someone he considers an enemy be liberated from suffering. The joy inherent in this wish and its accomplishment also bounces back on ourselves because it is in profound harmony with our basic nature.

And then we must recognize that often it's the idea, the mental representation of the effort to be supplied, that is painful for us, more than the effort itself. Once we launch into the action with its concomitant difficulties and satisfactions, we see that we are one with the effort, and the hour of cogitation is over. To take the sports example again, when athletes train it might be hard physically, but they experience the joy of making progress, bettering themselves, staying the distance, and performing well. We also experience a kind of jubilation from having completed a long hike, despite the fatigue.

CHRISTOPHE   Moreover, the efforts connected with a mountain hike are many and various. The effort to get up very early, at two or three in the morning (scheduling that is always necessary if you want to climb quite high and get back down before the snowfields soften up), is sometimes painful. But once you get into the right rhythm, the effort of the gradual night climb rapidly becomes automatic, regular, not very tiring, and it becomes satisfying almost because it's hypnotic.

Then the first rewards appear: the day dawns, little by little the magnificent landscapes are revealed, and the effort becomes meaningful. Arriving at the summit is the supreme gratification. There's a feeling of freedom and intoxication, even more delicious because it occurs in the aftermath of major effort, because the pleasure registers in a body that still harbors all the willingly undertaken pains of the climb. The well-to-do tourists who get themselves dropped off on the summits by helicopter will never taste this same intensity, this same quality of happiness, unless they have made long and passionate efforts.

MATTHIEU A just measure of effort makes it possible to enter into the experience of flow that I mentioned earlier. When the flow is carrying us, even the idea of effort is forgotten.

If we want to change our habits, it is ineffectual to go at them head on. We must work with them thought by thought, emotion by emotion, with intelligence and skill. Little by little our moods, then our character traits, will end up changing. We will have eroded our habitual tendencies. We will no longer need to control our anger, because it rarely survives this process, and then only feebly. This accomplishment marks a high degree of inner freedom.

CHRISTOPHE There are very interesting studies on the state of mind we're in when we accomplish efforts. I very much like Christian Bobin's words here: "Whatever we do with a sigh is stained by nothingness."[2] These words were a revelation for me and became a kind of mantra that I repeat every time the temptation to grumble comes over me: Don't spoil the present moment by sighing and grumbling. Instead say to yourself, "Whatever you're living through at this moment, you are living! Would you prefer to not exist?"

Not only is what Bobin says beautiful, but it's scientifically accurate. The same effort, if it's perceived as a chore and performed with grumbling and complaint, will be more painful, bring less pleasure, and be less fruitful. This is the influence of what is called one's mindset, one's state of mind, which was shown particularly well in a study of eighty chambermaids in luxury hotels. The researchers separated them into two comparable groups chosen at random. They told one group of maids that they were studying the impact of their work on their health. They gave a different message to the group they wanted to evaluate: "We think your job is good for your health because it's a job that requires physical exercise on the level recommended by scientific studies." (The statement is somewhat true, on the condition that the work doesn't have to be done at too hectic a pace.) At the end of the four weeks of the experiment, it was observed that the group that had received the educational message benefited from a small amelioration in their health: they lost weight and their blood pressure went down. Experiencing their efforts as something beneficial for their health had done them good.

MATTHIEU A study conducted by Richard Davidson and Jon Kabat-Zinn showed that persons vaccinated at the end of an eight-week program of mindfulness-based stress reduction (MBSR) produced 30 percent more antibodies in response to a flu shot than a control group that had not participated in the MBSR program. Thus, pacifying the mind brings a reduction in stress, which in turn translates into a more robust immune system.

CHRISTOPHE True, and yet meditation requires effort! To highlight the playful, interesting, stimulating side of these efforts, I often say to my patients who are apprentice meditators, "The bad news is that meditating is work. And the good news is it's interesting work, because observing how your mind works is truly fascinating!"

MATTHIEU One day someone said to me, "I'm afraid to look at my mind, because I'm afraid of what I'll find there." I related this remark to the Dalai Lama, who answered, "Still, it's much more interesting than going to the movies—so many things go on in your mind!"

Effort Is Not Mental Orthopedics

ALEXANDRE Another danger lurks for those working toward wisdom and freedom: turning the path into a house of correction or into mental orthopedics. It's unconditional acceptance of our wounds that leads us, as by the hand, to detachment. To climb a stairway, it's helpful to look and see where the steps are, catch your breath, lean on the railing. Each *progrediente* has his resources, frailties, baggage, and necessities for the road.

For my part, I practice "KakaoTalk therapy." KakaoTalk is an app similar to WeChat and WhatsApp, and it lets you record vocal messages up to five minutes in length. The ascesis here is very simply to dare to take stock at the end of day, to unburden oneself to a friend in the good about the moments when we've stumbled, identify what got us over that rough spot. We are invited, without falling into the swamp of guilt and narcissism, to confide the ups and downs of the day to a compassionate ear.

KakaoTalk therapy also invites us to lay down our burden, let go, lighten up. The teachings are clear: we are buddha nature. Therefore, there is no point in adding a layer; instead we must clear away, empty, throw out. By the same token, there's no way to fabricate silence. It remains there, always present, included beneath the racket and turmoil.

What would lead me to despair, without the thousand and one arms outstretched to support me, are the force of inertia, habit patterns, tenacious emotions that emerge on the path day and night. If I only look at my past, I'm a goner. Progressing, very precisely, is daring to take one step after another, opening oneself to the unknown, to the new. And nothing stops us from raising our eyes to the sages, to the everyday heroes who bear testimony to the possibility of peace, of a mode of life that is cheerful and calm.

MATTHIEU Buddhism does indeed hold that we cannot fabricate the perfection of buddha nature. We can only reveal it, actualize it. If we look at the root of our consciousness, we find this awakened presence, this pure awareness, untainted by the content of thoughts, which could be called "original goodness," which is another way of expressing the idea of buddha nature. Hatred, jealousy, or any other mental event cannot adulterate pure awareness. This original goodness transcends the distinction between good and bad, but on the relative plane, we can nonetheless speak of goodness in the sense that this fundamental state of awareness is not affected by ignorance or contaminated by mental toxins.

If we didn't possess this buddha nature, our efforts would be futile. We can extract gold from its core, but we would just be wasting our time spending years washing a piece of coal hoping that it would end up shining like gold. The Buddhist path does not consist in fabricating buddhahood, but in doing away with everything that masks this perfection within us. In this sense, we don't repair and we don't fabricate; we just eliminate veils. But we can't do that just by waving a magic wand!

ALEXANDRE   What do we ask for from practice? Why do we wear ourselves out with effort? Are we running after some ideal in order to extricate ourselves from self-contempt? What are we trying to compensate for? Inevitably, we come back to the question of motivation. What is the motivating force that drives us to embark joyfully into ascesis? Think of those Zen practitioners who spend hours raking a garden to get it perfect, never ceasing to apply the precept "Do everything perfectly, and remain detached from the result." A gust of wind and a few falling leaves, and it's time to do it over again.

With a physical impairment, effort is constant, crushing sometimes. Some days, getting up, twisting open a tube of toothpaste, and getting into a bathtub is like an obstacle course. This is why it's necessary not to make too-heavy demands on oneself.

In my eyes effort — the art of living, the inner itinerary — consists in providing oneself with the means to move through life far away from bitterness, to create conditions that help us stay on course, to sail on without sinking. It's a runway for taking off, a springboard, not a ball and chain or a burden.

The First Step

ALEXANDRE   If we want to jump in the water, to embark on a path of action, where do we start? The first step, so crucial, consists perhaps in daring a lucid and very factual diagnosis of the situation. Epictetus, who described himself as a slave on the way to becoming free, helps us to look *without flinching* at our inner enemies, our areas of struggle — or better, the points where we have to be vigilant — our life's big challenges, not to mention all the akrasic areas of our being. Here is a viaticum for this adventure: patience without limits, cheerful and lighthearted perseverance, and unbounded compassion.

Entering deep within ourselves beyond the agitations of everyday life and giving our attention to our inner compass protects us against many dangers. Knowing that we are vulnerable, influenceable, identifying the situations in which we tend to crash, are already big helps. Ignoring the existence of toxic relationships that drag us down is keeping ourselves in bondage.

CHRISTOPHE When we speak of a first step, in effect that presupposes that there are going to be many more steps to be taken afterward. We are not talking here about minor isolated changes — even those are also necessary and sometimes followed by major results — but rather about big changes of direction in our lives: changing jobs, moving to a new place, changes in mental or behavioral habit patterns. It's like trying to immediately go in the right direction, rather than responding to an impulse.

MATTHIEU Yes, the first step contains the following ones *in potentia*. If I begin practicing meditation, I envisage the possibility of deepening this practice over the course of years. If I buy a piano, it's with the intention of devoting a certain number of hours a day to playing it, not with the intention of putting it in the garage. If I volunteer to work for a humanitarian cause, I foresee giving a part of my life to it. If I decide to take a tour around the world, it's the first step that starts off this big journey. It doesn't matter if the road is long if we are enthusiastically determined and have the feeling that we're going in the right direction.

CHRISTOPHE But all the same, sometimes we take these first steps, and they don't lead anywhere. We try something, and it doesn't work; then we give up and try again elsewhere, in another way. It seems to me that in the course of a lifetime we have to be ready to take lots of wasted first steps, and that's the way we learn to live. First we get to know ourselves by learning to accept failures and the fact that we've gotten lost along the way. That doesn't exempt us from having to think before we act, but when our thinking doesn't result in anything clear, when our intuition isn't working too well, when the advice we receive points in a variety of directions, what do we do? It seems to me that at that point it's better to launch into some kind of action, even without guarantees, than to remain inactive.

MATTHIEU   True, the optimist is always ready to take a whole variety of first steps, trusting that one of them will lead to a satisfactory destination, even if most of them lead nowhere. The pessimist, by contrast, says to herself, "Why should I bother putting one foot in front of the other? There are big risks of failure."

CHRISTOPHE   That's a professional hazard for me. Since I'm under the impression that with most of my patients, inhibitions (thinking too much before daring to go ahead) create more damage than impulses (acting without thinking first), I have the tendency to prefer failure to avoidance. At least failure teaches us something about ourselves, about others, about the world.

Microchoices

ALEXANDRE   I don't know about you, friends, but often in everyday life I suffer from "peanuts syndrome." No sooner do I eat one than I have to have another, and the whole package is soon history. Not touching the first peanut would have been enough to have gone whistling by this addictive behavior. How can we sustain the gentle vigilance we need to avoid getting sucked into the gears of such behavior and to be aware when dangers and temptations are cropping up? Perhaps liberating ourselves here is more a matter of microsteps than major resolutions, a matter of paying attention to the little things that trigger old habits. As I see it, the effort here is climbing back up the hill, getting out of the vicious circles, putting a stop to the forces of inertia, escaping from resignation because action is what supports letting go, being able to quit. When I miss a train, instead of squandering a quarter of an hour being mad at the train company (or whomever), the real point—the spiritual exercise, the action that helps us to tune into the fluidity of life—is finding the way to catch the next train. We have to cut short the mental blah blah blah and have to tune out Mental FM. It never solves anything.

MATTHIEU   Yes, it's a good idea to be aware as often as possible of what is going on in our mental landscape and to use the right antidotes at the right time to avoid losing emotional balance. One of the jobs of vigilance is becoming aware of microthoughts at the very moment they show their noses, so to speak—that is, when they can still easily be controlled by catching them in time. If we don't, chain reactions will be triggered, and we will be in big danger of tumbling down the slope of the passions, just as when you miss your footing on a mountain.

CHRISTOPHE   Yes, it's true. Many important things play out in our lives during these kinds of harmless moments. If I spent my whole life stressing out for fear of missing trains or cursing them when they're late, in the end that would add up to a fair number of hours of my life spent hyping myself up with stress—and those close to me as well—to no purpose.

And here, as long as I haven't identified the problem (my tendency toward anxiety and complaint), as long as I haven't set myself a goal to free myself of it, I can spin around and around, thinking that the world is screwed up, when, in fact, it's my vision of the world that's screwed up. Living means adapting to adversity when you can't change it, and doing it as lightheartedly and joyfully as possible. Microefforts, microchoices, but macroconsequences in life!

MATTHIEU   The way our mind translates external circumstances into well-being or misery considerably influences our quality of life. Now it is possible to educate this translation process.

ALEXANDRE   I was talking a little while ago about the difficulty of leaving one's doctor without anything at all in the way of an answer, not the faintest hope of progress. How do we stay on course when we start spinning around ineffectually, when we aren't making any headway, just bumping into walls everywhere? Where do we find the force to persevere without exhausting ourselves?

It still seems to me that what you have to do is make your life part of a dynamic process. What helps me is to transform helplessness, fatalism—in brief, whatever resists us—into a spiritual process. In very concrete terms, as I say goodbye to the doctor, I almost immediately ask myself, "What could be an opening for me, here and now? What could I accomplish on the level of greater health?" As you were saying, Christophe, we must do something. That's vital.

CHRISTOPHE Yes, when one is a caregiver, what one fears the most for sick patients is that the feeling of helplessness and despair will get the upper hand. Our job is always to encourage hope, because we never know what is going to happen in advance—never! The development of an illness can be unpredictable. Even degenerative illnesses, for example, follow very different rhythms. Things can happen in a flash or go very slowly. The amyotrophic lateral sclerosis (ALS) of the famous astrophysicist Stephen Hawking should have taken him very young. On average, that degenerative disease only gives you four years to live. So he shouldn't have gone past the age of twenty-six. But Hawking died at seventy-six, after an incredibly full life—and doubtless an incredibly difficult one as well.

It's very important for us to remind our patients of that unpredictability and to support them in everyday life by giving them concrete things to do daily, like movements or activities, to counter their illness. We must tell them how to eat, to breathe, to meditate, to turn themselves toward life and happiness rather than solely toward illness and fear. We must always go in the direction of relief, more control, more action, whenever suffering and discouragement throws them for a loop. They are continually confronted by microchoices: giving up or continuing the fight.

ALEXANDRE Don't look for anything exceptional from these microsteps, from your daily ascesis! Always it's a question of decentralizing, of coming back to the essential, and of opening—blowing away the boundaries of individuality. What could be better at that point than making a call to a person in distress, not to assure ourselves that there are people worse off than us but to cause life to circulate, to practice generosity, just simply to give oneself? In moments of trial, there is a kind of reflex that makes us withdraw, that shuts ourselves in, that turns us back on ourselves. The spiritual practice, liberation, causes us to expand.

CHRISTOPHE When we are suffering we need to rely on others, either for consolation or to forget ourselves, to forget our excess of suffering. This is a difficult effort because suffering is a centripetal force that keeps pushing us back on ourselves—and not for the better! It's not a question of fleeing suffering, but rather of expanding our consciousness so that suffering doesn't fill up all the space. When we can't reduce the pain, we have to enlarge the space around it.

In the course of my life I have left the offices of medical colleagues with bad news about my health. I also remember that each time I sat down on a bench in the hospital corridor, I took the time to breathe, to listen to the birds, the noises of the city, and the life around me. I made an effort to smile and say to myself, "Up till now you have experienced many beautiful things, and maybe, in spite of everything, you still have more of them ahead of you. Do your best to smile, out of gratitude, out of hope, and because it's good for your health!" In hindsight, I see that that's the best thing I could have done in those moments, and I did well to undertake those little efforts immediately instead of starting off with worrying and complaining.

ALEXANDRE I believe that confidence, peace, and joy are not the fruit of psychological orthopedics, which can perilously veer in the direction of abuse, but precisely the fruit of exercises that are repeated every day. One foot after the other, each person with the means available to them enters deep within into yea-saying, the fullness and the giving of self.

MATTHIEU Giving a box of tools to an artisan or tillable land to a farmer incites them to effort by giving them the means to succeed in it. It's not enough to say, "Get it done. Scratch the soil with your fingernails." Mind-training utilizes the inner tools with which we will be able to cultivate our latent good qualities.

Toolbox for Putting Joy into Your Efforts

MATTHIEU

In order to be sustained in the long run, effort must be combined with enthusiasm and contain a quality of joy that is born from the meaning given to that effort. It is neither a punishment nor a duty; it is not in vain. It represents the most constructive means of accomplishing what is really in our hearts.

Overexertion makes no sense. Once the ocean has been crossed, what's the use of carrying the boat on your back?

Face the results of your efforts with equanimity. Rejoice in what has been accomplished. Dedicate the benefit of it to all beings. Let go of what has proven to be beyond your abilities or unachievable due to adverse circumstances.

ALEXANDRE

The blessed Buddha Shakyamuni, like a brilliant doctor, speaks of "right effort." Before getting started on the path, to guard against exhaustion, it is perhaps good to ask myself about what it is that inclines me to practice, where I will get the strength to make progress, and how I will feed my effort so it is not exerted ineffectually.

Enjoy yourself fully in your ascesis. What makes us fall into the abyss of the false passions is doubtless our inability to be good to ourselves and to be genuinely happy. In the Sutra of Inconceivable Liberation, Vimalakirti praises the pleasures of the practitioner. Yes, there is happiness in devoting oneself to virtue, to becoming detached from attractive objects, forgetting rancors, doing away with negative emotions. Let's go for these exquisite pleasures—without moderation!

Gently hurry up and rest. Succeed in your efforts. Be there for the long haul. Run easy in the marathon of life. Be outrageous enough to take time off, grant yourself breaks, dare to not struggle if you don't want to end up rolling on the rims of your wheels. Undertake an ascesis with this oh-so-liberating question: How do I let go of my tensions?

Commit yourself to working with friends in the good. Along the way, there are struggles that get us down, that leave us exhausted and drained. Alone, we may be swamped by discouragement and be incapable of getting ourselves out of it. Sharing our problems with others, telling them about our relapses, opening ourselves with complete transparency to them, and finding solutions together is a powerful antidote to despair and to the severity with which we sometimes judge ourselves.

CHRISTOPHE

Society encourages us in the direction of least effort, at least as far as our personal life, daily activity, and lifestyle are concerned. We should be wary, because our era is, among other things, the era of excessive consumption. A principal consequence of lack of effort is changing our approach from that of an actor to that of a consumer.

The notion of joyous effort is no joke! At least at times it's a reality under several conditions: that we accept as a principle that living means effort (not all the time, but often), that we choose goals that are meaningful for us, and that we properly gauge our efforts because often what is unpleasant about effort is that it isn't properly dosed and we make it either too easy or too hard.

Sometimes our efforts lead nowhere; they are wasted efforts, like when we're trying to find our way on a hike and there's no path. It's not necessarily a tragedy or a mistake, but some moments in our life are just like that. Sometimes we have the good fortune to make a discovery along the way — about ourselves, about others, about the world or life — that we never would have imagined if we'd stuck to the main highway of easy and pre-delineated efforts. At certain times the most appropriate effort consists in not making any further efforts, in just letting go!

12

Training the Mind

In midsummer, we were joyously gathered around the table with family and friends, celebrating life. Suddenly I had a horrendous anxiety attack. Obsessed by death, illness, I was afraid of losing my family. Dark, almost macabre images passed through my mind—the faces of the dead, grief-stricken. My chest tightened, even though I couldn't find any reason for my malaise.

During a bathroom break, I noticed that my hosts were using the same perfume in their house that my friend Joachim, the undertaker, uses at his morgue. This innocuous odor of roses had awakened in my psyche the memory of the bodies I'd seen, of the mourning families I'd met. The experience of my funeral visits had passed among us like a shadow.

This was very liberating. Today I use it as an exercise, a practice. I notice what it is that is acting like a remote control on my states of mind. I identify the thousand influences that weigh on my moods. I explore my traumas, memories, external influences—anything that does not depend on me.

Our famous "I" resembles an iceberg. We definitely only know the conscious part of it—not the unseen bulk of the iceberg below water level. Training the mind means ceasing to function on automatic pilot, breaking out of one's bubble and living in the world, meeting people in the flesh, and loving reality however it presents itself.

—Alexandre

CHRISTOPHE Your effort to elucidate where your anxiety was coming from allowed you to ease its grip on you. The very point of training the mind is to help us in dealing with, the events of life, quickly and effectively, to increase our inner freedom.

What Is Mind Training?

CHRISTOPHE What is "improving" one's mind? Who hasn't dreamed of having a better memory and attention that is more stable and resistant to distractions? Who hasn't dreamed of being able to understand their emotions and use them to their best advantage, of having more willpower and insight, of being more generous and altruistic? But what can we do to develop these qualities? Is that what we call "mind training"?

You are the one I first heard this expression from, Matthieu, a long time ago. You were talking about bodybuilding, about the many people who spend their time sculpting their bodies, and you asked why they didn't also do "mind building," why they didn't dedicate the same amount of energy to improving the function of their minds? This image first amused me, then made me think.

MATTHIEU This is an imperfect image, because the idea of building muscles in your brain is too simplistic and reductionist. But this image shows that, like our muscles, our good qualities and faults are not forever fixed. Training the mind makes it possible to cultivate many qualities that make us better human beings. It would be odd and contradictory to impugn this process while at the same time recognizing the need to learn to read and write, to play a musical instrument, or to acquire knowledge. What mysterious thing would make training human qualities any different? They are as malleable as any other skill that can be improved by practice.

CHRISTOPHE　For years and years, despite the fact that I am a psychiatrist, a brain doctor, the goals I had my patients work on were in the area of alleviating their suffering but not very much on developing their mental faculties. Finally today, however, we understand that psychotherapy ought also to be regarded as a discipline for training the mind, training it to suffer less, but also to better cultivate all its good qualities. The second of these two goals can be a big help to the first, because a great part of our suffering resides in our underdeveloped faculties or in our ignorance of how our mind works. Anxiety or depression, anger or discouragement gain traction if we are ignorant of the laws of how our mind and emotions work—even though they're quite simple.

ALEXANDRE　As I see it, spiritual practice, meditation, and mind training proceed from an inner change of address. We have to descend within ourselves a level—or even several levels—to reach the core of our being, far from agitation and our habitual anxieties. Training one's mind is, in sum, deprogramming it, deconditioning it, seeking compassionately to expose the crazy logic of conceptual mind—it's often a bit paranoid and a hell of a tyrant—so as to expand and progressively get beyond our preconceptions. On the surface, where the famous ego holds sway, the lure of gain, fear, projections, and the most highly persistent discontent rule the day. Deeper within our being, buddha nature awaits us: calm, peaceful, and inconceivably free.

To inaugurate ascesis, let us dare to look at our diagnosis head on; let us recognize that quite often it's our fears, complexes, and deliriums that hold the strings. Just one step further, and we would be totally like marionettes, puppets, even weird robots. Happily, the practice is there to allow us to learn to dance in the chaos without adding layers to it. Far from being a chore, it is almost like a game: track the spoor of the inner blah blah blah of Mental FM, look at the inconsistency of our most tenacious desires, dispel the illusions that cut us off from the world of our freedom.

CHRISTOPHE　To a great extent, transformations of the mind obey the same rules as those of the body. You cannot wake up in the morning and decree, "From today onward, I'm going to have more energy, be more flexible, and have stronger muscles!" But you could say, "From today onward, I'm going to run regularly to improve my energy, do yoga to become more flexible, and lift weights to add some muscle!" In the same way, the statement "From today onward, I'm going to have less stress and be happier and more generous" doesn't work, or not for very long. What is effective is training every day.

This is the principle of mind training. In order to stand up to the passage of time, fluctuations in motivation, and the destabilizing forces of adversity, all change must be habitual—rooted and thus resistant to being wiped away. (And it's not easy to stress less when you're dealing with stress factors or to remain generous when you're passing through periods of personal need.)

Although most of our behaviors and emotions arise out of the goals we set ourselves, the values that inspire us, or our will, they can also be the result of unobtrusive and humble work and regular practice, which do not bear instant fruit. But like all learning processes, these have a significant impact over the long term.

There are two big mistakes concerning effort. For one thing, many people think that it's hardly possible to change psychologically, that our basic nature always comes surging to the fore. They are wrong about the ineluctable quality of temperament: "I'm just like that" or "Hey, that's my nature." And their other mistake—just the opposite—is to overestimate the power of their will: "If I want to, I can." People want to get ahead, decide to do so, but then fail because they think that merely making the decision and pulling the trigger will do it. Life is rather more complicated than that. We can't command a general mobilization of our will every moment of the day, every time a worry, a surge of emotion, or a difficult situation comes up. We need facilitating mechanisms, or "good" reflexes, but we still need to be able not to go along with them when necessary. To me it seems that this is what mind training is about.

MATTHIEU   Isn't it possible to experience the world in a truer and happier way than is our usual daily lot? Isn't there anything about our life that's worth improving? Is it true that our quirks and conflicting emotions are indispensable to the richness of life and make us the one and only person of our type that we're so attached to? Aren't we victims of Stockholm Syndrome when we become fond of the mental states that hold us hostage and deprive us of our inner freedom? Being free of our habitual conditioning does not take away life's richness—quite the contrary. Such freedom expands our horizons and reveals neglected possibilities. It opens us to other people because we are less preoccupied by our own vulnerability and the exacerbated feeling of self-importance.

Cognitive sciences, especially neuroscience, teach us that we can transform ourselves and that our brain changes as we cultivate new skills. We can learn to juggle and also to become more compassionate and inwardly free. The seed is not the shoot, and the shoot is not yet the flower or the fruit. And we have much to learn about these emotions of ours, which, on the slightest provocation, create the spark that sets fire to a pile of dry grass—and then to an entire forest.

Moreover, most of us are not familiar with the fundamental aspect of consciousness that can be discerned behind the curtain of thoughts. When we speak to someone about the "nature of mind," this notion often doesn't mean much. But it is important for us to familiarize ourselves with the awakened presence, the pure awareness devoid of mental constructs, that is at the core of our experience. It is by residing within this pure awareness that we become capable of freeing our emotions at the very moment they arise.

What does this have to do with freedom? If we want to liberate ourselves from the various causes of suffering, we must show discrimination as to what to cultivate and what to refrain from in relation to the most subtle aspects of the law of cause and effect. To this end, we must master our mind as a sailor masters his ship or an equestrian her horse.

One might argue that life teaches us enough as it is, and that it's unnecessary to impose the further labor of training our minds. On my trip to Korea, I had a discussion with the abbot of a Zen monastery. He said to me, "You speak of cultivating altruistic love and compassion, but people already have so much to do! You're just going to add to their stress. What is necessary is to empty the mind of all concepts." I permitted myself to suggest that it was quite possible that compassion would reduce people's stress rather than adding to it.

ALEXANDRE   The urgent thing—the big challenge—is to purge the mind of the will for power that we can exercise over others without realizing it. In this regard, Anthony DeMello, in his book *Awareness,* hotly assaults caricatured acts of charity, denouncing the kind of good deeds that are done for one's own personal comfort in order to avoid the pangs of bad conscience. This has nothing to do, he points out, with authentic compassion, which is devoid of all narcissism, of all desire for a return on investments.

Zen invites us to undergo "the Great Death," to let go of everything, to dare complete renunciation in order to be reborn as a child again. Naturally this baptism by fire is more than a little unsettling. However, this precarious process—which, if one goes astray, can lead to fanaticism, even to stony indifference—leads to freedom, to an innocent and limpid heart that relates to the other without calculation.

MATTHIEU   According to Buddhism, for a virtue—generosity, patience, or perseverance—to contribute to our progress toward inner freedom or enlightenment, it is important for it to be devoid of attachment to concepts of the subject (me, the generous one), of the object (the other, who receives my gift and should be grateful for it), and of the action involved (being hyperaware that one is in the process of "giving"). Giving should be motivated by a pure feeling of disinterested love and done with the fluidity of a mind free from any form of grasping. The same goes for patience, which should not arise from a cramped sense of martyring oneself and being patient about it. It should come from a joyful and confident sense of invulnerability arising from inner freedom.

CHRISTOPHE   Just as training the body allows us to run for a long time without having to strain or "bust a gut," training the mind allows us to function in everyday life with equanimity and therefore more freely, without being absorbed by this effort or being preoccupied with how hard it is. It's a paradox, but our inner freedom needs mechanisms and good reflexes in order to fully manifest.

Mind training doesn't come simply from wanting to change, and it doesn't arise out of an intellectual process either. Just reflecting on one's limits and one's goals isn't enough. That's why, for me, mind training is very much connected with the discovery of mindfulness meditation. The more I meditate, the more clearly I see the difference between thinking about something—having intentions, making resolutions—and being *exposed* to it in the space of open and fluid awareness that one is able to create by placing oneself in a state of mindfulness. Through the very specific mode of brain function obtained through mindfulness meditation, we become more receptive, more malleable, and more open, and I think there's a process of personal change that completes the kind of change arrived at through will and reflection. There is something here that is more on the order of receptivity, of letting go—more on the level of greater profundity that one is able to reach. The process doesn't stay at the level of the cortex, of the intelligence, of the rational; when one meditates, one tries to bring it into the innermost area of oneself, into one's body, into the deep cerebral networks of the emotional brain. And this deep impregnation facilitates putting the adapted behaviors into practice repeatedly later on.

MATTHIEU Aristotle said that this balance is respected when we express the right emotion—rightly adapted to a particular situation and with the right intensity—not too much and not too little and for the right duration. We can tame our emotions with patience and gentleness, as one would tame a wild animal.

The Emergence of Inner Cohesion

CHRISTOPHE It is also important to understand that both wisdom and inner freedom, which go hand in hand, are emergent skills or abilities—that is, phenomena that we can't decide to unleash at will, but whose appearance (emergence from our minds) we can facilitate by bringing together certain conditions. It's the same as for sleep: we can't decide to go to sleep, but we can bring together the conditions that make it possible for sleep to come.

MATTHIEU The new qualities of an emergent phenomenon are more than the sum of the constituents it emerged from; the whole is more than the sum of its parts. If we consider, for example, the fluidity of water and its other qualities, we cannot deduce them just by examining the qualities of the water molecule, H_2O, individually. In the same way, consciousness is far more than the simple addition of the properties of our brain neurons, the cells of our body, and the elements of our environment, even though these serve as a support for the expression of consciousness. In the case of human qualities, they emerge from a set of constituents that can each be cultivated individually. The feeling of fulfillment that constitutes authentic happiness, for example, is more than the simple addition of emotional balance, resilience, compassion, or equanimity.

CHRISTOPHE   Yes, but we have to regularly cultivate these constituents for this phenomenon to emerge—that is, arise from ourselves. We are not speaking here of qualities that fall from the sky. The constituents that facilitate the appearance of inner freedom are multiple: emotional peace and balance, self-awareness, proper comprehension of the dynamic of our emotions associated with appropriate regulation of them, and the habit of attentively observing our thoughts, especially when they present themselves in the form of certainties or convictions. As soon as you think something, look for the way in which the opposite is true, said Simone Weil. That's a good example of mind training in the realm of self-awareness and in the art of seeking the proper nuance if not the truth itself.

We cannot cultivate the proper functioning of our mind as a kind of overall entity, but we can work on its separate constituents. We should set specific goals, ones that provide an outline of the mental and emotional landscape we dream of living in.

MATTHIEU   Super imposition of all the colors of the rainbow creates white light. In the same way, if we bring about a cohesion of compassion, mastery of the mind, inner freedom, discriminating intelligence, and the joy of living, the various colors of these qualities together form the white light of wisdom. Wisdom is not a simple addition of qualities, but what emerges from them.

ALEXANDRE   Why is it so crucial to undertake mind training? First, the mind is the great interpreter that translates, organizes, and contextualizes the experiences and circumstances of our everyday lives. If it crashes, if it makes a mistake, if it understands everything the wrong way, what a mess we're in! Quite often, we are our own executioners, inventing worries all day long, a thousand and one troubles. It's as though there were two layers to suffering: first the tragic qualities of life (earthquakes, natural catastrophes, sickness, death) and second a heap of psychodramas, of woes fabricated by the conceptual mind, by comparisons, by illusion.

The good news is that we are not without power. Hence the necessity of transforming our mind and not relegating it to an ancillary level of activity that could help us spoil our lives less. We must give ourselves heart and soul to this training and not get completely lost in what's currently happening to us. Perhaps, along with love, this is the most important challenge in the world. How can we attain peace, joy, and balance if the machine that decrypts the world for us goes completely haywire? Adjusting ourselves, tracking down illusions and preconceptions, refining the way we look at the world—there's nothing sad in any of this. On the contrary, as Spinoza told us, freeing ourselves from error and the sad passions opens us up to tremendous joy. Why should we deprive ourselves of that?

Ongoing Mind Training in Spite of Ourselves

ALEXANDRE   Life is both tragic and comic. It's crazy that today, after just picking up the tools from you, I have the brass to give advice on daring to embark wholeheartedly on the adventure of mind training! In a not-too-distant time of my life, I was a totally loose cannon. I had lost control. This is why we must remain vigilant—on the alert—and stop continually forcing a high reading on the uptightness meter. Practicing ascesis means blowing away the forces of inertia, the various kinds of resistance, and maybe disobeying a part of the self. Philosopher Emil Cioran is certainly not a completely isolated case, as he conveys the idea that nobody can cultivate their own faults in such detail or with such passion as themself.

CHRISTOPHE   When we talk about training the mind, we think of a conscious and deliberate approach, and that is indeed the case. But that's not all there is to it. We have seen that our environments can also influence us and shape us through cultural osmosis. (For example, living in a culture of violence readily moves us to resort to violence without our having to make any effort or even be aware of it.) When a culture leads us to regularly practice certain behaviors and to regularly develop certain habits and automatic thought patterns, then we can also speak here of mind training. But it's a different kind!

Research in neuroscience shows that we are constantly learning. Every moment, every action, every interaction, is the occasion for our brain to develop in a certain way—to trace neural pathways and psychological trails, which, if they are regularly followed and practiced, become highways for our thoughts and emotions. One important question thus arises: What daily nourishment should we give our brain in the course of all of our activities? Our mind is training itself by itself all the time without our being aware of it. And it feeds itself on whatever we offer it through the objects that we put our attention on, through the environment we immerse it in.

MATTHIEU   Training in its most noble form is called "education." In a more prosaic form, it's "conditioning." Both education and conditioning involve the same process of neuroplasticity. We hesitate to introduce teaching of ethical values into our schools, but children are going to develop a morality in any case. It would be better if it were founded on universal values such as compassion, honesty, and integrity rather than formed by contact with television reality shows or incredibly violent video games. There they encounter arrogance, the will to provoke war on the five continents (shown by numerous American presidents, more or less consciously), the will to total power, and indifference to the suffering of others.

When I wrote my book on altruism, I was struck by training imposed over a period of time on US soldiers to overcome their repugnance to killing. The US Army noted that during the World War II and the Korean War only 15 percent of US soldiers fired on the "enemy" on the front lines—not out of laziness but out of natural repugnance to killing other human beings.

They either pretended to shoot or shot off the mark. However, since the beginning of the Vietnam War, military instructors have trained soldiers to stifle all feelings of empathy and shoot to kill without hesitation. During drills, with each step they had to chant "Kill!" They trained by shooting on targets in human form that appeared for only a short instant, obliging the recruits to fire without thinking. If they missed, the target disappeared. If they hit the target, it turned upside down and spurted artificial blood. The acknowledged goal was to desensitize the recruits. The results were spectacular. In Vietnam, 80 percent of soldiers fired at the enemy. But this same 80 percent ended up with quite serious cases of post-traumatic stress disorder (PTSD). The soldiers had been forced to act against their nature. After a few years, they were repatriated, then let go into society with little or no support. Many of them became depressives, alcoholics, or drug addicts.

Today the US Army has to deal with more suicide deaths at the front. Now aware of this lamentable situation, the US government spends a fortune trying to provide help as best it can to the victims of its own system. The same thing goes for child soldiers in Africa, who are desensitized by being forced to kill someone they know. In all these cases, we are dealing with mind training that makes use of neuroplasticity.

It would be better to actualize our potential for goodness, no? And this is not a case of cosmetic surgery of the mind but rather of implementing our optimal way of being. Let's not allow our potential to go bad before it has a chance to develop.

CHRISTOPHE Mind training allows us to choose, among all the capabilities latent within our brains, the qualities we want to grow. As human mammals, we have potential for aggression, egoism, anger, and so on. But we also have potential for cooperation, altruism, and joy. If I want to be free to choose, it's better not to let my brain be fed only by my cultural environment or by circumstances, but rather to choose to take charge of my education myself and to point it in the right direction.

MATTHIEU When we learn to play the piano, a teacher guides us and shows us the right fingerings. We train and we make progress. In the case that interests us here, the work applies to our own minds. How should we go about it? We are all in agreement on this point: if we wish to free ourselves from certain noxious emotional elements, we first have to identify them and perform a diagnosis. We have to acknowledge, for example, that we are hotheads, that we lack enthusiasm, or that we suffer from chronic jealousy. Everything does not have to be changed. We just have to identify the aspects of our mental states that bring us pain and put the appropriate antidotes in place. Training also consists in fostering the development of certain good qualities and then strengthening them—compassion and strength of mind, for example. A small heart becomes a big heart, and we end up an "altruist," as my mother used to say of a particularly good person.

Emotional Intelligence and Mind Training

CHRISTOPHE In the matter of emotional intelligence, training the mind consists of creating new habits and new responses to situations that trigger our emotions. In general, our difficulties come either from our emotions being too intense (fits of anger, panic attacks, critical levels of despair), or from emotions prolonged by rumination (dwelling on gloomy ideas, worries, or resentments).

What we must clearly understand right off is that none of our mental activities is harmless. Every time we brood over something worrying us, we add muscle to our ability to worry; every time we dwell on a grudge, we muscle up our ability to carry grudges; every time our mind is seized by a distraction, we buff up our capacity for distraction. This is involuntary mind training, but sad to say it is effective. Similarly, every explosion of anger or panic attack paves the way for another return the next time we're in similar circumstances.

So it is important not to run these programs in our brain. We should stop ruminating as soon as we notice we're doing it and should engage in an opposite activity such as walking, talking to somebody, or even putting the thoughts in writing in order to clarify them and be rid of them. If a fit of anger occurs, get away from the scene and proceed as above. It's more difficult dealing with panic attacks—for that we may need a therapist's help. A therapist will explain how to hinder such attacks on our own: by breathing slowly and by remaining attentive to the external world instead of centering on oneself or getting involved in anxiety-producing interpretations of one's state. So the first phase is to cut off these mental programs and put the kibosh on this "wild" mind training that sustains emotional suffering.

In the second phase, test new programs "for real." In behavioral therapy, for example, this means confronting situations that trigger fears, but without obeying the fear. If you are afraid of empty space, stay with the empty space, breathe calmly, and don't run away. Every time you succeed in your confrontation with a situation without running away, the chosen program (facing it) scores points over the training program you succumb to (running away). That is why it takes so long. In my life I've had forty panic attacks. It took me at least forty successful confrontations with "panicogenic" situations for the anti-panic and pro-panic programs to reach equilibrium, and then, little by little, my reflex became to remain calm and breathe rather than to panic. The same goes for anger. The more I confront irritating situations without getting upset, the more my emotional-regulation program becomes robust and functional and goes into action first. For instance, once I might have reacted by saying, "If you keep up like that, I'll knock your block off!" Now I can calmly say, "That ticks me off."

It's the same principle in positive psychology: developing your optimism or your capacity for gratitude requires that you first observe what spontaneous, unidentified training your mind is submitting to. In the case of optimism, don't we have the tendency never to feel joy because we are too cautious? That is, we're well trained to put the brakes on any form of enthusiasm by immediately putting up a firewall: "Don't start rejoicing too fast—you never know." Or in the case of gratitude, don't we focus our attention on the benefits that come to us from others?

Once you have identified these tendencies, you have to run the optimism or gratitude programs regularly. For example, every evening recall three events that merit your gratitude; if possible, write them down and express them. The more the exercises are embodied and the more the emotions are genuinely felt and accompanied by acts such as writing or making phone calls to express your gratitude, the more the neuronal pathways are activated and strengthened. It's like with memory: mental repetition helps — as does repetition done out loud, in writing, or spoken to other people. The best way to remember jokes, for example, is to tell them several times.

There is definitely a biological substrate to mind training that is related to neuroplasticity — in other words, the ability of the brain to reconfigure itself and to remodel its synaptic pathways in response to cerebral networks being regularly activated by mental events, actions, emotions, and life experiences, and all of it repeatedly.

ALEXANDRE   One of the great tasks in working on oneself, it seems to me, is disarming the time bombs planted by the past: traumas, wounds, unfulfilled expectations, emotional needs, betrayals, disappointments. A dive into oneself allows one to revisit the thousand and one ordinary and forgotten incidents, the treasures and the ghosts of former days, to identify their subterranean impacts, their influences on today, on our current states of being, on our present way of being in the world. How long are emotions revived by a simple memory going to be allowed to continue smacking us upside the head? When Zen speaks of the "Great Death," it is inviting us to start anew, to be completely reborn. We could also amuse ourselves by ferreting out the thousand old refrains we carry around in our mental repertoire: "You're happy — you'll pay for this!" "Sooner or later you're going to croak, so get ready to go under!" "I need more. Gulp it down!" "Give me some food. I'm hungry!" All these hooks yank us out of the present, tempt us, hunt us down. The practice is to stay on course and not fall into the trap.

All the Same?

CHRISTOPHE   The argument that is sometimes raised against mind training is the fear of being formatted, that we'll all end up resembling each other. This is strange, because the same teaching — for example, in school — does not produce the same effect and the same results in everyone; it depends on the personal individualities of the children. Perhaps the fear of uniformity has other roots? Perhaps it's because we're afraid that our faults are what make us ourselves? Do people believe they stand out more from others on account of their egoism, their anger, their pettiness, their foibles, their faults?

But we have an excuse for thinking like that. It's a recurrent theme in Western culture. We all know the famous opening words of Tolstoy's novel, *Anna Karenina*: "Happy families are all alike; every unhappy family is unhappy in its own way."[1]

MATTHIEU   For certain, suffering is exciting; rich in twists and turns, it gives spice to life and an incandescent quality to our boredom. Our faults are supposedly myriad fascinating little beasts swarming in our minds, whereas virtues resemble pompous damsels, dressed to the nines. Doesn't this approach come from the fact that it is easier to deride good qualities than to make the effort necessary to acquire them?

ALEXANDRE   Conceptual mind always has to be gnawing on some bone, sharpening its teeth, feeling itself existing by toughing it out against adversity, by finding an inner or outer enemy to justify its existence. Are we sufficiently initiated into the art of resting, of self-recreation, of non-struggle, of living without the need for inner roller coasters so we can feel ourselves vibrating?

CHRISTOPHE   There is the idea that happiness would level everything more than unhappiness would and that we could be more creative in the expression of our faults than in the expression of our good qualities! That hasn't been studied very much, but the small amount of data that do exist does not confirm this idea. Rather the pleasant emotions are associated with greater attentional openness and greater psychological flexibility. This does not substantiate those stereotyped reactions. Moreover, we might note that the diversity of pleasant emotions experienced is associated with better health. (There is such a thing as "emodiversity"—emotional diversity—just as there is biodiversity.)

Finally, we can still be different from one another in our way of being kind, generous, and optimistic! Some people express their kindness overtly; others express it discreetly.

MATTHIEU Even the great spiritual masters manifest their kindness differently. Having acquired great wisdom and being perfectly free inwardly does not prevent them from having different characters and different ways of teaching. Some aren't very talkative; others are inclined to chat. Some are hermits you can only meet at their remote retreats; others, like the Dalai Lama, tirelessly share their vision of compassion with countless numbers of their fellow beings. They resemble each other in essential things—wisdom, compassion, contentment, self-control—but not in appearances, not in aspects more peripheral to their character.

It's curious, because among people who still have fairly far to go on the path, the magnitude of their differences reveals the infinite variety of possible faults, while their qualities of wisdom and compassion tend to resemble each other in their concordance with reality.

Some people imagine that if all beings were compassionate, patient, free from jealousy, and so on, it would be a dreadful bore, and they would be bored to tears in a drab and monotonous paradise. Inner peace seems so remote. I've always found it strange that people associate equanimity, calm, and silence with boredom. But in fact, the feeling of fulfillment that comes with inner freedom brings out the richness of every moment. Inner peace goes hand in glove with joie de vivre, enthusiasm, openness to others, and strength of mind. It brings the best in us to the surface. Nothing boring about that!

The Default Mode

MATTHIEU Neuroscientists speak of a default cerebral network to designate the mode of activity of the brain when one is doing nothing special and not directing attention to any particular object. On the psychological plane, this is the state of mind that prevails most of the time when a person is not engaged in any particular mental or physical activity. Subjectively, one's default could be equanimity, freedom, and inner calm but it could also be sadness, boredom, or mental agitation.

ALEXANDRE My default mode would be pretty much based on the old refrains that keep recycling again and again: "I'm screwed anyhow, so I might as well . . . ," "I'm never going to change," "It's a crazy waste of time to try to fix what's basically twisted." One of the great tasks of mind training consists in contemplating and observing the forces that are present and in identifying our default mode.

I call the habitual state of my mind its "idling state," which is what I feel inside when I'm no longer taken up with tasks, when distractions and preoccupations have subsided, or when I find myself alone without a book or the TV—without any chance of getting away from myself. Is it anxiety, fear, mortal boredom, peace, confidence? Identifying one's idling state is a considerable step forward. How can we not instrumentalize other people, blame the world, or keep running away from ourselves if deep within us we constantly feel need, conflict, or existential discontent?

Moreover, it is a definitive step to understand that our brain's custom is to be distracted, not to meditate. Basically speaking, equanimity is not its thing. It is programmed to judge, condemn, compare, worry, flee into the past, anticipate—in short, to lose it and go on wild goose chases. A singular practice recommended by Mingyur Rinpoche is this: ten times a day stop and observe, "Hey, I'm completely not meditating" or "I was completely distracted." Noting that one is distracted is in itself a powerful exercise of vigilance. And there you are, freedom is already happening!

Meditation provides a royal road that allows us to subject our flood of ideas and passions to a lucid, compassionate gaze and cut through our illusions, one by one. But we should not absolutize any particular practice; we should remember that when a person is up to their neck in the sad passions, meditation is not always within their reach. We also have need of people who will reach out to us and help.

Toolbox for Training the Mind

CHRISTOPHE

Taking care of yourself is taking care of your body *and* your mind. This means training the mind to cultivate its good qualities and nourishing it with good experiences. (There is also care for the soul, in addition to care for the body and mind, but we'll get to the soul later.)

In praise of repetition. If there's one rule to remember with regard to the way the mind works, in my opinion it would be this: many small repetitions (concrete) transform us more effectively than a single big decision (abstract).

Thinking that it's impossible to change is a mistake. This is confusing something difficult with something impossible. If you chase away your nature, will it come back at a gallop? Maybe, but your nature, like a horse, might *not* come back at a gallop if you take the time to teach it to move at a walk and if you don't try to "chase it away" but to tame it instead.

Watch out for invisible mind trainings. Exposing yourself regularly to materialistic or egoistic social situations or contexts can effectively train you in materialism or egoism. Continually whining, grumbling, seeing things negatively, and complaining will make us into champions at grumbling, negativism, and complaint. This also, unfortunately, is mind training.

The key to freedom. The significant technological progress happening now makes it necessary for us to make equivalent psychological progress in order to control it and make good use of it—instead of becoming its slaves. Training the mind is one of the keys to our freedom in the world of tomorrow.

ALEXANDRE

Make good use of mental representations. As the philosophers of antiquity remind us, the way in which we judge and interpret the world is the area where we can exercise our freedom. And this is the basis of an ascesis: track down our prejudgments, try to stick to facts when our imagination exaggerates, and identify the bundle of projections that we are imposing on reality.

There are a thousand ways to have fun alone in one's room. Coming back to ourselves and descending below the surface is sometimes an experience of boredom, fears, the tyranny of desires, the crowd of expectations milling around at the bottom of our mind, and perhaps of loneliness. Finding the resting state, our default state of mind, is at the same time perceiving the heavy baggage that we drag around with us—fears, needs, fantasies—so that we can divest ourselves of everything that gets in the way of a wholesome encounter with ourselves and others.

It's not a defect to be a little bit allostatic. With this point of view, I can ask myself, without forcing anything: What do I really need to stay happy and embrace a generous approach to life? What am I bound to? Where am I being dragged by the needs of my heart and the prejudgments of my brain?

Return to the state before judgments set in. Observe a flower, contemplate a landscape, or feel wonder at the beauty of a face without cramping these incredible experiences—always so rich and dense—and without fitting them into categories, classifying them, or comparing them with past experiences, with the already familiar. Let life come to us without forcing it into the mold of our ideas. In short, rediscover the wonder of a child without knowledge.

Training the mind does not resemble cramming for a spiritual exam. There's no need to accumulate knowledge. It's more about liberating yourself from your reflexes, your clichés, your defense mechanisms, your self-deceptions. Why not use the Socratic approach to reach the following ideas: I know that I know nothing. I know that I don't know how to rest, forgive, appreciate life, or spend an hour without worrying. Those are all "I don't knows" that lead to progress.

MATTHIEU

Superficial seduction versus lasting satisfaction. Laziness, cozy comforts, and distractions are seductive at first, but we soon find them dull and get tired of them. Training the mind is not as attractive when we begin, but the more we practice it, the more it brings profound and lasting satisfaction.

Training the mind is not a succession of fireworks; rather, it is the slow growth of a mighty oak that takes root in the nature of the mind and unfolds its foliage in the forest of life.

A harvest that is beneficial to all. This training gives us tools to manage life's problems skillfully and bring together greater inner peace with greater openness to others.

13

Meditation

In 1970, I was in Darjeeling when a sturdy fellow showed up wearing a three-piece suit, carrying an attaché case, and speaking with a southern French accent. Getting right to the point, he said to our spiritual master Kangyur Rinpoche, "I've run into a wall. I don't know which way to go. Something has to happen!" As he carried on describing his situation, Kangyur Rinpoche, his wife, and his whole family laughed good-naturedly, but the young man remained extremely serious. They brought him a good lunch, and once he relaxed, Kangyur Rinpoche began teaching him the rudiments of meditation, of a view of life and a spiritual path that was going to inspire him for the rest of his life.

Later on this man did nine years of contemplative retreats. An engineer by trade, he supervised the construction of several monasteries in India and Nepal. Since this time, he has been one of my closest friends. He's a solid, jovial person, full of good sense, well grounded in life. Meditation, integrated into the whole structure of a spiritual path, made all the difference for him.

Recently, while my friend was in Nepal, the little house he owned in the Dordogne completely burned down along with his few possessions. He was not the least bit troubled and commented, "In any case, I'll surely find a

place where I can sit quietly!" That is the kind of fruit that a life devoted
to seeking inner freedom through meditation can ripen.

—*Matthieu*

What Is Meditation?

MATTHIEU   According to the etymology of the Sanskrit and Tibetan
words for *meditation,* the term means "cultivate"—close to the idea of
mind training—and also "familiarize oneself with." Thus, there are as
many forms of meditation as there are ways of training the mind. All of
them have in common presence of mind, attention, clarity, and stability.

If we are cultivating attention and compassion, we familiarize ourselves
with these qualities. Thus, there is the dimension of the aim of the practice
and a process of cumulative training: we gradually become more and more
attentive and compassionate. We can also familiarize ourselves with a new
way of being, of dealing with our thoughts, of perceiving the world.

Finally, we can familiarize ourselves with the nature of the mind, which
usually escapes us because it is veiled by the clouds of our mental fabrications, the Mental FM radio so dear to Alexandre. We can habituate
ourselves to apprehending the awakened presence behind the cascades of
thoughts and to resting in the nature of this pure awareness. In this case, it
is not a matter of active training but of direct experience. Here the practice
does not consist of mental bodybuilding but in clearing away the clouds of
confusion and contemplating the sky of mind nature.

Buddhist introspection makes use of two methods, one analytic and the
other contemplative. Analytic meditation consists in getting to the bottom of
things. Are things permanent or impermanent? Do they exist autonomously or
interdependently? What are the immediate and ultimate causes of suffering? Is the "I," the ego, a unitary entity, endowed with independent existence?
Or is it not rather a convenient illusion existing only as a convention? Once we
have arrived at an irrefutable conclusion, contemplative meditation consists in
letting the mind rest in a nondiscursive manner in this new understanding,
in such a way that the mind assimilates it like water penetrating the earth.

CHRISTOPHE   Perhaps it's my failing as a caregiver or as a meditator less experienced than you are, Matthieu, but I would like to add a third dimension that comes even before what you just described and that seems to me very precious: calming.

MATTHIEU   Yes, a calm mind, clear and stable, is an indispensable condition for any form of meditation. We cannot cultivate anything if the tool of our mind is perpetually distracted, confused, and agitated like a turbulent child.

CHRISTOPHE   This initial calming phase is also something of an initiation. It teaches our patients that meditating is not a matter of drowsing away or thinking with your eyes closed. To meditate properly, we have to be quite awake. If we have slept badly or taken too many psychotropic drugs, our meditative exercises don't go very well.

We also have to understand that in meditation we change to another psychological register: we don't reject thinking or manifesting our intelligence, but we do it in a different way, by another path. We start by taking an overall inventory: we observe our thoughts, their vividness, their nature, their influence on us. This is a detour that allows us to come back to our thoughts later in a better way, in what you call analytic meditation, characterized by—among other things—a functioning of the mind that is composed, stable, and nourished by calm and detachment.

There is another detour that is also followed by a meditative return: when we do mindfulness meditation, we draw back from the world for an instant (but without abandoning it) simply to observe our experience. I am very fond of these words by Christian Bobin: "For the moment, I am happy to listen to the noise the world makes when I'm not there."[1] This disengagement is only transitory. And after it we return to the world, but we now definitely approach it differently—more lucidly, with greater composure, greater calm, and also with more intelligence and resolve.

MATTHIEU   We say that in meditation, instead of being carried away by the current, we sit on the bank of the river and watch the water flow from there. We can also choose to navigate on the river, controlling our boat in an expert manner.

CHRISTOPHE   True, and staying with that analogy, if we choose to return and navigate on the river, we will have taken the time to recuperate and recover our forces, and also to map the currents (understand the external world) and identify our fears and our confusions about how to navigate (understand how our mind works in these circumstances). We will have refilled our tank with clarity and energy, so to speak. This sort of detour via contemplation is very valuable for facilitating action if action is later required. We are far from a vision of purely contemplative meditation at this point; we are only talking about turning toward our inner selves and retreating from the world. But regular times of retreat are extremely valuable, whether our life is an active or a contemplative one.

ALEXANDRE   What led me to the practice of meditation was a deep state of distress without the slightest possibility of a pause, a rest; a quasi-permanent state of slavery, to put it in the words of Swami Prajnanpad, a state in which alienation could invade every area of life. There was no end to the grip of the past, of traumas, attractions, prejudgments.

Meditating is opening oneself to contemplative experience, heeding the call of the spiritual traditions to relate to the real without trying to possess it, to grasp it, while not rejecting any of it. The Christian mystics take us by the hand and lead us beyond having or possessing, beyond grasping or rejecting. It's a singular experience. The habitual ego is sidelined, and we get a glimpse of another relationship with the world. Along with the Buddhists, we are invited to give ourselves to the world without having ego collect its perpetual toll. When we are in the grips of discontent, it's difficult not to consider other people, nature, and life itself as instruments, a crutch, a huge department store. Practice expands and clears the horizon.

How can we ever be done with the rapacity of conceptual mind? Arthur Schopenhauer speaks of a will to live, blind and fierce, that *wants* through us. Embarking on the spiritual adventure is perhaps leaving behind this unquenchable appetite, this state of want, little by little. It's crazy the way greed, desire, and expectation cut us off from the beauty, the lightness, and the freely given quality of each moment. If we are in the grips of hunger, how can we walk down a street, even the most beautiful street in the world, without ogling the restaurants, the fast-food joints, the corner pizzeria, without being closed off from everything else? At that point, it's impossible to connect with fulfillment, rest, peace.

Meditating is thus attempting another kind of relationship with ourselves, with others, and with daily life, opening to another quality—another flavor—of life, an inner accessibility.

Here is a sort of survival kit that I have used for a long time to get myself into the practice of mind training. First of all, reduce the racket of Mental FM and listen to the sounds of the world with precision: to the honking of horns, to the laughter of a child, to the silence—in short, to everything around us. Basically, this is a matter of exiting our inner cinema and opening ourselves to the entire universe. Coming back to the senses, to perception, is choking off the conceptual mind that analyzes, compares, and comments. In a second phase, following that, we are asked to turn our attention to each part of the body to relax it—to relate to our hands, our feet, our legs, our arms—to survey this vehicle, which, as screwed up as it may be, carries us to enlightenment. This is an occasion to stop regarding it as a weight, an idol, a load, a burden. Then, without judging, without either rejecting or grasping, we can watch the immense flood of thoughts, the feelings, the emotions that come through us. Finally, in a fourth step—and oh, what a very essential one—in order to make an offering of our practice and reach out to something greater than ourselves, we send out *metta*: love, kindness, and compassion.

Meditating—parting with the negative emotions, dropping the self—also, and even especially, means working for the benefit of all. Sitting on a cushion or lying down in order to collect oneself—this is not cutting oneself off from the world but giving oneself.

MATTHIEU *Metta* in Pali (*maitri* in Sanskrit) means "lovingkindness"; it consists in wishing for all beings to find happiness and the causes of happiness. *Karuna* means "compassion" (the counterpart of *metta*), in other words, the wish for all beings to be liberated from suffering and its causes. Lovingkindness embraces all beings, no matter their condition, and it transforms into compassion the moment it is confronted by suffering.

ALEXANDRE Training the mind to do away with the mental toxins, get rid of the parasites, and track down idolatries is sharpening our inner ear. And for the believer, it is making oneself accessible to transcendence. It is seeing the immense solidarity that unites us all with everything. This glimpse, this opening, can quickly pervade all of daily life and extend itself into a movement toward the other, a joy in sharing, in really listening.

In *Human, All Too Human*, Nietzsche provides us with a marvelous tool: the best way to start the day is to ask ourselves if we can make somebody happy that day.

Dealing with Thoughts in Meditation

MATTHIEU Distracted awareness, or the mind asleep in some excessive relaxation, is the opposite of meditation. The distracted mind resembles the wild weeds at the top of a mountain pass, bending in all directions at the whim of the winds. It does not even know that it is distracted. Dull and murky awareness can be compared to water at night: even though it is naturally transparent, it becomes opaque in the dark. By contrast, if many thoughts arise but we remain perfectly aware of what is happening, we are not distracted.

Wanting to stop thoughts is a vain fantasy. If we take the point of view that a "good" meditation must be devoid of thoughts, we are off to a bad start. The important thing is to remain lucid and conscious of our present state. Are we calm, agitated, clear, tense, or relaxed? Are we aware of being sad, joyful, full of enthusiasm, or bored? Distraction causes us to lose this awareness of the present moment; ten minutes later, we see that our mind has wandered through the whole world, and we have completely lost track of the object of our meditation. The goal, therefore, is not to try to make everything perfect, like an ever-immaculate sky, but to never forget the presence of pure awareness. We should be like a shepherd watching his sheep. He does not prevent them from roaming around but always keeps an eye on them.

CHRISTOPHE The gossiping mind, scatteredness, distraction, are always the first obstacles in the practice of meditation. But all of that is completely normal. Our mind works that way; our brain produces thoughts just as our lungs produce inhalations and exhalations. Each one of our organs does its job in its own way. It's up to us to go beyond, to allow those thoughts to be there but not to feed them, not to become submerged in them. As you point out, Matthieu, distraction is not having a whole bunch of thoughts in our mind, but it is listening to them, following them, getting stuck in them, lost in them.

In mindfulness meditation, the work consists in observing our thoughts and our reactions to those thoughts—how they attract our attention, how they influence our body, how they generate impulses, how they become associated with each other. Every moment in which we become aware of our distraction or our scatteredness is a very precious moment. Each one is training in quickly noticing that our mind has gone elsewhere.

But this scatteredness is not itself a problem if we accept its presence. It is like being out of breath when we are jogging; it's normal, and it doesn't keep us from running. We simply adapt our rhythm, and we keep training over time so that being out of breath is less and less an issue. Our scatteredness and our distraction should not dissuade us from meditating but encourage us to undertake simple exercises, first centered on noticing that we are scattered and distracted, and then each time we notice, returning to awareness of the breath, for example.

What is very specific to meditation is that after having become aware of mental scatteredness, we decide to observe it for a rather long time. We don't get into reflections like, "I'll never make it" or "This thing of theirs is impossible for me; you have to have a special kind of brain." Rather we stay with it, observing with full attention, mindfully, just what it is that constituted this experience of distraction.

Once again it seems evident that meditating is not thinking about something in the usual manner but rather begins with experiencing our experience deeply, fully, attentively—even annoying experiences such as distraction and boredom.

MATTHIEU In the beginning there is a targeted effort—diligent, somewhat forced. Then pure awareness becomes second nature. We no longer meditate intentionally, yet nevertheless we are not distracted. It's a kind of an uninterrupted flow of awareness, a way of being that is the ripened fruit of training.

Why Meditate?

MATTHIEU Some people might ask, "Why should I bother to meditate? I've got lots of other things to do." Or, as we saw when we were talking about effort: "Life teaches me enough stuff. Why add to it?" For that question, we could substitute the following one: "Am I functioning optimally?" You have to be very pretentious or dishonest to say that everything is proceeding ideally in your way of being or thinking. We are a combination of lights and shadows. A specific kind of mind training, meditation has been practiced for millennia, and the neurosciences have confirmed its effectiveness. Why not try it? We've already pointed out that we don't meditate in order to muscle up our brain but because we have to deal with our mind from morning till night, and it is quite frequently disturbed.

CHRISTOPHE Inasmuch as regular meditation does require effort, it is legitimate to ask the question, "Why meditate?" Some teachers answer this question by appealing to a strict ideal. But meditation, in order to really be meditation, should be without a goal; it should not be connected with any specific expectations. We meditate for the sake of meditating, period!

Most of us do not come to meditation through simple curiosity or an attraction to exoticism. We come to it because we have a need for it, because we are suffering, ill—because we clearly see to what extent our mental, emotional, and behavioral functioning is remote from our ideals of conduct. As you just pointed out, Matthieu, we know that we are not functioning optimally, and we just want to improve. Thus, we are ready to commit ourselves to the effort of meditation practice, through all its stages.

MATTHIEU Nowadays it is universally accepted that exercise is good for our health. Nobody would accuse you of wasting your time if you devoted twenty minutes a day to it. Even if we do sometimes exaggerate the benefits of meditation for our health, several hundred studies confirm its beneficial effects on our physical and mental health (in the prevention of relapses in cases of depression, for example). Therefore, if twenty minutes a day of meditation would improve the quality of the remaining twenty-three hours and forty minutes—including our sleep, our relationships, our ability to avoid burnout—then it seems rather like a good investment! The argument most often raised against it is, "Yes, but I haven't got the time." It's a bit as though the doctor told you, "In all candor, you're not well. You have to undergo treatment." And you replied, "Listen, doctor, I can't go through with this treatment. I don't feel well, and what's more, I haven't got the time. So I'll do what I have to when I'm feeling better and I've retired." We have to be smart enough to take the time to learn to improve the quality of our life.

How Does Meditation Liberate Us?

MATTHIEU In the beginning, our mind is very turbulent, so it is very difficult to complete an analytical meditation and to cultivate compassion, and it's still more difficult to observe the nature of awareness. We just have to deal with a whirligig of thoughts. The first step, therefore, as we have seen, is to achieve a certain level of calm. We don't do this by knocking out the mind the way we would knock somebody out with a stick; rather we give it a chance to become a little clearer, a little more stable.

That's why most meditations begin with observation of the breath. It is at the same time practical (the breath is always there), simple (a constant movement of coming and going), and subtle (it's invisible, and if we don't pay attention, it disappears instantly from our perceptual field). It is, therefore, an excellent object for refining our attentional faculty. This simple training is not necessarily easy, however. We can even be discouraged at the beginning by seeing that "I have more thoughts now than I had before; meditation is not for me." There are not necessarily more of the thoughts; rather we have begun to perceive what is going on, to be able to gauge the extent of the damages. However, like a waterfall turning into a mountain torrent, and then into a river, and finally a still lake, the mind calms down with time.

After a few weeks or even a few months, I can pass on to the next stage: "Now that I have a more flexible and accessible mind and can direct it like a well-trained horse, I can say to it: 'Apply yourself to compassion.'" This sequence of progression should be respected, and it is of no use trying to skip ahead. If you try to meditate on compassion when your mind still won't hold still, you won't cultivate compassion; you'll simply be distracted.

I can also ask myself, "In the end, who is meditating? The ego? Awareness?" I can analyze the nature of all that. In a more contemplative and direct fashion, I can deepen my questioning: "What is behind all these thoughts? Is it not awakened presence, the quality of pure awareness that is behind all mental events?" At that point, I begin to glimpse that which, underlying all thoughts, is always there like the unmoving sky behind the clouds. I can then let the mind rest in this pure awareness.

CHRISTOPHE Yes, the stage of calming, the first goal of mindfulness meditation, is similar to the warm-up phase for an athlete or like scales for a pianist—a way of maintaining optimal physical condition so as to be able to accomplish other actions. For meditators, as I explain to my patients, it's a nonspecific exercise for getting one's mind on the right track.

That's why we need to keep working regularly on simple mindfulness—first for cultural reasons (because our environment makes us scattered) and then for natural reasons (because our attention, the way it functions in our brain as a primeval mechanism for surveying our environment, leads us to distraction). Distraction is, in fact, a useful function; it permits us to react at the moment when a new event arises in our environment. If we are animals and this new event represents a threat, then being "distracted" from what we are doing—grazing, resting—can save our life. But if we are humans of the twenty-first century, distraction—a phone call, an internet ad—does not at all save our lives. Quite the opposite.

ALEXANDRE Conceptual mind prefabricates a vision of the world, of life, of love, of self, of happiness, of joy. It has an opinion on everything. With its suitcase full of preconceptions, it cuts us off from naked, immediate experience. Ascesis here is perhaps to identify what belongs to the ego sphere—worries, cares, troubles, the desire to please, discontent—in order to rediscover the primordial goodness of life, which, beyond all fears and expectations, is given in the fullness of the moment.

But how do we calm the beast? In the midst of chaos, I had to improvise a makeshift exercise: Notice and evaluate your thoughts, emotions, and fears on a scale from one to ten. On this scale of inner seismography, a number of one corresponds to a neutral, quiet idea that doesn't make me either hot or cold. At ten on the scale, I have to leap for the phone in order to avoid doing something irreparable. This technique, on the whole rather basic, has the merit of detaching us a little from our thoughts: "Hmm, let's see, there's a three. Here's a four! Oh, I'm looking at a six."

To our misfortune, we believe in an ironclad way in everything that appears in our mind: convictions, whims, phobias, fantasies, delirious ideas. Sometimes disobeying these commandments, daring to let them pass without acting on them, is one of the most effective expedients.

MATTHIEU   To the extent that our mind is prey to mental agitation, we are the slave of our thoughts. Mastery here is freedom. The sailor who is master of his vessel sails to the destination of his choice. A ship buffeted by winds and currents is in great danger of wrecking on a reef.

A person subject to distraction will set off after each thought like a dog chasing a thrown stick. The unmastered mind tends to amplify thoughts and let them proliferate. A thought occurs—"I'd love a cup of tea," "I need something at the store," "I have to make a phone call"—and the body follows it and executes it. The calm mind concentrates on a chosen object or rests in a vast and transparent simplicity.

CHRISTOPHE   What meditation contributes to our inner freedom is very important: stability of attention and emotion first of all—the keys to sound judgment. Then comes expansion of the consciousness: meditation is intentionally and calmly (not as in involuntary distraction) opening to others and the world, understanding their importance, as well as the associations and interdependences that link us with them. This is adopting a view of the world that is in some sense exterior to ourselves, liberating ourselves from the self.

MATTHIEU   Let's take the example of a person who is a prisoner of their reactions. Someone insults them. They take offense, get angry, or become depressed. They are far from being free. They are even a target who is vulnerable to criticism and praise, to loss and gain, and other ordinary considerations. Now, it is possible not to fly off the handle when somebody criticizes us or not to become arrogant and vain when we are praised. If we understand that ego is not such a solid target as it makes itself out to be—that it is, in fact, transparent by nature—then all the arrows in the world can no longer hurt it. We have rediscovered our freedom. If we broaden and deepen this inner freedom, disturbances pass through our mind, unwinding as they occur.

ALEXANDRE   It's crazy and at the same time marvelous to consider oneself transparent, to perceive one's own nature as a clear sky on which traumas, accidents along the way, and various trials and tribulations in the end leave no trace.

One of the purposes of meditation involves revealing that *it* is thinking in us, *it* is desiring, *it* wants, *it* is reacting. Meditation reveals that grafted onto our being is a host of defense mechanisms, extraneous desires, and fantasies. We are far from transparent. The aim of training the mind is precisely to return home, to separate ourselves from all external scaffolding. Yet all day long, ego fights to maintain its prerogatives, impose its rights, defend its ideas—to the point where there's a risk of general and complete exhaustion.

Zen speaks of the original state, of space, of an immense heart, vast and open. We have all been children unburdened by our present heap of preconceptions, complexes, social roles, free of the need to compensate. There continues to exist within us an unscathed, unharmed, untouchable element, sacred and pure. Meditating means returning to our true essence beyond all the intervening layers. It means entering into a state of intimacy with our true nature.

CHRISTOPHE   There is an instructive distinction that we caregivers establish between reacting and responding. Reaction is immediate and impulsive; response is composed and thought out. In life we have need of both. Sometimes we have to react fast; sometimes we have to respond with composure. Reacting requires no effort from us; it is instinctive: giving back blow for blow, for example. Responding, on the other hand, involves a learning curve, especially where our emotions are implicated.

Here again, regular practice of mindfulness meditation supports our efforts with a series of irreplaceable exercises and experiences. For example, when we meditate with our patients, we explain to them that if their nose itches or if they get a cramp in their calf, they can certainly scratch or move. But we also ask them not to behave habitually here: before doing it, they should take the time to observe what is happening, to explore their experience. Breathe, see exactly where the itch or the cramp is located, how intense it is, what thoughts it triggers ("I'm not going to be able to hold out. I have to do something"), and what impulses the body manifests ("Have I already stretched out my arm to scratch? Have I already begun to wriggle with the intention of moving?"). Then look to see if, after a few moments, the need to scratch or move is still there or if it has changed or even disappeared. Thus we are saying: try to respond rather than react immediately. It's amazing when patients see that through taking the time to be mindful before obeying an impulse, sometimes the situation (the itch or cramp) or their psychological feeling ("I have to do something") changes by itself.

This is good training, based on simple situations, that can help us learn to confront more complex situations, particularly in dealing with impulses that have been emotionally activated, especially in connection with fear or anger.

Meditation teaches us not to be enslaved by these impulses, these mental mechanisms: I itch, so I scratch. I see something that needs to be done, so I do it. I have a worry on the horizon, so I dwell on it, I chew on it. Somebody offends me when I'm feeling stressed, so I explode or I collapse. It's always the difference between reacting and responding. Meditating regularly gives you a space of freedom that makes it possible to choose between the two. This space of freedom consists in being present, observing what is happening, and then taking the time not to do anything hurriedly so we can discern more clearly what is important at this moment.

On the neuropsychological level, through this non-active, nonreactive practice of being present to the world, meditation can help us to inhibit certain automatic behavioral, emotional, or cognitive programs (our automatic thoughts). And this is extremely valuable for patients, because it inhibits the automatic triggering of rumination or inappropriate behaviors, but is not a case of blind or blanket repression. We're not in the "keep yourself from doing that" mode, but rather in a mode something like, "Observe the experience that consists in having the urge to do that and remain in a state of observation before going on to act or not." The exercise about the cramp or the urge to scratch your nose while meditating may be kind of dumb, but it represents a phenomenological discovery for most people. They understand that they can choose to do or not do something that seemed irrepressible to begin with.

MATTHIEU When I was learning sailing from my uncle Jacques-Yves Le Toumelin, who sailed solo around the world in a motorless sailboat, we were cruising off the Brittany coast on a day of heavy swell. When you're at the rudder and a wave takes the boat from the side, the boat deviates from its course. At that point, you want to pull hard on the rudder to make it come back on course. Once that's done, you want to bring the rudder back hard in the opposite direction. My uncle corrected me: "Stop fidgeting around! Keep the rudder steady in the middle!" When you do that, the boat will move a bit to starboard and a bit to port, and so on and so on, but overall it will stay on course. There's no point in tiring yourself out reacting. In life, keeping a steady hand on the rudder means staying in a mindful state without spending your time attracting or rejecting experiences.

CHRISTOPHE The attraction-repulsion mechanism is important to understand. We are attracted by experiences that seem good to us. Meditation is not going to make us indifferent to those experiences, but it will help us to savor them without becoming attached to them (without worrying every moment that they're going to be interrupted). Meditation will also allow us to check out whether savoring what attracts us is really a good idea because it might be something toxic or addictive like sugar, alcohol, or tobacco.

We also tend to reject what seems unpleasant to us. Meditation will help us do a better job of accepting the fact that unpleasant experiences exist (instead of dreaming of never having to confront them) and to get through them in the best way, without necessarily trying to avoid them (they can sometimes be useful to us). This means in some sense suffering less or suffering "better," without becoming fully identified with our suffering or being permanently under its thumb.

ALEXANDRE   Zen talks about everyday mind, saying that freedom, peace, joy, and detachment can be found in the very midst of conflict and chaos. So why not consider anger, impatience, and negative tendencies—all those feelings we would like to tear right out of our hearts—as occasions to practice wisdom, exercise virtue, and grow?

In *Beyond Good and Evil*, Nietzsche speaks of a fated spiritual state that resists all instruction. At the core of our being are there not preconceptions, but also hardcore aftereffects, memories, and traumas that stubbornly persist and block progress and change? We can break our teeth for lifetimes on these hardened kinks, large and small, that plunge us into discouragement. The binary way of reading the world, in terms of attraction and repulsion, for example, is really tough and tyrannical—it's as hard as granite.

To move in the direction of freedom, perhaps it's a good idea to identify this deep-lying stratum of rock.

MATTHIEU   In winter, ice hardens the lakes and rivers. Water becomes so solid it can support men, beasts, and vehicles. In spring the thaw comes. Ice is hard and sharp, and water is soft and flowing. Water and ice are neither identical nor different. In a similar fashion, it can occur that the mind freezes hard, especially when it imposes on reality intrinsic attributes that it is devoid of (friend, enemy, attractive, repulsive, etc.) and is tormented by attraction and repulsion. Meditation then allows us to melt the ice of mental fabrications into the flowing water of inner freedom.

When everything in the mind seems to have solidified to the extent where you have the feeling of never being able to come to the end of certain tendencies or sources of pain, I understand how the idea would sometimes arise that there exists in you a piece of granite, a hard, intractable pit. This is a belief linked to certain experiences, memories, and traumas, such as you mention. But in reality, no enduring stumbling block exists at the core of our being.

To the extent that we learn to rest in the fundamental nature of our mind, it becomes inconceivable to succumb to profound anxiety or to hate and jealousy. These states of mind seem alien in this space of pure awareness. That which within us feels hate is not buddha nature. This does not mean, however, that we are not susceptible to going astray again, because we are far from the end of the path.

ALEXANDRE What is it that exiles us from this "big mind," to put it in the words of Shunryu Suzuki—from this fundamental mind nature? Trauma, suffering, fear of being hurt, a certain will to power: all these compete to give freedom the slip. Listening to you, dear Matthieu, I realize that meditation is not there to correct us but rather to help us come back to the ground of grounds, to true joy. We should devote ourselves to it with the lightheartedness of the prisoner who sees the dungeon door opening.

MATTHIEU Yes, the goal of meditation is not to correct us, in the schoolmarmish sense of the term, but rather to permit us to deepen our level of awareness to the point where we rediscover the total pure awareness, which is not this hard pit we were talking about but the natural transparency of the mind. I often cite the following example: after a fit of anger, people quite aptly say, "I was beside myself" or "I was not myself."

ALEXANDRE There are lots of different ways of being beside oneself or outside oneself. There is the rage or the hubris that carries us away and alienates us from ourselves. And there is also the giving of self, generosity, love, and compassion, *karuna.* On one side, the ravages of passion; on the other, surrender of self. Meditating is parting with the ego and plunging into the ultimate depths of our being.

CHRISTOPHE That is the image evoked by Simone Weil: "Look upon each human being (image of oneself) as a prison inhabited by a prisoner, surrounded by the whole universe."[2] Getting angry is breaking everything in our cell; pacifying this anger, without necessarily giving up acting upon what made us angry, is getting outside our cell a bit and seeing a little of what's going on around us. Once again, meditation is not, or not only, getting away from the world; rather, ultimately, it's always opening up to it, returning to it.

MATTHIEU As long as we are prisoners of our mental fabrications and continue to distort reality, we resemble a bee imprisoned in a glass bottle, as my teacher Kangyur Rinpoche used to say. It flies up and down endlessly without being able to escape. Inner freedom is not breaking the bottle, but rather understanding that our attachments are not as solid as they seem and that the glass of the bottle is only an illusion. At that point, the bee is free in the vastness of the sky.

Before and After Meditation

MATTHIEU Meditation should not stop when we get up from our cushion. If it did, what's the point? It would be like going to a Turkish bath: once you're out of the cocoon of hot steam, it's freezing outside, and you are no further advanced in being able to combat the cold. Even worse, you might catch a cold. After meditation (we speak of "postmeditation"), we therefore have to make sure that certain qualities last like the scent of perfume and allow us to enter into action while at least partially maintaining the mastery of our minds attained during meditation. This is a difficult but indispensable exercise. If we do not manage this, we are like the horseback rider who has little trouble staying in the saddle while in the stable, but who falls off the horse at the first obstacle in the forest. The more one is the master of one's mind, the less vulnerable one is to the ups and downs of daily life. The degree to which meditation and postmeditation are unified is a good measure of one's spiritual progress. It is said that at the end of the path, on the highest level of the bodhisattvas, there is no longer any difference between meditation and postmeditation. But we don't get to that point in just five minutes.

Nevertheless, something remains even for beginners who have some taste of daily meditation, like a landscape one remembers with one's eyes shut. Right in the middle of a traffic jam or a conflict situation, it is possible to reposition one's mind onto this experience. Reconnecting in this way calms the mind. It becomes less susceptible to boiling on the fire of adverse circumstances.

If one recalls in this way more and more frequently, at the end of a certain time the qualities of meditation form something like a trickle of water, thin but continuous. Little by little this trickle transforms into a river, and the current of pure awareness is no longer in danger of being interrupted.

CHRISTOPHE   In teaching mindfulness, that's exactly what we do. We very clearly distinguish three categories of practice: the extended formal practice (I sit and meditate twenty minutes every morning); the parenthetical interludes of mindfulness throughout the day, being present to oneself and the world for a few minutes (in a waiting room, on public transport, on the way from one place to another, during breaks) or being present to one's emotions (pleasant ones, in order to appreciate them more; unpleasant ones, in order to get through them better); and finally mindfulness in action (cooking, housekeeping, mindfully doing one's work; eating, walking, looking at the sky, observing nature, listening mindfully to others).

Little by little we reach the understanding that there aren't, on one side, moments when we are meditating and aiming for peace and understanding and, on the other side, moments when we are just living and are stressed, irritated, and scattered. Meditation is not just a compensation or a reparation; it has to be the basis for the transformation of our way of living.

ALEXANDRE   We have to practice here and now, with available resources, without obsessing about any particular result. The Zen masters never give up hammering it in: "It's nothing special." It's in daily life, as you were saying, dear Christophe, that we have to dare to give ourselves to acting mindfully: cooking, housekeeping, wiping away a mocking expression, catching a bus, fighting with an ornery computer.

Sometimes, caught up in an unhappy state, we might dream of a shock treatment, a horse pill, something that will do the job in a flash, but real progress happens millimeter by millimeter. The rich experiences of everyday life provide a thousand levers for opening ourselves to the world and dancing joyfully amid its tragedies. Why not dedicate ourselves to this very simple practice: contemplate and examine this nice little person — oneself — getting agitated and simply let it pass: "Hmm, look there, I'm stressed out," "Ouch, oh, oh, there I am in panic mode." There is perhaps nothing extraordinary in ascesis: brief inner retreats, small moments of mindfulness that little by little bring us back home, to calm, to peace.

MATTHIEU As for small regular exercises, there is this one proposed by Chade-Meng Tan, a former Google engineer: One day when we were with the Dalai Lama, the neuroscientist Richard Davidson, and a group of meditators, Meng said, "I'm going to tell you a big secret: ten seconds of meditation every hour!" At first we thought, "This is one of those Silicon Valley things, the height of superficiality." And then when he explained his idea, we began to change our minds. Everyone can take a break for ten seconds, look around or out the window, and for ten seconds generate an altruistic wish for unconditional compassion toward everyone who is within their field of attention. In the subway, at work, in the street we wish intensely for ten seconds, "May beings enjoy happiness, flourish in life, and liberate themselves from problems, from the mental poisons. May these obstacles disappear." Ten seconds. Even if we do it only six times a day, that's already much better than nothing.

The virtue of this very simple practice is that the effect of it lasts far beyond the ten seconds. If you open a bottle of perfume for ten seconds, the fragrance remains after the cork is back on the bottle. If these compassionate wishing times are close enough together, they will constitute a continuity, like a perfume in the atmosphere. And what's more, after having wished all good things to all people, there is very little risk that we'll end up slapping our neighbor the next minute.

Finally, this practice of Meng's is not very far from traditional teachings on meditation. Short repeated periods at regular intervals are much more valuable than big efforts very spaced out in time. In the neurosciences, moreover, it has been shown that to change the brain, it is preferable to repeat small efforts every day than to come up with a big effort every two weeks. In that case, the process of altering the brain is briefly engaged but does not last.

CHRISTOPHE That reminds me of a little exercise that I recommend to my patients—especially the female ones—to do in the evening, after work. I tell them, "When you get home, the first thing you should do is sit down on the living room couch and allow yourself ten minutes to compose yourself, recenter yourself, and breathe. Inevitably you will be assaulted by thoughts like, 'There's dust on this piece of furniture. I see it. I have to tidy up, cook dinner, answer my emails.' This is normal! Definitely don't obey those thoughts. Observe the pressure they put on you, ordering you to obey them, filling your mind and body with malaise, guilt, the feeling you have to get moving, go into action. Don't forget that you are doing something very important that nobody can do for you—taking care of yourself. Others can help you with the housecleaning, with the cooking, and all the rest of it. But taking care of yourself is something you alone can decide upon and do." So, for five or ten minutes, these patients stoically experience doing nothing. And understanding that this is possible, that it is a plausible existential choice, is very valuable and beneficial.

Real Changes Occur Imperceptibly over Time

CHRISTOPHE There is another big misunderstanding concerning meditation. Many people think that getting into the realm of meditation will transform their way of being, make them more "Zen," more this or more that. As a result, they think they are failing when they don't feel more "Zen" or don't succeed in feeling that way all the time. I then tell them, meditation will not immediately transform your way of being, but it will enrich your possibilities for responding to life. You will still get angry. You will still get sad or worried. You will still get distracted. But perhaps these things will happen less often, less overwhelmingly, and to better effect. There might also be moments in which you will succeed in not having these things happen. The goal of meditation—in any case of therapeutic meditation—is not becoming a full-time sage, but rather to train in adopting new ways of reacting and to become a part-time sage! Instead of saying, "Before I was doing this, and today I will do that, which is completely different," it is better to say, "Before I was doing this, and I will continue to do it from time to time, maybe more effectively. But I'm also going to try some other things, and then I'll make up my mind." Meditation is an enrichment and expansion of our lifestyle, rather than a radical transformation.

MATTHIEU   It's somewhat the same situation in Buddhist centers. We see that someone is behaving obnoxiously, and we get upset about it: "How dare that person behave like this in a Buddhist center!" Now, if people like that have come to attend the teachings, it's precisely because they find themselves imperfect and have the laudable desire to improve. It would be unreasonable to require them to instantly manifest all the marks of perfection!

In the case of meditation, the goal is to make progress over the course of months and years. Rather than trying to make sudden leaps forward in our practice, we should look for slow but reliable progress. If you stare fixedly at the hands of a watch, they seem immobile, but if you look at them every now and then, you see that they've moved. Thus, we should be diligent without being impatient. Haste doesn't mix well with meditation, because all genuine transformation takes time. It doesn't matter so much that the way is long; what is essential is that we feel we are going in the right direction. Moreover, it's never a question of all or nothing. Each stage contributes to our inner development and brings its share of satisfaction.

CHRISTOPHE   Yes, that's true in therapy as well. We don't set an immediate goal of radical change. In the first phase, we recommend to patients that they add new ways of responding intelligently to certain life situations, test them out, and see if they want to adopt them. In a dentist's or doctor's waiting room, is it better to practice mindful breathing, play video games, or read magazines? Any of those is fine; the point is that we should be ready to try out and practice new possibilities in order to find out what is useful to us at different times and in relation to different needs of ours.

ALEXANDRE   In a waiting room, at a bus stop, when I'm upset, I can always give myself to an ascesis: "Ah, see there, I'm getting into that thing. . . ." This has greatly aided me in pacifying the infernal machine. Fundamentally, meditating is profiting from every moment without speculating about the future, parting from the calculating mind and just being in the world.

MATTHIEU   One day I spent a long time sitting in a waiting room with two friends of mine, one of whom was a long-time meditator. The third fellow finally said, "I'm sorry you're having to wait such a long time." The meditator replied, "But I'm not waiting." He meant that he was not frustrated by the length of the wait because his mind was disengaged from waiting for what was not happening.

ALEXANDRE   But how do we get out of the grips of our accountant-like brain and from our inability to be comfortable in the here and now?

MATTHIEU   We have to know how to rest in the freshness of the present moment, at the core of which there is no waiting. But there is also another form of waiting that is more serious in tone, where we not only have to dispel the heaviness of boredom but also have to prepare ourselves in a concrete way for good or bad news, in the case of a medical examination, for example.

CHRISTOPHE   We have to make the effort to immerse ourselves in the experience of waiting, seeing that, on the one hand, there is the fact of sitting there in a state of expectation with regard to an event that is to come and, on the other hand, the fact of being in a particular mental state. If I say to myself, "I'm wasting my time. Time is passing. What are they up to in there?" then the experience of waiting is not the same as if I say to myself, "Okay, I see these thoughts and this impatience that are trying to take over the way I am perceiving this moment. I can also experience it differently. I can profit from the waiting to feel myself alive, become present to myself and to the world, take advantage of it to compose myself, breathe, observe, smile." The consequences are different. In the second case, we will not have wasted our time; we will have lived it.

MATTHIEU   If we don't enter the vicious circle of expectation, then what is the problem? People complain that they don't have time to meditate. We could take advantage of that twenty minutes of quiet!

Does Mindfulness Necessarily Mean More Altruism?

CHRISTOPHE   To date, there are at least three studies that show that simple mindfulness practice, even in which compassion is not specifically taught, augments our capacity for empathy and altruistic behavior. For example, a brief exercise of mindfulness causes volunteers to give up their chairs to a person on crutches more often than those who haven't meditated. Always after even brief experiences of mindfulness practice, results on empathic sensitivity scales are significantly increased.

The hypothesis is that emotional calming, attentional openness, and detachment in relation to ourselves naturally open the door to compassion. We are more attentive to what is going on around us, and our natural inclinations toward empathy and compassion are facilitated because they are not obstructed by possible painful emotions and self-centered preoccupations.

MATTHIEU It is, in fact, reasonable to think that diligent practitioners of mindfulness would be naturally more open to the needs and aspirations of others. In general, if meditation is well taught and practiced, compassion occurs naturally. But we should be wary of the idea that such compassion will automatically come as a guaranteed secondary effect of meditation. We're better off making compassion a core priority of ours from the beginning.

This seems to have been confirmed by the only serious longitudinal study (one that is carried out over a long period of time) performed to date on the effects of different kinds of meditation. At the Max Planck Institute in Leipzig, neuroscientist Tania Singer and her team of thirty researchers followed 150 volunteers over nine months. These subjects carried out three months of mindfulness meditation (not the full MBSR intervention, which includes compassion), three months of considering the point of view of other people, and three months of *metta* (lovingkindness) meditation. These meditations were all done at the rate of thirty minutes per day, five days per week, plus two hours with an instructor every Saturday. The volunteers were divided into three groups, which practiced these meditations in different orders to determine whether the order in which the practices were done influenced the results. Different volunteers served as a control group and participated in a nine-month program of memory training. All sorts of tests and measurements were carried out on all the groups: behavioral tests, questionnaires, physiological and immunological measurements, and various scans, including functional brain scans (fMRI).

The results showed that the three months of mindfulness meditation did indeed improve mindfulness (attention, presence, etc.) but in no way augmented prosocial behavior—that is, helping, sharing, cooperative, and consoling behaviors directed voluntarily toward other people. Considering the point of view of other people improved the volunteers' ability to understand what other people think and feel but only weakly augmented prosocial behavior. By contrast, after the three months devoted to loving-kindness meditation, prosocial behaviors considerably increased. Moreover, the structural changes observed in the brain were different for the three types of meditation and affected specific neural networks. It therefore seems clear that if we wish to increase lovingkindness, we must work on lovingkindness itself.

ALEXANDRE If meditation doesn't make us more generous, it's not worth an hour's worth of effort. To descend into the heart of our inner being is to discover that an indestructible link unites us with each other. The proof of this is the impact those around us have on our joy and peace. The most consuming passion also shows that beyond the cramped state of ego we are all creatures of communication—open to, reaching toward, and offering ourselves to others.

Meditation also means discovering the bundle of projections, complaints, and resentments that live like parasites on our relations with others. In this sense, we could say that mind training lubricates our human relationships and pulls out, one by one, the barbs and spines that arise among individuals. Descending into oneself is daring to go naked, to cast off one's armor, to drop all disguises in order to give oneself without reserve. It also means discovering that there is no territory of one's own—no personal turf—to preserve. It's up to each person to blow to pieces the rigid walls that separate the outer from the inner, ego from other, me from you.

MATTHIEU That's true. If meditation consisted only in taking breaks with our gaze lost in the clouds, surrounded by plumes of incense, and contenting ourselves with relaxing as if we were at a spa, ten years later we'd be more than likely to remain just as ill-tempered, tormented, and incapable of managing our emotions as before we started. We will have totally wasted our time.

In the beginning, meditation runs the risk of being too self-centered. I remember the words of Ajahn Amaro, an English monk in the Theravada tradition, during the course of a day of mindfulness practice in California. He described a family father who had decided to begin meditating. He ate his breakfast very slowly, tasting each flavor in his spoonful of muesli, while his children were going nuts around him trying to get his attention. He ignored them. All he wanted was to shut himself up in a little bubble of individualistic tranquility.

CHRISTOPHE   One thing is sure: today we are at a pivotal point as far as meditation is concerned. This practice that we are encouraging so much has at this point acquired an impressive level of visibility and popularity. But there's still a lot to be done! On the scientific level, we have to continue working to better understand the effects of different types of meditative practice (as we were just saying with relation to mindfulness and meditations on compassion and altruism), to whom they should be recommended, in what order, and so on.

And with regard to spreading the word about meditation, we must continually remind people that meditation is only one element in a whole set of changes in attitude and ways of thinking and behaving that can contribute to the favorable development of our world. For example, meditating at the hospital where I work makes no sense unless the caregivers also alter the way they provide care (more presence, more listening, more compassion) and the patients change the way they take care of themselves (being kind to their bodies and not waiting to get sick before paying attention to their health). These changes in caregivers and patients have to inspire political decision-makers to legislate in such a way that caregiving sites are spaces where it is possible to take the time to listen, to console, and to meditate, and not just places to push getting as much work done as possible in the shortest possible time.

The same thing goes for business and schools. Individual meditation brings great benefits to each person and those around them, but it also has to be part of a big change in perspective in educational and managerial practices.

I am convinced that individual practice facilitates these changes and decisions related to the community. A director who meditates directs differently, a caregiver who meditates gives care differently, a teacher who meditates teaches differently, parents who meditate raise their children differently. And that's the reason why seeing politicians interested in meditation makes me happy. We have recently begun mindfulness sessions for a small group of deputies and senators, and the fact that they have practiced and experienced something of their inner nature will, I hope, have an impact on the way they carry out their mission.

Dangers and Misuses of Meditation

MATTHIEU   I think dangers and misuses arise when the type of meditation we practice is not adjusted to our mental dispositions and capacities. It is not generally recommended that beginners meditate too intensively, in environments that are too isolated, without being appropriately informed as to how to remedy faults or manage the experiences that might arise, and especially without the supervision of an experienced guide. If we fail to respect these conditions, we are in serious danger of becoming like a runaway horse or a car the driver has lost control of. The risks are similar to those of self-medication; instead of taking one pill, we swallow the whole bottle.

The absence of appropriate reference points comes from the fact that in the West many people meditate without the guidance of an instructor with more experience than they have, and without the benefit of being part of a community of practitioners who are familiar with the process of meditation. In the traditional context, students receive step-by-step guidance over many years; they can confer whenever they wish with a teacher much better informed than they are and ask, for example, "This is the kind of experience I had practicing meditation these last few weeks. What do you think about it?" The seasoned instructor will understand immediately if the person has gotten sidetracked and will reorient the person, adjust their approach, or tell them, "Watch out, you're too tense," or "You are letting yourself get carried away by your sensations or your imagination." In this context, the meditation master is like a doctor adjusting a treatment and advising a different approach to meditation.

In the absence of such precautions, if a student is fragile or takes a meditation book and uses it to dive headlong into intensive practice, there is the danger that mental fabrications will take over and carry the novice meditator into a vortex of disturbing experiences caused by his or her somewhat anarchical efforts. Sometimes people can go completely off their rocker! A mind inclined toward ruminative brooding will brood even more heavily than usual and thus exacerbate the situation. It's all a matter of using the right tool at the right time, with the right amount of force. If the practice takes a bad turn, it's not because of the meditation itself but because the person is making inappropriate use of this tool.

CHRISTOPHE There are several stages, as in any learning process. First there is the stage of discovery. You run across an article, a book, a CD, or an app that allows you to try out the practice and see if it suits you, attracts you, or does you any good. If you decide to go further, it's better not to do it completely on your own. You will be able to avoid mistakes through the guidance of teachers and by sharing your experiences with other meditators. At that point, joining a group is important so that you can learn correctly, continue to practice, and benefit from the practice in everyday life. Then there is a third stage: that of deepening your practice further, which tends to apply to fewer people. At this stage, it is really very important to prudently and patiently choose the right path, the right method, and the right teachers for *you*—for your aspirations, capacities, and needs.

ALEXANDRE Shunryu Suzuki inoculates us against the danger of seeking extraordinary experiences in Zen. The idea is not to take off from the ground but to take root in it. He goes so far as to compare sitting in meditation to the simple act of going to the toilet. Practicing Zen, for example, is purging oneself of ideas that might become harmful. It's disencumbering ourselves, emptying ourselves, in order to return to our original state, our buddha nature. Life has ended up throwing a lot of unseemly crap into the well of our inner life. Letting go of these parasites, this inner pollution, these preconceptions, these thousand and one uptightnesses, is like making a little trip to the water closet. And the playful sage adds that we have to keep this practice up as long as we live. I like this down-to-earth quality: to achieve upliftedness and edification, there's nothing better than leaning on reality.

CHRISTOPHE There are also "guardians of the temple" who stand up and denounce the instrumentalization of meditation—meditation at the office, meditation in schools, meditation for couples, meditation at the hospital, meditation for confronting cancer, for example. Is this a denaturing of the practice? Their arguments are based on the idea that limiting meditation to a specific use reduces it to the rank of simple tool in the service of the well-being of the individual, used for reducing stress or anxiety or for providing quick, cheap access to inner peace.

This utilitarian conception of meditation with definite, concrete goals intended to improve our daily life—is this a legitimate first stage in your view, Matthieu?

MATTHIEU Sometimes it doesn't hurt to keep things simple. Not everyone is inclined to commit themselves to the spiritual path. It's more the exception. It is clear that, on the condition of not considering mindfulness practice to be the apogee of meditation, it can be beneficial in a number of areas.

It would be a misrepresentation and a deception, on the other hand, to present these simplified techniques as the essence of meditation and of the Buddha's teaching. In short, if we consider the path of Buddhism as a whole, two essential points are missing in mindfulness meditation as it is usually taught these days: the motivation and "the view." Most people do not practice mindfulness in order to attain enlightenment and liberate beings from suffering. They are not necessarily seeking either to understand "the view" as Buddhism defines it—that is, the fact that the individual self and phenomena appear, but they are devoid of independent existence. This is what we call emptiness.

There is nothing wrong with that, because the goal of mindfulness is different from that of Buddhism. For the anxiety sufferer, the sick person in the hospital, for someone who has difficulty managing their pain, their chemotherapy, their psychological suffering, their burnout, Mindfulness-Based Stress Reduction (MBSR, the program created by Jon Kabat-Zinn) is extremely beneficial. People who undertake this training are therefore not trying to attain enlightenment or liberation; they simply aspire to be able to deal with illness and suffering. If meditation helps them to get better at dealing with their daily life and to become more serene and compassionate, one can only congratulate them on that.

CHRISTOPHE   At the Sainte-Anne Hospital in Paris, where we conduct groups for patients who suffer depressive relapses, we give as clear an explanation as we can. To those beginning a program, we basically say, "Meditation is a vast universe, a door that opens onto a multitude of practices. In your case, there is a need: the diminution of your suffering and better regulation of your emotions. That is an absolutely legitimate goal, a first stage. For that, we propose teaching you to meditate following an approach that is very simple but quite significant: mindfulness, which consists in being able to become present to all your life experiences, pleasant or unpleasant." Then at the end of the program, we tell them the following: "There, we have given you training in a form of meditation you can use in everyday life. If it interests you, you can go further, but not with us. We are caregivers, not teachers of this or that tradition of meditation, secular or religious."

The same goes for school. If mindfulness helps children to stabilize their attention and pacify their emotions, it's a good thing, even if it's a simplification of all that meditation can make possible.

MATTHIEU   Being more attentive to others, achieving better emotional balance, accentuating prosocial behaviors—these are essential points. But we are not about to do a course in Buddhism for children or, for that matter, for anyone who has not asked for it.

ALEXANDRE   To put an end to all danger of instrumentalization and to elucidate the desires and the motivation that bring us to the practice of meditation, why not go ahead and review the expectations we have for self-transformation? Is our problem that we're afraid that without the help of some effective method, we're going to totally bomb, go under? Are we scrambling to get hold of a life buoy? Can we introduce a sense of altruism into this movement? First of all, I think we have to renounce all idea of a miracle cure, all hope for a magic wand. Once again, it's a matter of being cured of the idea of a cure.

We also have to give up any idea of meditation as a means of recovery, as in the case of Japanese companies that provide their highly pressured employees with a short course in zazen so they can hold out and keep working longer. Putting aside the political issue—working conditions in this case—there is a big danger there of applying a bandage to a wooden leg and loading even greater burdens onto the backs of these salaried workers. Meditation is a path to liberation, not a means of increasing performance, making people work till they drop.

MATTHIEU   Yes indeed, there is a danger here. At the World Economic Forum at Davos, Switzerland, I found it encouraging that for the last four years, the first item on the agenda, every morning from 8:00 to 8:30, has been a meditation session. Generally about a hundred people show up, among whom I saw a Japanese minister, major economists, a swimming champion, and many others. When I was asked to lead this meditation session, I said, "You've come here to do mindfulness meditation, and I propose that you practice caring mindfulness." If you put in a component of care and compassion right from the beginning, at least you avoid the worst of disasters: instrumentalization of meditation for selfish ends.

To understand the risks we run by failing to specifically cultivate compassion, let's take two examples that are somewhat caricatured but still revealing: the hit man and the psychopath. If we stay with the technical definition of mindfulness—keep your attention in the present moment, on the experience unfolding moment by moment, without being judgmental—then this applies to the professional sniper, whose mission is to shoot somebody down and who has to keep himself in the present moment without being distracted by his emotions. He remains completely nonjudgmental and doesn't ask himself whether it's good or bad to kill somebody. A psychopath can also concentrate on the present moment nonjudgmentally so he can exploit others unmercifully. However, there is no such thing as a compassionate professional killer or psychopath. Therefore, if we speak of "compassionate mindfulness," it's not just to make things more complicated, but to avoid instrumentalization and exploitation based on purely utilitarian, or even negative, purposes.

To come back to meditation in business environments, the idea is not to transform employees into lemons that can be squeezed to get more work hours out of them by keeping them from burnout. In truth, this does not seem to be the way things are in existing programs. I have met a number of CEOs who have used meditation, not as a tool for exploiting employees, but with constructive and benevolent intentions. Sébastien Henry, an entrepreneur and a pioneer of meditation in the workplace, put questions to a large number of CEOs. He learned that in the beginning they were afraid that meditation would cause their employees to become too soft and that it would be a waste of time. But little by little they saw that not only was this fear unfounded, both the CEOs themselves and their employees developed better judgment because they saw things in a larger context with greater composure. And, most notably, human relationships significantly improved. In the beginning, that's not what these business leaders expected, but in the end that's what they observed.

ALEXANDRE I'm not sure that you can use forceps to achieve equanimity, complete acceptance, and a sense of saying yes to life. A Zen proverb says that it's futile to tug on a blade of grass to get it to grow! The spiritual path is made of mistakes, relapses, groping. I confess that it took me a long time to return to meditation and see something else in it besides a straitjacket, a futile attempt to repair something fundamentally twisted. As I already told you, on the chaotic path that leads us back home, beyond fear and torment, I went on a three-month retreat. I had hastened to join the school of a spiritual guide in somewhat the same way you enroll yourself in a psychiatric hospital, with a superhuman demand: "Cure me in three months." Obviously this was not a good plan! And what followed did not for one moment bring me any closer to peace and joy. To tell the truth, it turned into a nightmare, and being unwilling to come out and admit that I didn't belong in that situation, I ended up in the hospital.

The last day, one of the disciples told me straight out that if I left the retreat, it meant I was possessed by a demon. In five seconds, I took a taxi and put an end to my Zen career. Today, when I hear talk of spiritual masters and disciples, I can't help but think of the ways in which that whole thing can go wrong. Even with the best will in the world, it is difficult to relate to that spiritual granite in oneself without resorting to an arsenal of therapeutic aids and a host of heroic measures.

MATTHIEU   Maybe you were stuck in a system that was too rigid for you, a system of the "kill or cure" type?

ALEXANDRE   That terrible dictum, "If you leave here, it's because you're possessed by a demon," followed me for a long time, and I believed that my basic being was vitiated, cursed.

I think that along with meditation, there is another indispensable remedy: unconditional love. Accept your relapses, your mistakes; nurture infinite patience toward everything recalcitrant that remains beyond your control. That's why, with all my being, I dream of playful sages, antic masters who dispense their teachings with a great roar of laughter and with enormous relaxation.

MATTHIEU   In Tibetan Buddhism, as I mentioned earlier, we recommend examining a potential spiritual master for years before entrusting yourself to him or her, so as not to be very sorry later. It's not a matter of being cynical or negative, just cautious. In the same way, it is said that a teacher should examine for a long time a potential disciple before accepting him or her. A spiritual commitment has major consequences for our lives. Of all the teachers I've known, none of them tried to attract or keep disciples. I knew a teacher who was a hermit who lived on the Tibetan border: Sengdrak Rinpoche. Two or three hundred meditators, men and women, lived around him. He said, "They come and go as they like. If they want to receive teaching, I offer it, but they are entirely free to come or go."

Toolbox for Meditation

CHRISTOPHE

Meditation is not only a religious or spiritual practice; it is also a form of mind training. It can help us cultivate attention, detachment, understanding, and emotional balance. It can also help us to develop our basic human virtues, which otherwise might lie dormant deep within us and not express themselves. I'm talking about kindness, compassion, generosity, and so on.

Meditation is simple. It only requires us to regularly pause and observe the nature of our experience—our breathing, sensations, emotions, thoughts. Everything starts with that.

Starting with very simple kinds of exercises like those recommended in mindfulness meditation (the kind of meditation we use in health care and education), there are many meditative traditions that are much more demanding and complex. As with the piano, we can very quickly learn to play a few little pleasant tunes; then we can go on to cultivate virtuosity for the rest of our lives.

ALEXANDRE

Let things pass. If I had to sum up the practice in three words, without hesitation, I'd go for "Let things pass." In the midst of chaos or deep in one's inner battlefields, dare to make the experiment of not controlling, of dropping the self. It's mayhem, but there's no problem! Far from giving up and far from resignation, letting things pass means distinguishing between the psychodramas (the problems created by conceptual mind) and the genuine tragedies of existence, which call for solidarity, commitment, and perseverance.

Enjoy the journey of meditation. As Shunryu Suzuki saw it, we might be missing the essential point if we are waiting for enlightenment to start feeling better and enjoying being alive. That would be a little like thinking we absolutely *had* to win the lottery in order to relax and appreciate life. This teacher spoke of illumination and Illumination. The point is that the fruits of meditation appear incrementally. Nothing prohibits us from enjoying the landscape all along the way.

Be at home in the present moment. Sometimes when worries and fears of the future are raging, I try to come home to the present moment, to open myself to the here and now so as to see and savor the fact that at this moment I am not the victim of cardiac arrest, that I'm not totally screwed up, that a vast potential for progress always lies before me.

Meditating is stripping down, daring to live nakedly in order to give oneself, contributing to the welfare of the world, giving one's share. Why don't we look at the day that lies ahead of us not as a store where we can acquire things, but as a clinic, a dispensary of the soul, where together we can recover and advance?

MATTHIEU

Many forms. The term *mind training* covers a large number of practices whose modalities and goals differ according to the needs and aspirations of individuals and their views of the world.

Meditation requires diligence, which should be nourished by enthusiasm, by joy in the virtues, by inner peace, by compassion, and by the feeling of having a clear direction in life.

Pure awareness. Meditation in its most essential form aims at experiencing pure awareness, which is always present behind the swarming of thoughts but is too often forgotten due to distraction.

Meditation, in itself, does not have harmful effects. Meditation is not contraindicated unless it is not properly understood or properly used—used in the wrong conditions or at the wrong time. Whether we like it or not, from morning till night we are dealing with our mind. Who wouldn't want their mind to be functioning in the optimal fashion and to be providing them with inner freedom rather than playing rotten tricks on them?

14

From Transformation of Self to Transformation of the World

When Karuna-Shechen started a mobile clinic in Bihar, India, the local farmers were suspicious. They had been exploited for a very long time by big landowners and burned by the duplicity of politicians. They therefore came to the conclusion that we were raising lots of funds, giving them only a small amount in benefits, and filling our pockets with the rest. They accepted care and medicine from us, but were not very open.

One day during the monsoons, our mobile ambulance got stuck in the mud while coming into the village. All the villagers came over to where we were stuck, but what did they do? They asked us for money for their assistance in getting our vehicle out of the mud. They wanted us to pay them so that we could reach the village and provide them with medical care!

Rabjam Rinpoche, the abbot of the monastery, remarked, "One really has to be a bodhisattva!" Because basically we had only one goal: to give them medical care, no matter how they treated us. In this case, a minimum of inner freedom permitted us to react not with resentment or irritation, but to laugh at the situation and especially not to lose sight of the compassionate goal we had in mind.

—Matthieu

Is Inner Freedom a Prerequisite for Action?

MATTHIEU If we wish to act on the world in a proper manner, with understanding and compassion, it is indispensable to prepare inwardly. Through the Karuna-Shechen nonprofit organization, we have been engaged for twenty years in humanitarian projects relating to education, health, and social services, and we help more than 380,000 people annually. We do our work in problem countries such as India, Nepal, and Tibet, and we have partnered with a number of nongovernmental organizations (NGOs), both large and small. Often we have observed that in the beginning, these organizations do some good work in accordance with their intentions, but along the way, many of them fail. Too small a percentage of the funds collected ends up being used for the people they were intended to help, for all kinds of reasons. Sometimes it is because the organization is the victim of ego conflicts or, worse, because its members are subject to greed or corruption. Or it is because they impose solutions on populations that are not suited to their needs or aspirations. According to one expert, the average life span of an NGO is ten years. They disappear not because of a lack of resources or of missions to accomplish; they collapse from the inside, worn down by conflicts and bad management.

Beside management skills such as organization, planning, and accounting, the best training that candidates for humanitarian action could have would be a meditation retreat of a few months, which would enable them to develop compassion and strength of mind, to learn not to react to the slightest provocations of those they are helping or collaborating with, and to cultivate the inner spaciousness they need not to be destabilized by the first obstacle that comes along. One should not join an NGO for the sake of building a career or boosting one's self-esteem but for the sake of helping others. For that, it is important to know how to manage one's toxic emotions.

In short, before attempting to change the world, it is desirable to develop the human qualities associated with inner freedom. This allows people to respect their primary commitments and at the same time be less vulnerable in dealing with the difficulties that will inevitably present themselves. Such freedom is not only a guarantee of equanimity, of knowledge, and of the ability to land on one's feet, but also an indicator of success. Because if our thoughts are monopolized by stress, doubt, animosity, and despair, then our energy and our minds will not be available for the work that needs to be done. It is true that helping others also is beneficial to ourselves, but if we are too fragile inside, the work is very likely to be beyond our current capabilities.

CHRISTOPHE The idea that we have to change ourselves before changing the world is not an obvious one. Is the ability to change things limited to people who have completed the work of inner liberation? Can't people who are uncomfortable in their own skins also do their part? One can work for the improvement of humanity without necessarily being in great shape oneself. Every one of us has experienced this on the individual level; even on days when we're not feeling tip-top—when we're sad, stressed out, or irritated—we can still do things that are helpful for others. We can comfort them, lend them a hand. Do political leaders necessarily have to feel great in order make positive changes in the world? When we look at the biographies of admirable people like Martin Luther King Jr., Gandhi, or Albert Einstein, we also discover a dark side, such as infidelity and verbal violence in marital relationships. That doesn't take anything away from their greatness as public figures; it simply reminds that they are human beings and not icons.

ALEXANDRE If we are required to be impeccable to reach out a helping hand, we will never take the plunge and embark on the adventure of compassion. In this area, we are always *progredientes*, individual progress makers on the path. The essential thing is to go forward, to listen to the best in ourselves without dreaming of illusory perfection or sinking into a fatalism of the type "After me the deluge!" This a beautiful and magnificent exercise in balance.

Developing our freedom and offering it to this stumbling world is the great challenge. Self-improvement and genuine love for our neighbor go hand in hand. Looking at our weaknesses, our foibles, our contradictions, and our ambivalences without reducing ourselves to them is making progress on the path.

For now, we have to go forward in the midst of paradoxes, in the midst of our conflicts and uncertainties. If we wait until we have put an end to all our wounds and the least traces of ego to roll up our sleeves and work compassionately for others, we might have to wait a very long time.

CHRISTOPHE   Maybe we can manifest compassionate and altruistic behaviors at any time and under any circumstances, even in the midst of suffering. But to manifest them over time and in an impactful and effective fashion, without doubt it's better also to be in as good a state as possible.

MATTHIEU   It's completely true that it is not necessary to wait to be in a perfect state to put ourselves at the service of others, provided that we are conscious of our weaknesses and our own challenges and that we take care that they do not interfere with helping others in the most appropriate way.

Moreover, doing something for others can help us improve our own state of being when we are too shut up within ourselves. I remember a woman visiting in Nepal who would tell me on and on in infinite detail how she was feeling morning, noon, and night. Nothing else seemed to matter to her. In the most diplomatic fashion possible, I suggested that she try working as a volunteer for two weeks in our humanitarian projects, saying that she would feel much better afterward. And that turned out to be the case.

We can certainly help others even if we are not doing too well ourselves, and so much the better. But I have also seen extreme cases of volunteers who were in very bad shape throw themselves headlong into humanitarian work in order to forget their problems. These were people suffering from real pathological conditions. Sometimes that works, for a time at least, but most of the time, these people broke down.

That said, in ordinary life, whether you are in good shape or bad, it is always good to be altruistic. Everybody wins, since altruism is the best way to bring about benefit for others and ourselves.

How Inner Change and Outer Change Are Connected

CHRISTOPHE   We might also raise the question of the relationship between changing ourselves and changing the world. We can look at what mechanisms connect them. It seems to me, to put it simply, that there are three levels: the level of our thoughts and our speech, the level of our actions (insofar as they are transformational), and the level of our example (insofar as it is inspiring).

Everything begins with our thoughts and speech. What we have going on regularly in our heads, the remarks we repeat, even ordinary ones (little pessimistic or optimistic comments, critical or encouraging observations)—all of that influences us, but also influences others. It is important to notice all these things that we don't pay attention to: the little unscripted comments that make up the daily verbal bath that permeates our brains and those of the people around us. The first way we can change the world is through our speech.

Then there is action, the concrete acts we perform or fail to perform, and that have an influence on our environment: throwing a piece of paper in a trash can or on the sidewalk, helping a person we don't know carry a heavy package or ignoring her, participating in some club or ignoring the people around us. All of these things don't have the same level of impact, obviously. But changing the world is not necessarily a gigantic enterprise. We can already have an influence on our little world, our immediate environment, our family, our workplace. It begins with very small gestures. Everybody does their part, at their small level. And that contributes to changing the world.

Finally, there is our own example—what we embody. This dimension is based on our speech and actions, but it goes beyond that. We can always lie or pretend. It's easy to lie in words, to say things we don't really believe or give advice that we don't follow ourselves. We can also lie with actions, by doing things purely for show to cause ourselves to be seen favorably. An example is being nice because everybody around me is nice and I don't want to be seen as a bad egg. But even that action is still helpful for others, and perhaps it will get me to taste the happiness of being nice!

It is more difficult to disguise our basic state of being: in the long run, something of us gets through to others—our sincerity, our genuineness, our presence. This is rather clear in medicine and caregiving. Over the course of my career as a doctor, I can remember having seen very marked differences among the nurses, both male and female, with whom I have worked. Some of them had a particular gift for being able to soothe patients suffering from anxiety, aggression, or just nerves. That came from their basic being as much as from their good words or their good actions. They were deeply calm, compassionate, respectful, and trusting of the intelligence and humanity of the patients living and breathing in front of them. Patients would feel this, and things would get better. To train others in our values, it is essential for us to embody them, not only to recommend or advocate them.

Education is a good model for understanding this process. We transform our children through what we tell them to do, through how we teach them, and through what we show them by our example—especially in those moments when we think they're not looking at us. At those moments we transmit to them what we are. And that is also true in relation to our family, our colleagues, people we don't know.

MATTHIEU The world begins with your family and your neighbor. The danger is saying to oneself, "I don't have that much trouble being compassionate toward humanity as a whole. But don't talk to me about that neighbor of mine!"

ALEXANDRE Abstract love and nice feelings are not enough when it's time to get your hands dirty, to engage, to help through actual deeds.

Christophe, you give us quite a valuable tool when you speak of the verbal bath that our brain flounders around in day after day. In this regard, the philosophers of antiquity tirelessly recalled to *progredientes* the need to control their inner discourse, their mental representations. What is that stuff that our Mental FM churns out all day long? What station is it that we're permanently tuned in to? Is that Radio Ego blaring away at us?

Between the neuronal blah blah blah and the nagging pains in the body, we really have no choice but to follow the call to freedom. We are not thinking things. A thousand influences can turn us away from the ideal. The essential thing is to actualize the high aspirations that dwell in our hearts like so many stings and prods waking us up, guiding us, inviting us to go beyond ourselves.

The main challenge is, gently and with infinite compassion, *to attack* that granite, that akrasia, those conflicts that paralyze us and leave a bitter taste behind in those who fail to have absolute fidelity to the best in themselves. What the Roman poet Ovid saw (before Saint Paul did) and expressed in *Metamorphoses* stays with us: "I see the best, I approve of it, and I do the worst." There are so many hazards and obstacles to prying oneself loose and living free! The first step is perhaps humbly to recognize one's contradictions, to dare to be transparent, and above all to set forth energetically— new every day—toward joy, peace, and disinterested love.

CHRISTOPHE Sometimes the idea that we are somehow responsible for the way the world is going can seem overwhelming. Where will we get the energy to do the best we can? Taking care of yourself and arousing in yourself as often as possible moments of joy, pleasure, happiness, admiration, and gratitude is not only a source of well-being, but also a source of energy and openness to the world.

MATTHIEU Emotional resonance, the power of example, and the quality of relationship with others are all heightened in the presence of a person who is balanced and calm.

ALEXANDRE *My* happiness, *your* happiness, *our* happiness. What if we were to take away these little possessive adjectives and embrace a challenge common to us all—the challenge of really lifting us all up together using the means we have available right now? It looks like this: *Do good, remain joyful, and go forward toward freedom.*

Toolbox for Transforming Ourselves and the World
CHRISTOPHE

Transforming ourselves, improving who we are as persons, can help and contribute to the transformation of the world. It's like the sound of a choir: it's always possible that a few people are not singing, but if nobody is singing, nothing will happen at all! And if no human beings make an effort, the world won't change. Moreover, like in a choir, it is enjoyable to act together, to see that we are not alone in working on ourselves so that the world will be more livable.

Changing ourselves in order to change the world is not something we do out of self-interest, nor do we do it expecting to see immediate results. We do it out of principle, out of generosity, out of intelligence.

All our efforts count. Even if it's no big deal, even if it's not all the time, even if it's not perfect, each of our efforts counts—all of them!

Transformation of the self *always* facilitates or enriches transformation of the world, no matter what logic we apply. It could be transforming oneself *in order* to transform the world (the two processes linked in the spirit of a global human ecology) or transforming oneself *and* transforming the world (two separate processes: psychological and political).

MATTHIEU

Any action performed sincerely for the welfare of others merits our support and admiration. As far as we are concerned, let us begin with compassionate actions that do not require us to leave our comfort zone. Then **let us gradually increase the frequency and amplitude of these acts.** In this way, let us set in motion a process of transformation.

Over time, this transformation of self will spontaneously translate into a transformation of the world.

ALEXANDRE

Making inner progress in order to give oneself to others—now there is something revolutionary. I am speaking of a gentle revolution that takes the form of unlearning distrust, calculation, and the me-first mentality.

Feeling communion with others breaks our isolation. Repairing ourselves, devoting ourselves to spiritual exercises, or embarking on an ascesis is not worth an hour's worth of effort if we don't become fervent workers for peace, enthusiastic artisans of freedom. Practicing is always, ultimately, moving forward in a profound linkage with all beings—those who are suffering, those we love, those we can't even see. Feeling this communion blows away the duality that erects barriers everywhere: my happiness, your happiness; my joy, your joy; my practice, your practice. Why do we always have to compartmentalize reality?

Let us embark on an adventure that takes us beyond the narrow frontiers of self-interest. Getting up in the morning with the sole intention of pleasing others, obeying the desire machine hidden in the recesses of our individuality—this is dooming ourselves to a persistent discontent that will leave us completely drained, worn out, and riddled with neurosis. Let us embrace a less individualistic and altogether vaster project: let us work for the joy of all, mobilize against inequality, lighten people's sufferings, do whatever is necessary so that everyone can find his or her place, his or her equilibrium, in the bosom of the great "we."

What gift can I offer to the great human family? Marcus Aurelius, good Stoic that he was, invited us to consider ourselves members of a great body, part of an immense whole. Starting in the morning, we should ask ourselves what actions we can accomplish with the available means of the day to contribute actively and generously to the great whole that gives us life. Here and now, what can my joyful participation be?

Part IV

the fruits
of freedom

MATTHIEU What are the fruits of freedom when they have fully ripened? How does the wisdom that accompanies that freedom change our attitude toward life and death, toward ourselves and others? What impact does it have on our way of being and acting?

A sage is supposed to be liberated from the yoke of delusion, confusion, and malevolence; from dependence on craving; from jealousy; and from many other mental states that are a source of torment. Being free, a sage is not susceptible to being distressed in the deepest part of the self, torn by perpetual inner conflicts, wrecked by existential anguish. If that were not the case, what is the point of being free?

The sage is not unaware of joys and pains, but they do not cast doubt on the freedom and peace that reign in the depths of the inner ocean. Wisdom gives greater dimension to the mind and liberates it from the causes of suffering. It makes resources available that enable the sage to navigate the highs and lows of life with ease and skill.

Being free, we are less vulnerable, which makes it possible for us to open ourselves generously to others. Wisdom, unobstructed by delusion, also supplies the reference points needed to make decisions that affect our own lot and that of others around us. It reflects an accurate view of reality, free from the distortions created by mental fabrications.

One of the most precious fruits of wisdom, therefore, is inner freedom. This freedom is a source of peace.

15

Inner Pacification

A few years ago, when I was vacationing in the UK in the Cornwall area, I was taking a walk by myself along a hillside path when I came to a small bench at the top of the hill, overlooking the sea. On the bench was a small plaque that read "R. I. P." and mentioned a gentleman from the area who liked to come and sit on that bench daily right up to the end of his life.

I sat down, like him, and I felt incredibly good. It was as though I were connected directly with an immense reservoir of inner peace. I had the strange feeling that, even though the environment was very favorable, it only played the role of waking up the aptitude for peace that lay within me. I felt that this feeling came from the inside.

I took a moment to observe what was happening to me. I felt peaceful but also full of compassion, equanimity, detachment, and lucidity concerning what really counts in life and what is just chaff. I had an impression of lightness and deep-rooted freedom, anchored in the reality of life and death. These impressions were not illusory like the ones that can arise in states of euphoria or excitation. In this state of inner peace, I did not feel cut off from the world or from people, but even more connected with them.

I thought about the gentleman whose name was engraved on the bench. I thanked him and dedicated that moment to him.

— Christophe

Inner Peace, Calm Energy

CHRISTOPHE   Pursuing inner peace is not renouncing conflicts but making an effort not to live in a state of permanent struggle, always butting heads with reality. It means seeing when it is necessary to make war and when it is necessary to make peace, even imperfect peace. It's attempting to use force and firmness without anger or blindness. Quite a tall order!

But maybe we do better to pursue a process of inner pacification rather than the state of peace itself, which is necessarily unstable and transitory. This would mean regularly undertaking the work of pacifying the toxic emotions within us, or the excess of anger or resentment in us that pushes us toward action but also toward acts of aggression.

How could sages not also be tormented sometimes? And shouldn't they be? This would be a sign of their involvement in the world, where everything is not just happiness — far from it.

MATTHIEU   The sage is the first one to be touched to the quick by the suffering of beings. It is said that he or she is sensitive to the suffering of others like someone who gets a speck of dust in their eye, whereas ordinary beings feel it only like someone who gets a speck of dust in the palm of their hand. Self-centered hedonists give little place to others in their thoughts; sages do not exclude anyone from their hearts.

The Dalai Lama told us that practically no day went by in which, during his daily meditation from three until seven in the morning, tears did not come to his eyes as he thought of the suffering of beings. These were tears of love and compassion that did not shake his inner peace. Paul Ekman, PhD, one of the great experts in facial expressions, said that of all the people he had observed, the Dalai Lama was without a doubt the one who expressed his emotions — joy or sorrow — with the greatest transparency. But these emotions arise in the heart of an unshakable wisdom.

The sage perceives the needs of others with great acuity, and he or she is always ready to act for their welfare, yet his or her mind is not caught up in the maelstrom of their afflictions. In 2008, before the Olympic Games in Beijing—at a time when more than two hundred Tibetans had been killed by the Chinese army and thousands had been imprisoned for demonstrating in the streets—the Dalai Lama declared that he had not felt so impotent in his ability to do anything helpful for the Tibetans since the year he had to flee from the Chinese invasion of his country. Nevertheless, in contrast to what he experienced in 1959, the most tragic moment of all, he did not lose his inner peace. Wisdom and spiritual maturity had given him great freedom from the influence of afflictive emotions.

ALEXANDRE The luminous example of the Dalai Lama is enough to dismiss the lamentable minds who believe the sage has sealed himself off from the world, that he leads a cool and cushy life, far away from the vicissitudes of common mortals.

Advancing without hesitation toward freedom perhaps means daring to develop an art of living that applies antidotes against egoism and the other navel-gazing pathologies. Wisdom, inner freedom, is acquired through two main lines of work: a science of mind, an ascesis repeated over and over again to purge our being of all the afflictive emotions, and the practice of generosity, the way of the heart and the path of altruism.

When I was battling addiction, it was immensely comforting for me to know that on my bedside table were books by skillful healers who were ready to provide the help I needed. Meister Eckhart leads us toward surrendering the self and teaches us to lose ourselves, to abandon ourselves. Friedrich Nietzsche is a great pacifier who invites us to say yes to everything, including the gigantic chaos that often threatens to eat us up raw. Chögyam Trungpa demolishes our illusions and temptations one by one and puts a chokehold on any kind of artificial, contrived peace or cheap, bogus security. And precisely regarding the point we're looking at, this remarkable teacher provides us with what is perhaps a key instruction: "You have to work hard to help others, directly, without even wearing rubber gloves to clean up their vomit."

It's enough to say that the sage, the man or woman who is completely liberated, never gives up. It is in the midst of our chaos and torment that we become students of wisdom, develop freedom, harvest tiny bit by tiny bit the fruit that comes to those who make progress on the path. What a sad misunderstanding it is to believe that the work of inner pacification amounts to irrevocably curbing all sensibilities, becoming a total wuss, a soul already dead walled up in a cell.

CHRISTOPHE Science shows, as you just said, that wisdom is not the sterilization of our passions. The few studies we have at our disposal show that people considered "wise" (on the basis of evaluative questionnaires) experience as much emotion, both pleasant and unpleasant, as other people do—sometimes even more. But they are less enslaved by these emotions and less under their spell. Inner peace leads to outer calm—but not apathy!

Nevertheless, many people think that strength lies in anger and agitation. When we try to visualize a person who is full of energy, we don't imagine someone who is calm and composed. According to Western clichés, engagement in the world is a source of agitation and not tranquility; it puts us in a state of war rather than a state of peace.

Is it possible to utilize the energy of anger without ending up with its aggressive tendencies? Many studies in experimental psychology show that there is a link between body and mind. That means that a mind at peace does not naturally push us into energetic action. But perhaps we should rehabilitate what I call "calm energy." I am convinced that it is possible to cultivate states where we are full of energy without being agitated or overexcited.

And listening to you talk, Matthieu, I would question the common clichés of "necessary anger" and "just war." And even though I'm sure their point of view is not valid, I sometimes lack arguments in responding to people who claim that inner peace turns us away from the concerns of the world and the desire to act.

MATTHIEU Without a doubt anger incites us to action. It has qualities of clarity, vigor, and effectiveness, which in themselves can be useful—as long as they are not associated with malice. But in most cases, anger degenerates very quickly. It goes from irritation, to loss of control, and finally to desire to harm or gain the upper hand. Anger becomes toxic. A study of several hundred students who took a personality test measuring their level of chronic anger and hostility showed that, twenty-five years later, the most aggressive ones among them had twenty-five more heart-disease incidents than the least angry ones.

ALEXANDRE   This is why we have to get to work in order not to end up completely rancid and bitter. Let us not overlook violence either, which turned on ourselves causes enormous damage.

What is the challenge here? To identify deceptions, betrayals, failures, and traumas—the various time bombs left behind in us. To embark on the work of self-liberation—on an ascesis—we need fuel, we need deeds repeated in daily life, we need joy, and we need friends in the good.

One of my friends who is kind of a Stoic told me that every time he feels criticisms, anger, or the slightest seed of discord arising in him about his relationship with his partner, he lies down on the floor and lets the sparks float off before any actual fire appears. I like the fact that self-transformation is a matter of small acts in the midst of everyday life. Liberating oneself requires ingenuity, perseverance, and a whole lot of humor.

MATTHIEU   From the point of view of evolution and the survival of the species, as Charles Darwin pointed out in *The Expression of the Emotions in Man and Animals,* every emotion has its use. Jealousy contributes to the maintenance of a couple by inciting the partners to drive off rivals, thus increasing the chances for survival of their offspring. Anger can help us rapidly surmount obstacles that stand in the way of the realization of our desires or that constitute a threat. Craving incites us to seize what we need. But these emotions become a source of pain when they intensify to the point of getting beyond our control and no longer being applicable to a given situation.

By regularly allowing our emotions to express themselves in a disproportionate manner, we reinforce our habitual tendencies, and we will again be vulnerable to these emotions the moment their emotional charge reaches the critical level. Moreover, as this threshold becomes lower, we will get angry more easily and more often. Freedom consists in establishing an intelligent dialogue with one's emotions and letting them unravel by themselves as they come up.

By doing this, we are not suppressing anger, but we are avoiding having it transform into a cause of suffering. Here again, wisdom is a synonym of freedom.

As to the calm energy you were talking about, Christophe, the Dalai Lama in his humorous way gave the example one day of someone who is in the grips of strong anger and who wants to hit the object of his emotion with his cane. If he is overexcited and swings the cane in all directions in order to land a blow on the other person, he is in danger of hitting himself in the face. The Dalai Lama added, in a playful tone accompanied by the appropriate gestures, "If you are perfectly calm, you take the cane and—bonk!—you deliver a precise blow to the end of his nose." It is completely possible to carry out a firm and determined action in order to neutralize a dangerous person without feeling the least hate or indulging in cruel and immoderate violence.

CHRISTOPHE   In the end, the ideal of inner peace is the starting point of engaging with someone or something. It leads to an action carried out with an economy of means. It's action without all the waving and gesturing.

MATTHIEU   A determined action accomplished with calm will often be more effective than an explosion of haphazard actions or words. In cases of emergency, when vital decisions are necessary, isn't it better to stay calm? In the case of a technical incident in an airplane, if everybody starts shouting at the pilots, there is little likelihood that the right decision will be made. A hero is never hysterical.

CHRISTOPHE   For you, that's obvious, but for many people it's necessary to get past a first reflex that associates outer action with inner agitation. That's the whole difference between peace and calm. One can be a calm person of action. But how can we explain that it is possible to engage without feeling anger or inner discomfort?

Inner Peace = Outer Calm

MATTHIEU   It seems to me there are different forms of discomfort. It is very desirable to be passionately concerned with the well-being of others and to consider the suffering caused by injustice, discrimination, oppression, and cruelty unacceptable. Depending on the circumstances it would be preferable to resort to diplomacy, to dialogue, and to mediation or, if necessary, to more energetic forms of intervention. When it is the most skillful manner of proceeding, a sage can manifest a resolute indignation or a "holy anger" while still remaining perfectly in control. Blowing up obscures our judgment; we superimpose our projections on our adversaries and perceive them as totally detestable, whereas the reality is always more complex. We see the results of that in people like Donald Trump, who are incapable of controlling themselves. Day after day, they go back and forth between dithyrambic praise and merciless criticism. Speaking unguardedly, insulting others, fulminating with rage, or indiscreetly manifesting impatience will usually trigger an escalation of hostility.

Calm must be exercised in the heat of action, while inner peace is built over the long term. If your boat has sunk and you have lost everything, if you recover your equilibrium and equanimity instead of being devastated for months on end, that is an indication of your resilience and your inner peace.

ALEXANDRE   Anger, like the torments of the flesh, often results in flagrant akrasia. The challenge is to identify the warning signs, whatever might tip us off that the conflagration is imminent. Yes, it must be said that our psyche, the conceptual mind, is a fantastic pyromaniac that does its utmost to throw oil on the fire and gets up on its high horse at the least provocation. A passerby mocks my odd appearance as a person with a disability—which happens almost daily —and there it is: a fantastic opportunity for me to throw down the "What right do you have to treat me like that?" and "Won't they ever just let me be?"

CHRISTOPHE   Working regularly to calm our minor ires and our small resentments prepares us to react better in more intense circumstances. The idea is not to wear down our ability to react but to get in the habit of associating it as much as possible with a state of inner calm. Calm thus becomes one of the behavioral and psychological benefits of inner peace.

MATTHIEU   In other words, calm is an expression of the peace of mind bestowed on us by inner freedom. People who are constantly agitated by wild thoughts enjoy only a very small degree of freedom because they jump as soon as an impulse arises in their mind. People who are free inwardly are exempt from the sore points that provoke hyperreactivity and from the wounds that make them cry out the moment anybody touches them. The sage is neither dull nor indifferent; it's just that his or her mental space is so vast that provocations do not challenge his or her inner peace. He or she ignores tempests in teapots.

ALEXANDRE   The Buddha, Jesus, Spinoza, Epictetus, and many others make clear what the highways to freedom are. Always it's a matter of uncluttering one's mind, stepping out of our narrow representations, liberating ourselves from worrying about what others think of us. *Progredientes* work to identify their prejudices, to get rid of their attachments, and to love more and better. In order to get out of the washing-machine drum of emotional storms and move rapidly toward ataraxia—that absence of inner troubles so dear to the schools of antiquity—maybe it would help to listen to Epictetus: "If someone turned your body over to just any person who happened to meet you, you would be angry. But are you not ashamed that you turn over your own faculty of judgment to whoever happens along, so that if he abuses you it is upset and confused?"[1]

Is Inner Peace Outmoded or Totally Up to Date?

ALEXANDRE   Someone told us recently: "Wisdom, inner peace—in the end that's pretty boring." Don't all the things we've been saying go against the trends of the times? Aren't these times of constant movement and change characterized by a continuous flow of information and distractions and incitements to react quickly rather than to think things over slowly? Inner peace presupposes regular relative withdrawal from all that. And inner freedom requires regular critique of the flux we are confronted with. Every piece of information has an influence, masks possible manipulation, and arouses desires, thoughts, and emotions in us that do not necessarily make us freer. Instead, those emotions tend to make us more dependent and leave us with less detachment and less discriminating intelligence. Therefore, we need wisdom to help us see everything more clearly! I'm not talking about giving things up; I'm talking about regularly questioning ourselves on the relationship we have with all that, especially with regard to our freedom: Are we capable of doing without all those things?

MATTHIEU   Quality time is not dependent on constantly new, intense, and exciting high-power experiences. The sage is content to watch the leaves falling from a tree, a little bird landing on a branch for a few seconds, and so on. Not seeing anything at all is as satisfying for the sage as looking at a lush landscape all the time. The so-called successes of life don't add anything to the sage's serenity, and their absence doesn't take anything away from it. Inner richness is self-sufficient and regenerates itself as it is experienced. In the end, the exhaustion of our inner resources comes from attempting to make what seems monotonous exciting, speeding up what is peaceful, and burning the candle at both ends. With inner calm, there is no need for smoke and mirrors.

CHRISTOPHE   Calm is not apathy, as we've said. And it is not monotony either. It helps us appreciate reality, its nuances, its subtleties, without the need of dressing it up. It sharpens the way we look at the world. It makes us less dependent on thunderclaps and drum rolls. But it requires additional efforts from us. The easy way is to let ourselves be bought by consumerist society and its stimulations, which are manipulations. The hard way is to cultivate calm and increase our discriminating intelligence and freedom, part of which is the freedom to choose what upsets us and what excites us.

ALEXANDRE   Ego is always involved in struggle, in the profit motive, the hunt for betterment. But there's no easy remedy. How can we undo the habits of a mind that is always on the prowl, crippled by hope and fear? How do we learn to slide easily on the slide of life when we have the mentality of a grand financier who is speculating night and day, to say nothing of the inner conflicts of ours that seem to resist the best will in the world?

It was always with envy that I encountered in Spinoza his *acquiescentia in se ipso*, his "self-contentment." As long as we don't find happiness at home, with ourselves, the temptation will remain great to continue running around instrumentalizing others, trying to turn them into automatic dispensers of rewards and affection. The author of the *Ethics* seems to be guiding us toward a love of self that has its origin in the foundations of our being. This has nothing to do with narcissism, which is confined to loving only a truncated image of our being.

For Spinoza, self-contentment is born out of intuitive knowledge of God. The brilliant point here is that we don't develop self-compassion in front of the mirror but by casting ourselves into the world, by giving ourselves to others, by living. On this path we can recognize already that we are impoverished creatures, very needy beings, who think that they can find a balm for their wounds, for the void within them, in excessive consumption. That feeling of want, of emptiness, makes us run after false goods—at the cost of considerable expenditures of energy. And there we are in the end, on our last legs, totally drained, and not very happy. How can we live simply in this world, letting the greed of a wounded and demanding ego fall by the wayside?

MATTHIEU   Simplicity goes together with economizing our emotional resources. It is not necessary to wear ourselves out managing our inner and outer conflicts all the time. We can cease being convinced that the entire world is against us, that everything has to be dealt with, utilized, and maximized. Our ego doesn't have to yearn to be pampered and feel threatened at every turn. As a result, we can save a phenomenal amount of energy. We can coast along in a state of inner serenity.

CHRISTOPHE   Inner peace is the source of great economies of energy. Our inner forces are more intelligently mobilized; we waste them less in flurries of inapplicable action. They get less exhausted. This is important because we have a limited daily energy allotment, whether for physical or psychological efforts. Past a certain threshold, we get drained. Another advantage of this economizing is that we don't pollute others with our impulses, our irritations, our demands and petty hang-ups.

In addition, inner peace is good for our mental ecology. It not only reduces tensions between people, but also within them. Because of that, it is conducive to their making the right decisions: consuming less, getting less worked up, taking the time to reflect on their real needs.

Through lightening our baggage and quietly and compassionately weeding our inner life (in the face of the constant growth of worry, dwelling, obsessions, dependencies, etc.), we use less and less time and energy and, over time, we liberate ourselves for all the rest—for everything that is not us.

MATTHIEU   It's a lasting harmony. Being in harmony with oneself, one is also in harmony with all others and with one's natural environment. There is no excessive consumption, either internally or externally.

ALEXANDRE   Such an inner conversion in the end is quite a humble thing. It's not a question of a grand 180-degree turn, but rather small acts carried out day after day. What makes me happy in my ground of grounds? How shall I keep life moving?

Toolbox for Working on Inner Peace

CHRISTOPHE

"May the Force be with you." To this very famous formula—repeated many times in the *Star Wars* movies—we might add, "and may peace be established within you, because you will use much less of your force!"

Inner peace does not bring passivity, but calm engagement. It does not lead to monotony, but to sharpened perception that is sensitive to nuances that are invisible to agitated people.

Inner peace increases our freedom. It makes us less dependent on the stimulants and sources of excitement of our consumerist society (ads, social media, facile and gratifying distractions).

But we remain imperfect. It's not a question here of self-censure or self-sterilization, of denying ourselves all forms of craziness, loss of control, excesses, or impulsiveness. Anything can happen, and sometimes loss of control can even be enjoyable for the moment (drinking too much alcohol, overspending, saying bad things about people, etc.). But the art and habit of working on inner peace will bring us back quickly to the path of our real life choices and values. It will only have been a momentary loss of control and not of driving right off the road.

ALEXANDRE

Identify the battlefields. To attain authentic peace of the heart, let us identify what we are at war with morning, noon, and night. Let us have the courage to put down our arms, to throw away our armor and coats of mail. Let us deliberately opt for gentleness, tenderness, and nonviolence.

Dare to be ourselves. How many of our fears and frustrations come from a life lived hidden behind our fantasies, external trappings, daydreams, inauthenticity? Reconciling oneself with one's being, moving toward serenity, is taking the risk of dropping all these postures, daring every day to live with a balance that never gets stuck in weighty fixations or false securities. It also means living our freedom in our life as it is—with this body, these traumas, these wounds, these thousand and one resources. In short, it means making peace with everything that I am without getting drawn into dreaming that I am somebody else.

Accept imperfection, and the ambivalence might dwell in our hearts, including our inner roller-coaster rides. Who said that we have to liquidate all our problems in order to enjoy happy times? Peace and joy are attained with our available resources. Let us not fabricate overwhelming ideals that are too much for us, that discourage us and sap all possibility of progress.

Identify what it is that truly brings us peace, what comforts us, nourishes us, and gives us rest: a film, a show, a date, an act that reconciles us with our daily life and restarts a dynamic process. Let us pay heed to what our inner compass points to.

MATTHIEU

Expand our inner space so that our joys and sorrows have ample room to unfold without either being ignored or disturbing our profound peace.

Gain a good understanding of our emotions. How do they come up? How can we acknowledge their usefulness without getting drowned in their excesses? How can we establish an intelligent dialogue with them so that they don't trouble our mind inordinately? And lastly, how can we become experts in liberating the afflictive emotions so that they unravel the very moment they arise?

Savor the freshness of the present moment, the natural simplicity of a mind at peace.

Become less inwardly vulnerable. That will permit us to open to others without fear.

16

Our Basic Nature

A few months ago, I found when getting up from the table that I could no longer walk. A meniscus had ruptured and wedged itself against my knee joint. It was very painful, but luckily, thanks to my friends, I was able to get an MRI that same day and be operated on the following day. For the operation, whether I liked it or not, I had to submit to a general anesthesia, and I remained unconscious a little less than two hours.

Unexpectedly, when I woke up, I had a very enriching experience. I had the impression of not being completely there. I was in a light and luminous state of mind. My first thoughts went toward my spiritual teachers. For a good hour, their presence illuminated my mental landscape. I experienced a state of bliss, of devotion, and unalloyed trust. I was alone in my room, and I began softly to chant verses that reminded me of my teacher. My thoughts also went to other people who are dear to me.

I said to myself that if things go this well at the time of death, it won't be too bad! Could anesthesia be a kind of dress rehearsal for dying? Could such a moment show us what is present in the profoundest depths of our mind when the thought processes that clutter the field of consciousness have been silenced? All in all, I was very glad to have gone through this anesthesia experience.

Later, I wondered if such experiences could be revealing about our basic nature. This feeling of lightness and bliss could perhaps result from not immediately reifying the world around us when waking up from the anesthesia. At that moment the mind is not yet distorted by myriad conceptual constructs. This is the antithesis of dwelling on thoughts; it is perfect simplicity. I felt like a young child discovering the beauty of life with a fresh and transparent mind.

—Matthieu

The Ground of Grounds

CHRISTOPHE I had an experience of the same kind two years ago, following a major operation. I woke up from the anesthesia in a very amazing state, pervaded by a profound sense of well-being—almost a feeling of euphoria about being alive—as well as a sense of gratitude toward the surgeons, the nurses, and medical science. This was unusual for me, since I am a rather anxious person. I could have been upset about the pain, the operative procedures, all the tubes and catheters stuck in my body, or uncertainty about my health and future. But no, serenity and gratitude were effortlessly there in the foreground.

I never felt gratitude so strongly, so physically, and, especially, so easily. This state lasted a rather long time, a good hour, as long as I was in the recovery room. Then it continued gently in my room all through the afternoon. No doubt that the arising of this state was facilitated by the anesthesia, the absence of pain, and the relief. But I then remembered your similar experience, Matthieu. Couldn't I also take it that the anesthesia had a clarifying effect, revealing a basic ground that exists beneath all the worries that could possibly arise?

And with that thought, what I was experiencing no longer seemed artificial but like a sort of immersion in a possible basic nature, like that described in the Buddhist tradition. The chemistry of the anesthesia, then, would not have created that state but just facilitated it, allowed it, revealed it.

MATTHIEU It would be interesting to know how frequent this kind of experience is. Years ago, I was accompanying a Tibetan teacher, Nyoshul Khen Rinpoche, who was having an appendicitis operation. I was with him when he woke up. He said the word *rigpa* three times: "awareness, awareness, awareness." This word does not refer to waking up from sleep or from anesthesia, but to waking up to the basic nature of the mind. He then asked me to read him some sublime verses from the great masters of the past. After a few minutes, he said, "Good, that's fine," and then he remained silent.

In Buddhism we speak of buddha nature, which is the true nature of the mind. It is not simply an optimistic vision of human nature. It is the fundamental nature of the mind, a kind of "original goodness," which becomes manifest when the mind is freed from the veils of mental confusion, from ignorance, and from distortions of reality.

CHRISTOPHE Afterward, I looked up studies on this subject and didn't find very much. There are other moments where this kind of state can arise, under certain medications, during powerful moments in life in which we are face-to-face with nature or a starry sky, or during moments that are ordinary but in which we are perfectly present and these kinds of feelings arise in us. These are incidences of serenity that come not only from favorable circumstances but arise from the deepest part of us.

What is our true nature? During my career, I've had the privilege of ending up under the knife on several occasions. When I woke up, I in fact felt extreme gratitude. I was opening to a fullness, to the unbounded experience of interdependence. The miraculous quality of life, that immense gift, was my dominant impression. I also thought of all those people who had passed over that same operating table but had not had the good fortune to be able to get off it again in a state favorable to greater health. The great spiritual traditions never tire of reminding us that at the heart of human beings there is a fullness, a fundamental state of health and sanity, and inconceivable resources. However, when we are not stimulated by an activity or sustained by friends, then the idling state, the normal tonality of our being, can be spoiled by the tyranny of desire—or by boredom. Is there a wall or a floor that prevents us from drawing on the treasures that dwell in the depths of our hearts? How do we descend into it completely, become one with the joy, the peace, the immaculate sky of infinite consciousness? This is the inner movement we are urged to make by the sages and philosophers. Where have we chosen to reside? In conceptual mind or in our inner depths, drawing upon which we are called upon to live?

MATTHIEU I remember a woman who told me, "When I look deep within myself, I find sadness." It's very disarming to hear such a statement. We cannot cast doubt on what that woman felt in the deepest part of herself. It would be cruel and unconscionable to take her experience lightly and say, "Hey, try to cheer up." The woman would like nothing better than to cheer up, but she doesn't see how to get to that point. Another time, I met a young man who told me, "Though I have looked within myself again and again, I still cannot find any reason for wanting to go on living." You feel quite helpless when you hear such tragic statements.

We can suggest that such people look and see if, behind that sadness or total lack of meaning, they might not glimpse a more fundamental element in their experience: the primary knowing faculty, not impaired by sadness or by any other specific state of mind. This pure awareness or open presence is the space of awareness in which all mental events occur. By relating with this space, it becomes possible not to identify with sadness or any other afflictive mental state.

We have to be delicate and patient in recommending this change in approach. We should not ask too much from people who see no reason to go on living. But it is possible, in spite of everything, that this approach might open the door to freedom just a crack for people like these who are prisoners of their own minds. Once a person has gotten their foot in the door—and this should preferably happen in the presence of an authentic spiritual master—they can gradually become more and more familiar with this pure awareness that lies at the very core of our being by learning to liberate themselves from mental projections.

CHRISTOPHE We have already spoken of the default mode of our brain, the basic way it functions when at rest—what our brain does when we are doing nothing. It probably corresponds, at least on the emotional level, to the cerebral networks that we activate the most often. But it is not associated with the same content in everybody. We observe hyperfunctioning of this mode in persons suffering from schizophrenia, depression, or autism—pathologies in which the patients are victims of automatic running-on of painful mental contents, which cause them to withdraw partially from the outer world.

This is why it is important to provide training that will orient this state of our mind, when it is idling in neutral, toward a more open, accurate, and balanced vision, and away from being entirely self-centered and caught up in worries. The more we are able to hold in our minds a certain way of looking at the world—composed, calm, and inclined toward objectivity, truth, and freedom—the more chance we will have that this will be what spontaneously emerges when we are making no mental effort at all and our brain passes into default mode.

MATTHIEU   Right, our habitual tendencies are the result of the accumulation of our thoughts and emotions, added to our genetic predispositions.

CHRISTOPHE   And if we are continually moaning and groaning, wallowing, tormenting ourselves, flagellating ourselves, that is precisely what our brain will shape as our default mode when we cease any effort. Those circuits will run all by themselves. In the long term, nothing we let run on in our minds is harmless! Our inner freedom is also at stake in these moments: if we struggle not to let these dark feelings take over and if we also regularly bring to our mind calmer and more accurate ways of seeing, then little by little our efforts to attain the "tranquility of the soul" of which the Stoics speak will become easier and more spontaneous.

Neuroplasticity Again

ALEXANDRE   Can we change the idling state, or is it regulated like a thermostat to maintain an absolutely fixed temperature whether we have the windows open or not? In short, is it possible to change? Is it possible to bid *adieu* to our persistent habits and be reborn lighter?

MATTHIEU   Training allows us to change our baseline, the average degree of well-being (or ill-being) to which we return between the highs and lows of life. Whether a flat calm prevails or thirty-foot waves roil the ocean in the short term, the average level of a person remains the same. Training of the mind amounts to gradually modifying the level of the seas of our experience.

ALEXANDRE   Can a person who is stuck with a depressive or anxiety-ridden base even hope for modest illumination? Can we hope for a slight upgrade, a small improvement in our idling state? The default mode of our brain seems to be tough, stable, hard as granite.

MATTHIEU   It is stable as long as we don't do anything about it. If we allow our habitual tendencies simply to run on, they won't change by themselves. The psychologist Paul Ekman speaks of a platform, or baseline, which we keep to in our lives. If we make an effort to transform our way of being through training, we will continue to experience joys and sorrows, but the level of our platform will change. That will take some time, unless major upheavals in our life occur.

CHRISTOPHE   I think we don't have to view regulation by thermostat as something that cannot be changed. If you know how to work with your thermostat, you can change the setting. And the way to do that is to understand how it works — to understand that the more you dwell on negative thoughts, the more you strengthen your negative default mode. As soon as you are no longer performing some action or pursuing some distraction (like watching a movie), these negative circuits will once more start running all by themselves. But fortunately they are alive, flexible, and subject to modification, on the condition that we make certain efforts.

MATTHIEU   This baseline level takes time to change, thought by thought, emotion by emotion, reaction by reaction, mood by mood. A flare of anger lasts a few seconds, a morose mood a few hours, and an anxiety-ridden character years and years. But nothing is carved in stone. Studies on neuroplasticity confirm the possibility of such a transformation.

CHRISTOPHE   I think a big issue for the science of psychology in the coming years will be to teach people to do a better job configuring their own brain function by themselves. For example, in positive psychology, this would mean training people to "ruminate" on positive states of mind and positive ways of looking at the world. We mostly ruminate on what is not working, but it's important (still without making up stories) to also ruminate on the positive, to reflect again on the good moments of the day, on the good we have done or have had done for us. We should do this not only because we get pleasant experiences and emotions out of it but also because it will set up and activate constructive and realistic cerebral circuitry. I'm not talking about lying to oneself or trying to believe that adversity doesn't exist, but rather about constantly expanding one's ability to also recognize all that is going well, all the progress that has already been made, and everything that represents sources of hope, comfort, and lucid and intelligent energy. The more we multiply these kinds of experiences and efforts, the more chance we have that our default mode will be recalibrated toward the positive. However, it's a lot of work, and it takes a long time!

ALEXANDRE   The good news is that no permanent fate weighs *ad vitam aeternam* (eternally) on our inner life. Even the spiritual granite that constitutes us can be sculpted. Patience, time, and meditation have more effect than force and rage. Step by step, training the mind opens us to an awareness that, beyond psychological states, is suffused by peace, joy, and *indestructible freedom*! The challenge is to reach this in the midst of the storm.

MATTHIEU   On the surface, a tempest is raging, but in the depths of the ocean, calm remains. If we live only in our surface experiences, we will not cease to be buffeted by the waves of suffering.

CHRISTOPHE   Yes, but sometimes when we are rolling in the big waves, our tendency is to fight to stay on the surface and not to accept sinking momentarily to the bottom. We're too afraid that will be the end of us!

MATTHIEU   If you get in the habit of relating to the depths, you develop a confidence and strength of mind that allows you to traverse the vicissitudes of life with ease. Being able to return to pure awareness makes us much less vulnerable.

ALEXANDRE   How, in mid-chaos, in the midst of torment, can we not identify with the panic, the conflicts, the passions?

MATTHIEU   It's clear that in the full force of the storm, it is very difficult to relate to the pure awareness that observes the storm without being carried away by it. That which is aware of the panic is not the panic.

Looking at this approach over the long term, it is desirable to train in managing our torments, conflicts, and inner convolutions, beginning with the less intense mental states and accumulating expertise little by little. After that, we will be better equipped to deal with the kind of powerful inner disturbances often associated with tragic events.

In many cases, there is no choice but to work on these emotions after they have calmed down. With a bit more experience, we can work with inner disturbances before they become uncontrollable. We will be able to see them coming and apply the appropriate antidotes. In the end, when a certain mastery of the mind has been acquired, we will be able to work with the emotions while they are manifesting in such a way as to prevent them from sowing trouble in our minds.

Moments of Grace

CHRISTOPHE   But what about the worst storms of life? Parents who lose a child, for example, do not want to go right to the bottom of the ocean—to their profound nature of total peace—because that gives them the feeling of abandoning their child, even though the child is dead. Because the suffering of mourning, in spite of everything, is still a connection.

MATTHIEU   I've already told that story about the woman in Hong Kong who found her young son drowned in a swimming pool. During the hour that followed, she determined that she had to make a choice: either the death of her son was going to ruin the rest of her life, since there's nothing worse than losing a child, or she could decide to lead a constructive life that could bring her profound satisfaction but still in no way diminish the enduring love she felt for her child. She chose the second option.

ALEXANDRE What moved that bereaved mother, facing the worst of the worst, not to let herself be wiped out, annihilated, by grief?

MATTHIEU It happened like a revelation. She doubtless saw two roads ahead, one filled with inconsolable sadness and the other filled with love.

CHRISTOPHE It's not just an intellectual vision. In order to take effect on us, a thought has to be energized by a strong emotion. In cognitive psychotherapy, we often say, "The stronger the emotion, the stronger the cognition (automatic thought)." When a thought arises in our mind as self-evident, it's because an intuition, an embodied emotion, is pushing it from behind. In all these cases of "revelation," which are frequent, for example, in mystical experiences, there is always something happening on the physical and emotional level.

What happened in that woman's brain at the very instant when she suddenly and clearly saw, as you said, that before her lay a path of sadness and a path of love, a path of death and a path of life? We could doubtless identify particular neural substrates if we were to explore such moments by means of neuroimaging.

There are several ways to attain this feeling of harmony, at least momentarily. We were just talking about what amounts to an existential earthquake—that is, the path of bereavement, the emotional shock of which allows some people, afterward, to radically change their attitude. But there are also calm and discreet upheavals. Isn't the coming to the surface of this deeper nature also linked to what we try to teach our patients when we say, "Try to be present to small moments of grace, moments in which you feel in harmony with yourself, with other people, and with nature. These moments are very precious. And whenever you're lucky enough to experience one, stop! Open your mind, savor it, be present to it." By doing this, we create a small break in our continuity, a small opening between our little habitual world—where everything is logical, predictable, and explicable—and the mystery of being alive and conscious in an environment that we think we understand but that is beyond us. Fundamentally, all the repetitive practices we do, whether in a Buddhist context or a psychological one, create moments of opening to this deeper nature.

How do we reach out to this nature and allow it to touch us? Maybe by following the model of geothermal heating. We dig beneath a house to get the benefit of the warmth existing underground, the heat of the deeper layers of the earth. There we have an infinite heat resource, but only people who make the effort to drill down can get the benefit of it. Sometimes I have the feeling that meditation is to our minds as the geothermal heating principle is to our houses: it's drilling down to the deepest level of ourselves, putting ourselves in contact with resources that are always present but hidden and barely accessible without effort on our part.

MATTHIEU We are like the poor man who is unaware that there is a treasure under his hut. He is simultaneously rich, because the treasure belongs to him, and poor, because he doesn't know that he possesses it.

ALEXANDRE In his novel *Zadig, or the Book of Fate*, Voltaire recounts the story of a recluse who, in taking leave of his host, burns down his house to thank him. Under the ashes an immense treasure was waiting. I was a teenager when I discovered this story, and I experienced a sort of mini-awakening, an outright revelation. Voltaire seemed to be indicating that behind the blows of fate (such as physical impairment) and beneath our daily setbacks, a teaching could be concealed: wealth, an unimaginable gift. Here is a marvelous invitation to view adversity, hindrances, and obstacles as so many occasions to clear away confusion, to say goodbye to illusions, and, without falling into a neurotic fascination with pain, to descend toward the treasure found in the ground of grounds.

CHRISTOPHE This is a path to psychological change that we psychotherapists should explore further. However, it is not the same thing as many traditional therapists propose, which is to encourage people to dig down and get to the bottom of their problems by endlessly examining their past, which is a kind of navel-gazing. Here the point is to get to the bottom of one's human condition but in a radically different mental state—that is, by abandoning all pretense of control and mastery, by letting go and trusting, and by stripping oneself of one's certainties and making an effort to simply observe and feel.

Mind training is a little like gardening: we do the best we can with what we experience and with what we are. And from time to time, a gap appears, because we experience something powerful or otherwise vivid for no reason. This gap opens our eyes to the fact that the profound nature of our mind, of our being, of our soul—I don't know what the right word is—has revealed itself to us for a moment. We move back and forth from our little garden to the big world; we are at the same time on top of the mountain, in the heart of the forest, and in the middle of vast prairies. Is this the value of these particular moments, which are perhaps moments in which we are discovering our deeper nature?

Toolbox for Opening Ourselves to Our Deeper Nature

MATTHIEU

Keep your mind open. Experience the key moments in life with an open mind, welcoming the range of constructive possibilities for oneself and others.

Discriminate. Let what really counts come to the surface from the profoundest depths of consciousness.

Be confident. No matter what happens, you will find a way to utilize adverse circumstances as catalysts for making progress on the spiritual path and for manifesting greater compassion toward those around you.

Inhabit the space of interdependence. Resituate the events that affect you in the much larger context of the interdependence of all beings and all things, who like you, experience countless joys and sorrows.

ALEXANDRE

Contemplate the little persona that you play all day long. Look at the labels, the functions you use to define yourself. Examine the outfit that you dress up in from morning till night so that you can go naked to meet your deeper nature.

Be aware of the heavy weight of education, of the mass of prejudices, of the heap of illusions that have ended up as an overlay on reality. Just identify this factitious layer so that you can take in daily life as it is without the intervention of ego, of concepts, and of the thousand expectations that shape your world.

Discover the deep personal aspirations that inhabit you. What do you expect out of life? What is it that you are running after so avidly?

Accept losing your grip. Ego defends its territory tooth and nail. It sets up boundaries, busies itself delimiting its world. In its folly, it isolates us, confines us to solitude, to distance. Opening your heart, going beyond the bounds of narrow individuality, means facing the experience of leaping into the void, of swimming in the open sea of freedom.

CHRISTOPHE

Discover your inner resources. The deeper nature we have been talking about is not just a theoretical matter, but a very practical one. We should do our best never to forget all the strengths and resources we have within us. They are not an illusion. Our mindset is such that we quite often underestimate our personal capacity to deal with adversity. And then there are the strengths and resources all around us, the help and inspiration that others can supply us. We are better equipped than we think. To access these resources within us and outside us, the best thing is not to shrink back into ourselves and dwell on our fears and bitterness or on our certainties, positive or negative.

What if nothing happens? What if no tangible sign of the existence or emergence of our deeper nature comes along? Well, it's not that serious! In any case, it's there. Let's just not forget to live, act, love, work, and enjoy ourselves; to help others the best we can; and to continue to be open to this profound and universal aspect of ourselves that we all have within us.

17

Dealing with Death

It is told that the great Tibetan sage Drukpa Kunlek, who lived for a few years in the kingdom of Bhutan, was invited to offer auspicious wishes for the members of a particular household. So he said, "Grandparents die, parents die, children die." This pronouncement met with a respectful but somewhat awkward silence. After a few moments, the master explained, "Well, if they die in that order, there will be no heart-rending tragedies in the family."

—Matthieu

ALEXANDRE   So then the best we can hope for here is: Matthieu dies, Christophe dies, and Alexandre dies.

MATTHIEU   No wonder Alexandre is happy. Being the youngest of us, he gets off light!

CHRISTOPHE   What hurts us is not the occurrence of death itself but the feeling that it has happened too soon in relation to our appetite for life, in relation to all the things we feel we still have to do and experience. That is why we always require comforting when we are facing death.

Arnaud Desjardins explained that for our Western subconscious, death is frightening because it seems to us that it is the negation of life. We relate to death and life as a pair of antagonists. But in some cultures, particularly Eastern ones, when they speak of death, they speak of it mainly as a correlate of its opposite, birth. The benefit of this view is to make us perceive death as a transition, rather than a state, even if we don't have a clear idea of what this transition leads to.

A Prime Occasion for Letting Go

MATTHIEU   A healthy view of death leads us to understand in the deepest part of ourselves that it is inevitable and its time is unpredictable. Taking this obvious fact into account allows us to give each passing moment its due value, even if this moment is one of doing nothing or just seeing the birds flitting around on a tree in flower.

This recognition has nothing morbid about it. It allows us to live better and prevents us from wasting our time, like letting gold dust slip between our fingers. Let's be smart enough to recognize the inestimable value of each moment of life and decide to make better use of it for our own sake and for the sake of others. Seneca said: "It is not that we have so little time but that we waste so much of it." Let us dispel the illusion that we have our whole lives ahead of us. Let us not veil the face of inevitably approaching death. Since time immemorial, we have never heard of anyone escaping death. If we rebel against this truth or pretend to ignore it, we're making a mistake.

Among all the teachings of the Buddha, those that highlight the impermanence of all things are most prominent. Reflecting on death and impermanence is truly what turns us with the greatest force toward spiritual practice and encourages us to draw the very essence from our life rather than frittering it away on trivial pursuits.

ALEXANDRE   The fear of dying, of losing a dear one, of suffering—that's major material to work on! In the end we do not control our own destiny. We are not the masters of the ship; we are all riding a train that is hurtling toward the void or maybe toward God. This is enough to make shivers run up and down our spines. It's insane what we can do to flee this obvious fact, to fight off the inevitable, to try to build a wall against that which, sooner or later, will surely happen.

The challenge is to dare a joyful lucidity capable of filling our hearts and making us love this fragile and ephemeral life. But ego stiffens its resistance—the very idea of dying is intolerable to it; it clings, it resists. It seems to me that behind the fear of death lies hidden the fear of not having had enough of life. Wouldn't the best antidote to this be to learn to open one's arms, to welcome each moment like a gift, without the voraciousness and banker's mentality that only wants to hoard and speculate, to stockpile, accumulate, and amass? But everything seems to be against this inner freedom: fear, the self-preservation instinct, unbridled attachment to this precarious individuality, stupefaction in the face of the void, nothingness.

Thinking about Death in Order to Love Life

MATTHIEU Buddhist practitioners are supposed to ask themselves every night, "Which will come first, dawn or death?" The great sage Nagarjuna said that we should marvel after each outbreath that we are able to breathe in again. That doesn't mean that we should beat our breasts all day, crying, "I'm going to die! I'm going to die!" It simply means we should give full value to our time by using it to progress toward freedom from suffering. That doesn't amount to having to be obsessed with the idea of getting the maximum amount of things done in the minimum amount of time. What counts is living each moment of our lives fully, including when we are doing nothing. If you have only a few days to live, you're not going to darn your socks. You'll prefer to spend your time with dear ones, showing them kindness, as well as collecting yourself as deeply as possible. It's a sad spectacle to see people whose death is approaching get angry with their family, sow discord among their heirs, cling to their possessions, and quit this life with acrimony and greed.

It is desirable to familiarize ourselves with the notion of impermanence and with death so that we are not shocked when it happens and we can experience it calmly. For that, it's important to understand that although death is certain, the time of its occurrence is unpredictable. All causes of life can change into causes of death. Most of the activities we engage in daily—work, eating, sports, trips, and leisure pursuits—can go wrong and lead to our death. So it's important not to fail to appreciate the time we do have and to try to experience what is essential in human life.

CHRISTOPHE   In order to avoid tumbling into the void, an acrobat on a tightrope should never forget he is in danger, yet he mustn't focus on the risk of falling. That's how it is for us living beings: never forget that death is possible at any moment, but never focus on it either.

ALEXANDRE   Between denial and obsession is the precise point where we can develop a freer, lighter relationship with our mortality. Since everyone is going to go die in the end, what's the point of being over-serious or holding grudges? During the handful of days that we have at our disposal, why shoot ourselves in the foot and spoil our precious time with rancor, resentment, hatred, and anger? What we must do is reconcile ourselves with the idea of our own end and familiarize ourselves with our helplessness.

In Seoul, I heard talk of "funeral parties." It seems that certain businesses organized parties in which the clients celebrated their own burial. Lying in a coffin, optimally situated for enjoying the officiant's sermon and the speeches of their relatives and friends, the clients could familiarize themselves with the idea that they too would eventually end up between four boards. According to the organizers, this practice had nothing macabre about it. It was an opportunity to relativize one's difficulties, feel all the love surrounding one, and to consider what is really of value in life.

CHRISTOPHE   This coexistence of inevitability and pain with the need for happiness reminds me of the great misunderstanding that affects the way people perceive positive psychology. Its aspiration to make our life more pleasant is not connected with a naive logic but a tragic one: death, our own as well as that of those we love, is inevitable. It's because we're going to die that happiness counts—that it's not a luxury but a necessity, a driving force, a source of energy that gives us the strength to act, to appreciate life, to do as much good as possible or as little harm as possible in the world around us. Only by regularly accepting and taking into account the aspects of life that at first appear dark and disquieting do we develop an aptitude for happiness.

MATTHIEU Real positive psychology shows us that positive emotions such as joy, gratitude, wonder, enthusiasm, inspiration, and love are much more than the mere absence of negative emotions. Joy, for example, is more than the absence of sadness. This dimension is the source of profound satisfaction that allows us to build up our strength of mind, notably in relation to the approach of death. So this is not just a matter of saying, "Cool, I'm going to die!" Rather, it means approaching death with serenity and with the sense of fulfillment that inner freedom confers on us. This attitude keeps us from sinking into nihilism and despair. We do not have the freedom to escape from death, but we do have the freedom to die in peace.

CHRISTOPHE This reminds me of an experience I had during a conference on palliative care where I had been invited to speak on meditation. Among the other contributors, there was a priest who told us an upsetting story, demonstrating to what extent we have a hard time relating to death.

This priest had visited a woman suffering from metastasized cancer that left very little doubt about its final outcome. He was sitting next to her on her bed, talking to her softly. The husband was a short distance away on a chair, listening. The woman, who had already survived several cancers, said to the priest, "Father, this time I think I'm going to die." The priest understood that there was no longer any point in pretending, in telling her she was going to be fine, or in talking about anything else. He leaned close to her and softly said, "You want to talk about it?" But at that moment the husband leapt out of his chair, bent near his wife, and said vehemently and with anguish, "No, no, you're not going to die!"

With that, everything came to a halt. The priest did not dare go any further with that approach, which seemed to be unbearable to the husband. And the wife didn't either. She let herself be reassured that she wasn't going to die. They all refrained from uttering the truth. They talked about other things. Two days later she died, without having had an opportunity to confront her fears, without having been able to receive genuine solace that went beyond soothing, false words. She was ready, but her husband wasn't. He made the decision for her.

Further along in the discussion, the priest told us that he also often felt helpless in the face of death: "Since I'm not a doctor, I can't say to people, 'Calm down, I'm going to ease your pain and explain to you how things are going to go.' Because even as a priest, I don't know myself! I have faith, but God has never contacted me directly to explain it to me! I have to muddle through with my convictions, without certainty."

I recall how completely I drank in these words. I admired his goodness and humility. I was also blown away by the volunteers and caregivers there, who accompany their brothers and sisters in humanity right to the doors of death without ever knowing what lies behind them, thinking to themselves that one day it will be their turn. I left the conference in an altered state. I had the opportunity that afternoon to experience both the peaks and the abysses. I had the opportunity to hear what we never hear. I was both upset and fulfilled. We had talked about death the whole day, and in the course of that, without having sought it, I had tasted the taste of life.

From Fear to Acceptance

ALEXANDRE Can one learn to die? In the philosophical tradition, there are at least two major schools of thought on this. First, there are the Stoics and many others who tell us never to lose sight of the fact that we're all going to buy the farm. Our job is to defuse, by relating to it, all of our panic, fear, and dread and attain the state of freedom that made Montaigne say, "I want a man to act and to prolong the functions of life as long as he can; and I want death to find me planting my cabbages, but careless of death, and still more of my unfinished garden."[1]

There's Spinoza too. In the *Ethics*, he writes, "The free man thinks of nothing less than of death, and his wisdom is not a meditation upon death, but upon life."[2] According to our author, those who are moving in the direction of freedom will not burden themselves with sad passions and dark ideas. They concentrate instead on joy, on *conatus*—that is, our power to exist and act. In pure positivity, they give themselves to the present moment, the eternity of here and now.

But can I decide one morning when I get up to stop brooding? More than trying for 180-degree conversions, we have to do what we can with our current resources.

In Buddhism, we have what are called the five recollections. Here the practitioner is asked to remember that (1) suffering is inevitable—no matter what I do, I am going to suffer; (2) aging is inevitable, whether I like it or not; (3) sickness is inevitable—even if I protect myself against all the rabid weasels in the world, flee from the least virus, I'm going to end up getting sick; (4) death is inevitable—there's no way out—one day or another I'm going to croak; (5) being separated from dear ones is inevitable—it's tragic, but every human life must face bereavement, separation.

These reminders have nothing depressing about them. On the contrary, they free up the path, clear the ground, and do away with false hopes. They liberate us from vain struggles, relieve us of an immense weight, and perhaps lead us in the direction of a happy state of acceptance. Denial is gone; I know the rules of the game, the ontological laws, the nature of reality. And like the chess player who is an expert at turning situations of being trapped into a win, I can take the first steps into a state of freedom, of peace.

MATTHIEU In the West nowadays, death is hidden, covered up, sterilized. Since there's no remedy for this ineluctable occurrence, we prefer to remove death from our field of consciousness. Because of this, when it happens, we are all the more shocked because we are not prepared. And all this time, life ebbs away day by day.

Not very long ago, people died most of the time in the bosom of family and friends, and this also permitted children to see death as an integral part of life. In the Buddhist culture, if a spiritual master is present at the bedside of the dying person, that person usually dies in peace and his family and friends are comforted. If, moreover, the dying person is an experienced practitioner, people will not be too worried about him or her. Savoring the inestimable value of each moment is fundamentally linked with the ephemeral character of our lives. It's because life doesn't last that we must make the effort to extract its very essence and not fritter it away meaninglessly. We cannot escape the impermanence that is an inalienable element in everything.

CHRISTOPHE   Traditional societies were not stingy about myths about death. I remember when I was a kid being struck by the figures of the Three Fates, goddesses who decide human destinies, and especially by the oldest of the three, who with her scissors cuts the threads of our lives. I was also impressed by the Latin motto on sundials: *Vulnerant omnes, ultima necat* ("They all wound, the last one kills"), reminding us that each hour brings us closer to our death. A monk told me that Trappist monks used to often greet each other with the expression *memento mori* ("Remember, you are going to die")! I don't think these images or these messages made our ancestors any unhappier than we are. On the contrary, they made them more clear-sighted and motivated to cultivate what counted for them, as well as giving meaning to their life: happiness, lucidity, faith.

MATTHIEU   Yes, we completely feel what you are saying in this verse by Milarepa, the great Tibetan hermit of the eleventh century:

Frightened by death, I went to the mountains
So I could meditate on its uncertain hour,
I conquered the immortal bastion of the immutable
And now my fear of death has been left far behind!

ALEXANDRE   Dying to oneself, attending to life thoroughly as it goes along, is assuredly learning to espouse impermanence. A quick glance at a photo album tells us that the little fellow we were at age five and the adolescent who back then was racking his brains over his dissertation have disappeared and allowed the being we are today to come to be. It would amount to killing life to try to freeze oneself in a static state while existence is moving along.

MATTHIEU   Death, like the deterioration of material objects—wood rots, iron rusts, houses fall to ruins—is only the visible reflection of the subtle impermanence inherent in all phenomena. Nothing remains identical to itself for two consecutive moments, no matter how close they are.

ALEXANDRE Meditating on our finitude, on impermanence, doesn't have anything sad about it. On the contrary, experiencing the continuous changes in our existence is opening ourselves to the continual innovation that makes it possible to live in the here and now. But conceptual mind balks at this. It hangs on, tooth and claw; it wants to hold onto something solid. It seeks security, fixity, when everything is transitory and everything passes. And this is where all the suffering, the constant alarm, the relentless dissatisfaction, come from.

MATTHIEU The fact is that by distorting reality—that is, by clinging to the idea that we ourselves, our friends and family, and our possessions are going to endure, not change, and that they are really "ours"—we feed the causes of suffering. At the end of the day, even if we want to abandon our possessions and our life itself, it is they who will abandon us!

ALEXANDRE A Zen master told his disciples that every time they crossed the threshold of a doorway, they should leave behind their identities, their roles, their expectations, their wounds, and the bundle of mental representations that everybody lugs around with them night and day. This is a truly concrete exercise that invites us to make ourselves totally available to whatever comes along, to open our arms to it without holding back.

An Indispensable Celebration of Life

CHRISTOPHE Sometimes we have to experience a serious illness, either in ourselves or among our friends and family, to realize that these thoughts should be the object of repeated exercises from which we could gain intelligence, comfort, and freedom in relation to our obsession with death (which subjects us to fear) or our blocking it out (which subjects us to flight and the quest for distractions).

A few years ago, I was stricken by a potentially fatal illness. I was submerged in all sorts of reflections, preoccupations, and worries. I remember that I was not worried by the idea of dying—I was just sad. And that really struck me. I suddenly felt very strongly that I still had a lot of great things to do, to experience, to feel. It seemed to me that the regular work I've been doing for years to become less impulsive, less egoistic, more generous, and more attentive was going to be halted. "Damn," I said to myself, "I would have loved to see how far I could have gotten with that!" The benefit of that experience is that it has stayed with me. Still years later, I believe I think every day of how lucky we are to be alive and able to appreciate our life, even with its griefs and sorrows.

MATTHIEU Absolutely right — fully accepting the inevitability of death should not lead to resignation but to a celebration of life and of the extraordinary potential it offers us. For someone who is dedicated to the spiritual path that leads to inner freedom, each day is worth living. A Tibetan sage said that in the beginning the practitioner thinking about death will feel like a deer that is caught in a trap and struggling desperately. After having made progress on the path, the practitioner will become like a farmer who has cultivated a field with the greatest care and has nothing to regret, whether the harvest is good or bad. In the end, the practitioner is serene and satisfied, like someone who has accomplished a great task.

For a person who attains perfect inner freedom, when death comes knocking at their door, they open it up without the slightest hesitation, as for a friend. They are ripe, they are ready; they have never hidden from it and approach this transition with equanimity. This is why Buddhist practitioners wish to die with their lucidity intact if possible. This permits them to put in practice what they were able to assimilate spiritually in the course of their lives, without being destabilized by the throes of dying.

A great meditator I was very close to, Sengdrak Rinpoche, died of leukemia in a hospital in Nepal. He wanted to stay in his hermitage, but his disciples convinced him to go to the hospital in Kathmandu. Being very weak, he had to remain lying down most of the time. When he felt that the moment of death had come, he sat up perfectly straight in the lotus position, his eyes wide open, looking into the space in front of him. He took a big in-breath, then he breathed out, resting in the nature of mind. He had asked for his body to be brought to our monastery. He remained seated in the lotus position, as though he had just died, for over a week without any rigor mortis. His body exuded a sweet fragrance, not at all the odor of a body beginning to decompose.

Illness or Physical Impairment Change Our Way of Looking at Death

CHRISTOPHE   What I also found very interesting in my personal experience is all the things that came up in my mind after I had had a close brush with death and then realized that it wasn't going to happen this time. Many people have this experience and are led to reflect, not conceptually but experientially, about hearing from the doctor's mouth that they have a living threat in one's body. It's very powerful.

Having this experience can leave people with a permanent case of anxiety concerning recurrences, possible new incidences of the disease, the looming reality of the threat. In my case, I'm under the impression that it did me good on the psychological level, that it opened my eyes and caused some of my understanding of my fears to evolve. Beforehand, like most people, I had a low-level preoccupation about getting old and all the aches and pains and minor maladies that go with it. But living with a potentially mortal illness, potentially having a time bomb in my body, changed my attitude toward the onset of age. At this point, I'm only asking one thing: to be able to get old! I could never have sincerely said that before this illness.

And that reminds me of conversations I had a long time ago with one of my close friends, who is very much a Christian. In Christianity there is a very fertile line of thought about the relationship we can have with death and about the way in which faith can help us work with this idea in a tranquil and intelligent manner. My friend said to me, "Getting old is ultimately a blessing. That's what prepares you for death. You learn little by little that there are things you're going to have to separate from. And in case you don't get it or you don't want to get it, your body reminds you by saying, 'Hey there, get ready to let go of all that.' Not in a nasty or threatening way, but like a teacher who pulls a pupil's ear a little and forces them to look at realities they don't want to see." I found these words interesting and pertinent intellectually. But I never thought I might agree with them one day.

ALEXANDRE Being stuck with a permanent physical impairment as I am, I sometimes have trouble watching lightheartedly as old age gains ground. I already have to put up with fatigue, pain, and exhaustion some days. I have a lot of trouble taking a positive attitude toward a chronic debility, a body falling apart, and at the same time coping with daily chores. I contemplate this worn-out and exhausted body and use this as an opportunity for letting go, as an invitation to make the most of the here and now to make progress in my inner work.

In order not to die before our time, let us embark on a spirituality that will make us really alive, fully healthy, even with our physical impairments, wounds, and illnesses. Because as long as there is a breath left in our body, nothing is completely a lost cause. A friend of mine who was suffering from an extremely insidious pathology went so far as to speak of a happy decrepitude. He saw the decline of his body as a school for letting go. The great leap, the eventual extinction of our fires, can remind us of what is essential.

18

Ethics

*We psychotherapists make a habit of never judging our patients—or
we try hard not to. But it's sometimes difficult. I remember a man
who came to me for help against his pedophilic impulses. He told me
he had never acted them out but felt that it was becoming more and
more difficult to contain them. I didn't treat him myself because I had
no experience whatever with this kind of problem. Instead I referred
him to a colleague. But this encounter was a tricky one for me because,
like everyone else, I have a very unfavorable view of pedophilia, a
view that seems to me completely legitimate on a moral plane. But this
reminded me of the comments an American colleague of mine, Jonathan Haidt, made about these moral questions. He essentially said
that when dealing with a question concerning which you think there
might be several possible legitimate opinions and attitudes, this is not
a question of morality for you but a question of personal taste. If, on
the other hand, you think there's only one possible option, it becomes a
moral question for you. Thus, having sexual relations before marriage
is an option accepted by the majority of Westerners, who therefore no
longer consider it a moral question. But nobody, or almost nobody,
will say that having sexual relations with children is a question of
individual choice that must be respected; everybody considers it a
moral question.*

It seems to me that morality is indispensable not only for the proper functioning of society but also for the proper functioning of individuals. That's why I'm glad to listen to what you two have to say on this subject—a philosopher and a monk know a lot more about this subject than a shrink does!

—Christophe

What Are We Talking About?

CHRISTOPHE   In your view, is there a difference between "morality" and "ethics"? Do these two words definitely refer to two disparate dimensions? If so, how so? Is speaking of "ethics" just a classier and more modern way of referring to "morality," a word that perhaps sounds more outdated?

ALEXANDRE   The etymology of the two terms is close enough to be confusing. "Ethics" comes from the Greek *ethos,* which means "mores," and "morality" comes from the Latin *moralis,* which also refers to "mores." Over the centuries, the two words have taken on different colorations and connotations, but many contemporary authors consider them synonyms.

Nowadays, however, the idea of morality gets rather bad press because it often refers to a catalog of dictums, codes of conduct, dogmas, injunctions, and even prohibitions, when in reality what it has to do with is becoming more human, growing up.

On this subject, great books are not lacking. We have Aristotle's *Nicomachean Ethics* and Spinoza's *Ethics*—inexhaustible itineraries for liberation, veritable paths of light leading to happiness. It's as though these philosophers were taking us by the hand and leading us step by step toward freedom and profound bliss. And there lies the crucial issue, the big challenge: at this time of envisaging the fruits of wisdom, what is perhaps most fruitful is to focus on the question of the good life, on an art of living that will cause the gardens of the heart to bloom.

MATTHIEU   Like Alexandre, I think that "morality," defined as the knowledge of good and evil, is most often conceived of in a normative sense, under the heading of duty. The danger here is defining "good" and "evil" in an absolute, disembodied fashion and not taking into account context and human situations as they are in real life. It seems to me more appropriate not to base ethics on good and evil, considered as principles written in letters of flame in the sky, but on the good and ill we cause other beings in terms of their well-being or suffering. In those terms, ethics is a science of happiness and suffering, linked with a desire for moral integrity and consistency. An ethics marked by clear-sightedness, impartiality, and compassion requires that we be free from our biases, prejudices, and conditionings. It would thus be one of the fruits of inner freedom.

The problem with dogmatic ethics is that the principles it rests on are not necessarily just, equitable, and universal. In his book *What's Wrong with Morality?*, C. Daniel Batson recounts how members of the Ku Klux Klan brutally whipped people who didn't go to church on Sunday—where they would then listen to sermons on loving one's neighbor! During the genocides of the wars of religion, many torturers succeeded in convincing themselves that their victims merited their fate and that the tortures they were inflicting on them were a good thing. They also would deal with their guilt by associating themselves with a majority opinion or social order that preached oppression and persecution, and in such cases would claim that they were "following orders." History is full of people who have committed the worst of atrocities in the name of morality.

The absence of ethics is characterized by a failure to consider the consequences of our actions for the lot of others. It is a triumph of egocentricity, which, depending on the case, ignores others, exploits them shamelessly to promote its own interests, or harms them, either intentionally or by being heedless of their condition. At the end of the day, everybody loses by this because actions and words that harm others also end up having negative consequences for oneself.

ALEXANDRE André Comte-Sponville, in his *Valeur et Vérité* (*Value and Truth*), explains that morality is connected with the entire set of our duties. It responds to the question "What should I do?" and aims at universality. Ethics, in his view, is "the reflected-upon set of our desires." Its primary question is "How should I live?" From this question, we can see how ethics relates to an individual or a group. According to this philosopher, morality peaks in sainthood, whereas ethics is an art of living "that tends toward happiness and culminates in wisdom."

At the point where narcissism and egoism are leading us to instrumentalize other people, to consider them as a means, ethics and morality embark on a freedom that goes beyond the limitations of individuality and self-interest.

Embodied Ethics

MATTHIEU In a small work on ethics, Francisco J. Varela cites the Canadian philosopher Charles Taylor: ethics is not only what it's good to do, but what it's good to be. How should we understand this distinction? In situations in which we do not have an indefinite amount of time to weigh the pros and cons, we react spontaneously, in a moral manner or not, on the basis of our way of being such as it has developed over years.

In the light of this philosophical aphorism, we can understand the connection between ethics and inner freedom, the latter being free from the influence of hate, jealousy, and dogmatism. Dogmatism can take the form of rigid restrictions—the idea that one should never lie, even to save the life of a fugitive pursued by a murderer. Buddhism advocates a natural ethics based on inner freedom and inspired by compassion, an ethics that arises spontaneously from deep with oneself, free from unbreakable dogmas.

Individual freedom consists in doing whatever one wants as long as it causes no harm to others. One might try to follow a line of personal conduct based on behaviors that only affect oneself—they are rare!—as a means to avoid shameful activity. But the safeguard ethics provides is to dissuade us from deliberately harming others.

Religions generally have very entrenched viewpoints on the great ethical questions like euthanasia or abortion. In Buddhism, the answers depend on the actual context. Asked about these questions, the Dalai Lama often replies, "Describe the situation of this person to me. After that, I can think about it." Thinking about it consists in weighing the consequences in terms of well-being and suffering.

CHRISTOPHE Our morality certainly must have a definite form, but that form also has to be processed. Our behavior does not automatically flow from our moral values. Going to church, to a temple, to the mosque, to a synagogue, or any place of worship and being in agreement with the moral precepts of our religion does not guarantee that we will always behave well. We have to strive constantly to translate theory into practice. And others can also help in this through social control of moral behavior.

It seems to me that morality is neither necessary nor sufficient for doing good. Not sufficient because, as I just said, the stage of putting preformulated morality into action is often a weak link. And not necessary, either, because sometimes we can adopt moral behavior without having received any relevant teachings or undergone any prior moral constraint.

Taking the problem the other way around, I was thinking, for example, of the times when we might end up doing harm to others. It seems to me that we are more likely to do harm when we have cut ourselves off from certain inner watchers of ours—in particular from certain emotional safeguards.

I believe that when we are at our best, we are capable of being attentive to little emotional signals deep within us that regulate our aggressive impulses. If we are not profoundly out of balance due to suffering, our emotions are quite capable of warning us when we are in the process of doing harm. They often send us signals beforehand, as well as while it is happening. Unless we are psychopathic perverts, we don't feel right when we are harming others. And the emotions also send signals afterward—that's where guilt comes from. We never do harm to others when a serene and tranquil atmosphere prevails within us, and if we are more attentive to what is going on in us, the frequency of harming others will diminish considerably. Thus, the role of inner balance and freedom is determinative. It goes a long way toward making us more ethical animals. That's why we must make efforts that lead us in this direction.

Sometimes we harm others without realizing it. We don't pay enough attention to the fact that people may be having difficulties. Or we say things that we don't realize can be hurtful. Basically this is inevitable when we live in the midst of people; these are brushes with reality inherent in all social life.

The Difficulty of Sincere Ethics and Altruistic Ethics

MATTHIEU   C. Daniel Batson, whom I cited earlier, did a lot of work on altruism. His most recent book on morality surveys the many works of behavioral psychologists, whose results are quite intriguing. The research shows that if children are able to hide their behavior, they have very little hesitation in behaving in a way that would draw disapproval from adults, along with a punishment if they were caught at it—for instance, taking a toy away from another child. Most of the time, then, children don't pay much attention to morality in relation to their own actions. But by contrast, if another child steals *their* toy, they will generally protest long and loud, proclaiming that it is very "bad" to act that way. The conclusion? Children promote morality when it helps them make sure that others will behave decently toward them, but are not bothered by going against morality when they can get away with it.

Similarly, when children become adults, a fair number of people proclaim moral ideas but at the same time covertly behave in ways that contradict the precepts they preach. They become experts in moral hypocrisy. This requires self-deception to avoid feeling too much guilt, which is an unpleasant feeling. In order to stay at peace with ourselves, we find very convenient justifications. As Batson points out, in such cases, we feel the need to make our moral failings invisible to others and to ourselves.

Thus, according to the research presented by Batson, morality is most often used as an instrument to force others to behave ethically toward ourselves and to protect ourselves from undesirable behaviors that others might inflict on us. Certainly moral integrity does exist, but it is weak in most individuals, especially when it involves a loss in personal advantage.

At first I must admit that I found Batson's conclusion disconcerting, especially coming as it did from the first psychologist to have shown, through rigorous scientific protocols, that true altruism does indeed exist, and that no plausible explanation based on egoism can call into question the results of the twenty-five types of studies that he carried out over fifteen years. Moreover, Batson distinguishes morality from altruism, whose goal is not to act according to moral principles but to improve the welfare of others. In Buddhism, in fact, compassion does not proceed from a moral judgment; rather, it aims to remedy the causes of suffering, whatever form that may take.

A few months after I read Daniel Batson's book, I came upon an illuminating study about bullying in schools. It turned out that the bullies were just as capable of moral reasoning as those who defended the oppressed. It turned out that bullies felt a perverse satisfaction in abusing their victim and had no pity for them. The defenders, for their part, came to the aid of these victims *moved by compassion and kindness*. This indicates that morality without altruism and compassion is not sufficient. Morality needs altruism to fulfill its function.

A compassionate or altruistic morality would begin with the observation that, whenever possible, I myself want to avoid suffering. So, if I value this aspiration and am concerned to fulfill it, I should avoid that which can cause suffering and do that which liberates me from suffering. Compassionate morality itself then consists quite simply in applying the same reasoning to others: others do not wish to suffer; I value their aspiration; I am concerned about their lot, and I abstain from actions that cause them suffering.

It may often be difficult to predict the long-term consequences of our actions, but it is always possible to examine our motivation sincerely and make sure that it is strongly marked by altruism.

We could argue that the road to hell is paved with good intentions. We might truly want to do good and still completely lack discriminating intelligence about how to accomplish our laudable intention. That's why we must free ourselves from delusion and distortions of reality.

ALEXANDRE   "What should I do?" is the moral question. "How should I live?" is the ethical question. Both these areas of work on ourselves can open into an itinerary of liberation. Saint Augustine and his celebrated formula *Dilige et quod vis fac* ("Love and do as you will") clearly shows the centrality of love and of charity. In his view, if we remain rooted in love, we can only act for good. There is no longer any need for a moral corset, rules of life, or a set of instructions.

The rub is that a variety of motivations can pull us one way or another, and there we are again, back with the theme of akrasia. On one side, the best part of ourselves looks toward the good, approves of it, and desires it ardently; on the other, there is the pettiness of everyday life, the mistakes, the aberrations. And this is perhaps the reason we need an ethics, a morality, an inner compass in order to advance, to make progress. It's by practicing temperance, courage, justice, and moderation as we go along that we acquire these virtues.

Why do we act morally? Are we virtuous, obedient, and proper because we are afraid of rejection or are moved by a desire to please? Out of a sense of conformism? Or are we, as Augustine wholeheartedly declares, really inhabited by a boundless charity that leads us naturally in the direction of the good? These are definitely ethical and moral issues and represent the immense challenge of stripping away all protective coverings and giving birth to a freedom, a love, that gives itself fully, nakedly, openly, and with no frills.

MATTHIEU André Comte-Sponville tells us, "We have need of morality only because we cannot love."[1] If one is listening to a sense of unconditional compassion, the question of ethics is settled, because in that case, it becomes inconceivable to deliberately harm others.

ALEXANDRE On the way to freedom, we have to leave behind the narrow-minded point of view of our prejudices and expand our hearts so that we always experience ourselves in the context of the situation. Life presents us with choices every day—sometimes difficult, lose-lose kinds of choices. Ethics, as well as morality, has to do with happiness, with all of us getting along together, with the common good. If we neither get sucked into the dangers of the social jungle nor try to contrive a state of happiness curled up in our own little corner, then we are promised a life of solidarity.

Described in broad strokes, ethics consists of doing a good job of being a human being, growing up, making progress together, and letting all the potential in our hearts flourish and thrive. Ethics in this sense translates into an art of living, an ascesis, spiritual exercises that guide us toward a happy life. Seeing morality only as some kind of straitjacket—a bunch of prohibitions meant to bully us around—is forgetting that we can't live well in a state of selfish anarchy.

However, ethics and morality can't be reduced to simple obedience to external rules. They must have a root, an origin, in our inner nature, in our personal core.

Paying Heed to the Inner Compass

ALEXANDRE The freedom of being human finds its way around and through and beyond our various attempts to reduce our action to models and schemas. There is no set of instructions for right action. Always we are invited to go deep, to dare to enter the depths of our inner being to listen to our inner compass. Doesn't daring to tread the path of freedom mean disobeying the clamoring of ego in order to make oneself available to the inner compass that leaves plenty of room for the other and would never shut itself in on itself?

CHRISTOPHE I like that idea of an inner compass a lot. All the studies suggest that our inner compass naturally turns toward the good. Whenever we manage to connect with it, it shows us the right direction. When we do good, we feel good, and when we feel good, we do good.

The problem is that this compass can be thrown off by our emotional disturbances. When we let anger, fear, and sadness take up too much space in us, that creates new mental polarities that throw off the needle of our compass, which then leads us in the wrong directions. This can be transitory, and some days, months, or years later, we might say, "But I was nuts to go that way, to neglect my values, my ethics, the needs of others." Once again we come back to the importance of the clarity and peace that are necessary for detachment and good judgment, so that we can quickly become aware of aberrations in our inner reference points.

ALEXANDRE Heeding the inner compass is one of the major principles and motivations behind ascesis and meditation. Going beyond the narrow framework of our reference points, our whims, and our self-interests we dive beyond fear, beyond the distant echoes of the past, beyond conditionings, beyond habits.

We have to recognize that we are under the spell of all kinds of sirens: the lamentations of guilt, the dictatorship of "What will they think of me?," the voice of remorse, or of "Don't do this, don't do that." The whole challenge lies in the dialogue between our inner nature and the other voices, the universal and the singular.

CHRISTOPHE   Altruism and a sense of solidarity can easily be taught to a child because his or her brain is predisposed toward that. But predisposition does not mean a necessary result. Without education or with education in the opposite direction (in the direction of egoism and competition), these innate tendencies will remain dormant or can be permanently deactivated.

MATTHIEU   Morality regarded as binding is made up of a series of major rules adopted by all people and all religions: do not kill, do not steal, do not lie. But when these rules are graven in stone without being really interiorized in people's collective mentalities, and when they do not admit to any exceptions, the rules can become harmful. It is at this point that the inner compass has to show the right direction.

The example of the great Indian sage Nagarjuna comes to my mind. His conduct was ethically perfect. One year a famine fell on his village. While the villagers were beginning to die of hunger, a rich Brahmin was storing immense quantities of rice and other grains in his storehouses. Nagarjuna organized a raid on those storehouses and, while leaving the Brahmin enough to survive on, saved the village. Deontologically, it was theft. However, from the point of view of compassionate ethics, it was a necessity.

Aristotle also said that we become virtuous by *practicing* virtue, which makes it possible to internalize morality to the point where it expresses itself spontaneously in our behavior. But this internalization, like any other form of mind training, requires sustained effort. Making a systematic effort to imagine what others are feeling increases our concern for them and encourages us to behave in an ethical manner.

ALEXANDRE   The journey toward freedom perhaps inevitably passes through a little examination of our personal morality because the most disinterested act in the world can perhaps in part be motivated by a will to power, a very strong need for domination, a desire to be rewarded, or a need to get even. When I was a child at the institution for handicapped children, we received a once-a-year visit by a number of politicians. I still remember these men whose eyes looked around for signs of approbation because they were shaking the hands of a few poor, handicapped people. No sense of reciprocity, no sense of relationship, came into being on that day.

CHRISTOPHE In the beginning or from the outside, morality looks like a set of constraints, but those constraints need to be freely chosen and not simply imposed. Freely chosen, they open up a space of freedom that is bigger than that provided by the absence of moral rules. This latter state is what is called "anomie," an absence of norms theoretically described by sociologist Émile Durkheim. This kind of anomie seems to be prized by our modern, relativist societies — "Any point of view is defensible; we shouldn't be judgmental" — in which it is often prohibited to prohibit (*interdit d'interdire*). As has been shown in studies on materialistic societies (those characterized by consumerism and anomic relativism) anomie apparently leads to greater anxiety and egoism, which are two forms of loss of freedom.

MATTHIEU In order to be translated into consistent action, morality must be impregnated with altruism. But it is very important that, in addition to our altruistic efforts, we liberate ourselves from the yoke of ignorance, the mental poisons, and an exaggerated sense of the importance of self. In that way, moral behavior on the level of wisdom and altruistic love would be one of the main fruits of inner freedom.

Toolbox for an Ethics of Everyday Life

ALEXANDRE

Socrates invites us to know ourselves and sharpen our sense of what is true so that we can lightheartedly step away from whatever weighs us down or leads us into dead ends. Pay heed to our inner compass — this "daemon," to use his word, this inner voice that acts like an alarm bell, a messenger, and a guide.

The lesson of Nietzsche. Perhaps each one of us is wallowing in a quite personal mythology. It's possible that over time we have decreed to ourselves what is good and what is evil, where happiness lies, and what code of conduct we must doggedly follow. For Nietzsche, "philosophizing with a hammer" means examining our values and the points of view we hold to see if they uplift us and make us grow, or if they weigh us down, rigidify us, and dry us up.

A necessary compassion. Perhaps the feeling of guilt is a vital safety barrier that keeps us from smashing into stone walls, but shame and self-contempt never did anyone any good. How do we look at our mistakes and the foibles of others? Are we prosecutors, implacable judges? Wouldn't it be better to consider our relapses and the akrasic areas of our lives with the eyes of a compassionate car repairman who is wholeheartedly and nonjudgmentally engaged in fixing our banged-up fenders?

What is a good life? This is the ethical and moral question par excellence. What do we aspire to in the depths of our being? Perhaps it would help to engage in the Stoic exercise of imagining ourselves on our deathbed. What is really of value in our life? What behavior, what actions, embody the quintessence of who we are?

MATTHIEU

Sincerely examine your motivation. Ask yourself, am I about to act in an entirely egoistic manner, or am I taking the situation of others into account? Have I just got a few individuals in mind or a greater number? Am I thinking short term or long term?

Bring in discriminating intelligence. This leads to making the most appropriate decision for the good of the greatest number for the long term.

Base your ethics on unconditional compassion. What would be the best decision if my only aim were the welfare of others? Next, consider realistically how you can combine this vision with your actual capacity for action, your energy, the time at your disposal, and your aspirations for your own happiness.

CHRISTOPHE

Ethics is beneficial for us. Morality is indispensable for life in society, but also for our inner balance. Anomie, the absence of rules regulating our social behavior, necessarily results in anxiety in individuals—notice the psychological problems of a child "king" or "queen" who is inadequately restricted by parents and who refuses all rules and constraints—and in violence within groups.

Examine your conscience. If you are not a philosopher, a simple way of bringing ethics to life within yourself is by examining your conscience. This introspective process leads to moral illumination. Ask yourself regularly what good or evil you have done. How? Why? See what lessons you can learn from this inquiry.

Pay attention to your emotions. They often put you on the right track. If you have "acted badly" or if you have needlessly caused suffering, it's rare that you will feel good about it. By contrast, if you have done something good, you always feel better.

19

Unconditional Compassion

I hadn't been back long from Korea when I found myself nose to nose with a strange person who made chills run down my spine. I was going through a period of rather heavy emotional turbulence, and I was feeling a bit sensitive and, frankly, fragile. I was in the bathroom in a restaurant in Lausanne when some guy walked in. It was like a bar scene from a movie. Looking straight into my eyes, the guy hollers, "You're not a man, Jollien! The world is a war zone! We're sick and tired of being nice, being kind! We're sick of sweet little teddy bears!"

On the spur of the moment I didn't have the force to whip out a few well-chosen lines to let the guy know, for example, that generosity is anything but sappy, that on the contrary it comes from a sublime level of courage, that it's a kind of dynamite that can quite easily blow away egoism, brutality, and the thirst for vengeance. Instead, at that point I would have much preferred to come up with a Tarantino-style comeback: "Oh yeah, bud? Is that right? Button it up and move on!" Why do the shields come up when it's time to promote non-ego, giving oneself, and the end of all fighting? Isn't the revolution today precisely on the side of altruism, gentleness, and generosity? Do we have to be hard because the world is hard? What should we say to the sour minds, to the sheriff types, to the cowboys who exalt self-assertion and power? Why the devil should we associate not fighting with cowardice? Isn't there enormous fear behind the need to hide behind armor and declare a state of war? "You're not a man!"

Feeling extremely insecure, shaken, and tottering, I walked out of the bathroom with a feeling of immense vulnerability. So I practiced solidarity, considering the other fellow a crewmember on the same boat—I couldn't take all of that for granted. That night, I felt an immense sense of solitude.

—Alexandre

CHRISTOPHE Remember, friends, when we were promoting our last book, *In Search of Wisdom,* the number of times we were criticized (if politely) on the theme of naive compassion in a world where wars and ill will are not in short supply. It's always the same misunderstanding: because the world is hard, we have to be hard, or rather we should *always* just be hard. It's difficult for a lot of people to understand that it's possible to take an active role in changing the world while remaining compassionate and kind. And it's just because the world already has so much violence in it that compassionate people are also necessary to make it livable.

This is one of the principles of the new generation of positive psychology: happiness is necessary not to make us forget unhappiness (as a shield against it) or to inactivate us, but so that we can deal with adversity better and draw strength from it in order to act.

Is Being Compassionate Naive?

ALEXANDRE The cowboy in the bathroom shook the hell out of me. His reaction challenged me, stripped me bare, and perhaps revealed the danger of making nice—even in the realm of spirituality—and of adopting a facade of altruism like a shield to ward off blows when real compassion at that point is somewhere else: in a state of fundamental genuineness that couldn't care less about being ingratiating.

CHRISTOPHE   It's amazing how brief, unpleasant moments like that can make us think about important things. And it is really true that that kind of phony posturing is disturbing. I sometimes see it in meditation circles, where teachers or students wear a pasted-on, ethereal smile on their faces all the time, as if to show off their advanced Zen-like qualities. Sometimes it's just too much, too unctuous.

Compassion has nothing to prove; it's not something to show off or exhibit. And it doesn't preclude conflicts or disagreements. It simply works so that nothing is added on to the aggressive or negative dimension of them.

ALEXANDRE   Another occasion when I was pretty freaked out and unable to control my emotions happened in the middle of a totally packed subway car as I was coming back with my son from a wonderful, magnificently sunlit outing. All at once one of the passengers let me have it full blast with his suspicions. I am very tender with my children and, being handicapped, my gestures often may seem a bit backward. After looking me over from head to foot, the man blurted out, "Get away from that kid! If you get near him again, I'm warning you, I'll call the cops!" How could I explain politely to this fellow that there was no problem, that I was the lucky father of this boy?

I was completely devastated, sad, and shaken, and found nothing better to do than shout out in the middle of that crowded subway car, "You poor man! Do you have any idea what a load of prejudices you're carrying around? I'm his dad, I'm his dad! You hear me? I'm his father!" No, it's not enough just to put on a show of politeness and courtesy to be really good.

The cowboy in the bathroom and the guy in the subway were wake-up calls to me to take a bit of a genealogical survey of my actual motivations in relating to people. Politeness, civility, and forthrightness should not be used to get a return on our investment. To love with no reason, for free — that is the challenge of daily life that arises in the midst of conflict, friction, stress, and lack of mutual understanding, constantly.

CHRISTOPHE   As you say, it's a daily challenge, a continual labor, to be the butt of these aggressions without becoming aggressive ourselves. The people who attack us are not on good terms with themselves. They take it out on the people around them, on those only there in passing, as in your encounters with the cowboy in the bathroom or the guy in the subway, or on those who are around them all the time. Many people are very attached to their anger and hatred, and they pass them on to others as a way of legitimizing their view of the world. This is, quite simply, because behind their anger and hatred lie their fears and sufferings. And letting go of the former would force them to confront the latter.

Faces of Compassion

ALEXANDRE   One day you gave me a powerful lesson, Matthieu. I was giving a conference with you, and when the question period came, one guy was babbling on and on in a never-ending tirade. The irritation of some of the attendees was palpable, and being afraid of getting into a quarrel with this person, I didn't know what to say. I remember your words: "I don't in the least mean to interrupt you, but I think we're going to end it there. Thank you and good night everyone!" I had shut myself up in the posture of somebody listening, understanding, and accepting, whereas inner freedom, courage, and compassion called for a much more nuanced approach.

There are two kinds of independence with regard to concern about what others are thinking: there's the arrogance of a Donald Trump, who pretends he couldn't care less about the opinion of others, and the freedom of the sage, of the saint, who has really freed himself or herself of this concern. Zen masters often employ a gentle firmness to disorient the ego of disciples at a point when flattery would bind them forever to dissatisfaction without ever healing them of it. Infinite compassion definitely does not preclude a certain toughness that respects others, takes them seriously, and loves them.

MATTHIEU   I think it's helpful to distinguish affability from compassion, firmness, and harshness. Compassion must always be present, unconditionally. Even when we are confronted by a cowboy in the bathroom, we can't respond with hostility; we can't deliberately wish this person ill. Nothing good can come out of that, nothing but the escalation of violence.

Kindness is the normal expression of compassion when people are behaving decently toward each other, which is the case most of the time. Instead of showing a sullen face to all comers, we greet them with gentleness. Gentleness is the face of compassion. Compassion is an inner attitude; gentleness is an external manifestation that can be seen in our facial expressions, our bodily posture, and in the tone of our voice.

The ideal would be to relate to everyone with compassion and greet them with a smile. In your story, Alexandre, you're stepping away from the urinal, and before you are able to express the least warmheartedness, the cowboy lights into you. If you try to disarm him with a smile, there's little chance of it working—the guy is hell-bent on making trouble. Thus, firmness is what is required. You have nothing to reproach yourself for; you remain inwardly calm, compassionate but standing firm. There's no reason for the outburst of a crude person to make you question the rightness of your inner attitude and thus destabilize you. For sure, that's easier to say than to do when you're dealing with some boor who couldn't care a fig about compassion.

So in the right circumstances, compassion can manifest as firmness. It's futile to smile sanctimoniously at someone attacking you. It's better to be firm with that person, without animosity, so as not to encourage his or her attitude and behavior.

Harshness, on the other hand, wounds other people. You harden your mind and whip out a volley of cutting remarks. The other person is either going to be hurt or get angry. In the latter case, the violence is going to escalate.

As for tolerance, depending on the case, it might be an expression of constructive openness or of harmful passivity. A doctor "tolerates" a maniac rather than bashing his head in, because his mission is to provide care. But nobody is supposed to accept the unacceptable, and tolerance should not encourage a permissive attitude toward injustice, discrimination, or violence. Openness of mind goes hand in hand with a certain calmness and allows us to accept reality as the starting point for desirable change. If we are not carried away ourselves by the maelstrom of the passions, we will be more capable of thoughtfully considering the appropriate next step to take.

In the case of the incident in the subway, I find your exploding with indignation quite understandable. The rudeness and total lack of tact, maturity, and judgment of that person are painful just to think about—even if on some level his intention may not have been malicious.

So you experienced two extremes: not reacting to the cowboy and blowing a gasket with the guy in the metro. You realized after the fact that neither one of those responses was ideal. Reactions to these kinds of provocations are often indications of the level of progress we have attained on the path and what we still have to work on. Little by little, by increasing our inner freedom, we learn to retain our equilibrium and remain on the middle path, which is the path of quiet confidence and discreet but solid compassion. A few simple and well-considered words, accompanied by a confident smile showing that we have not fallen into the trap of aggression, can disarm the brutality and even hostility of a person who is provoking or attacking us. If that works, so much the better. If not, we at least avoid falling into the trap ourselves, of being caught in the upward spiral of violence in which everybody involved loses.

In the case of the subway, I imagine if you had said calmly but in a loud voice that could be heard by everyone, "Sir, thank you for your concern for this child, who happens to be my son, whom I love with all my heart," he would have been mortified to have acted in such a brutal and inappropriate manner.

An unexpected response, an all-out gut maneuver, can sometimes put off an attacker. An eyewitness told me a story about Trungpa Rinpoche, a Tibetan master whose writings you've read a lot of, Alexandre. He lived for a long time in the United States and didn't hesitate to go beyond conventional behavior. One day, the person who was driving him stopped at a freeway service station. For some trivial reason—he wasn't parked properly—a huge guy wearing a cowboy hat approached the open window on the side of the car where Trungpa Rinpoche was sitting and began shouting insults at him. It so happened that a child had left a water gun in the car. Trungpa Rinpoche grabbed it, pointed it at the man, squirted him in the face, and calmly said, "You, chicken!" (These were his exact words, according to the person who was in the car.) The mixture of stupefaction and no doubt fear—we know that in the United States many people have guns and unfortunately often make use of them—was such that the dumbfounded fellow looked at Trungpa Rinpoche for a few seconds and backed off without a word, allowing the car to drive away.

Thus, one of the fruits of inner freedom is being able to maintain perfect lucidity at all times, without letting ourselves be carried away by the troubled currents of mental confusion. That also leaves us with a spacious mind that can relate comfortably to all kinds of circumstances, favorable or unfavorable, without loss of composure. Moreover, this freedom endows us with reliable judgment about how to best deal with adverse circumstances.

Everyday Benevolence and Compassion

CHRISTOPHE Trungpa Rinpoche put his mental-compassion software on hold and instead activated his humor program! But for those of us who are not masters, let us consider the stages we must pass through on the way to greater compassion.

We have natural compassion for the people we love and the people we know. Our effort with them consists just in keeping it alive, even on days when we're tired and in a bad mood. Those days, moreover, give us the opportunity to notice that just coming across as calm and compassionate does us good and often raises our morale because it takes the focus off ourselves and in this way generally leads to pleasant moments and positive emotions.

Then there is compassion toward people we don't know, who we just run into and perhaps will never see again. This requires us to have our little compassion program already turned on in our heads.

Compassion is doubtless a bit more difficult toward people who differ from us in their behavior, their philosophy of life, and their culture. I recall a conversation I had with a patient of mine. He told me that he tended only to give spare change to people who *did* something—musicians in the subway, for example. He didn't give anything to people he passed who were just asking for change. And the more aggressive they were, the less likely he was to give. He told himself that he only gave to people who "deserve it."

This reaction, which I sometimes also observe in myself, has something absurd about it: it derives from our own needs rather than those of the other. Compassion has nothing to do with approval; in any case, it shouldn't be limited to people who follow the same logic as we do. And regarding donations, this logic is also somewhat absurd, because it's often those very people who can't be bothered to play music or show courtesy who are in the greatest social difficulty and are the most in need of help. So there is a paradoxical side to donating in accordance with our mood: if you're in a good mood, you give, and if you're not, you don't. All that represents obstacles to be overcome.

I understand very well the logic of the patient who told himself he prefers to encourage well-adjusted behavior rather than maladjusted conduct. But the mission of compassion is to correct inequalities and distress rather than to validate the social order.

MATTHIEU   The goal of the practice of altruism and compassion is not to reward good conduct, and its absence is not a punitive rebuke of reprehensible behavior. Altruism and compassion are not based on moral judgments, even if they don't preclude such judgments. The particular goal of compassion is to eliminate all individual suffering, whatever or wherever it may be, and no matter what its causes may be. Looked at in this way, altruism and compassion can be impartial and unlimited.

ALEXANDRE   When I was struggling with addiction, caught up in a secret life with death in my soul, I often dreamed of some clinic that would take me in with my whole load of hurts, projections, and attachments without any judgment. Sometimes daily life brings us doctors, mechanics of the soul who give us the strength to believe in the goodness of life and to set off on the path to greater health.

CHRISTOPHE   Another notion that interests me is that of a *duty* of compassion. Since there is a lot of talk of the "duty of intervention," for example, shouldn't there be a notion of compassion as a duty for all human beings in connection with all forms of life in society?

For a number of years, there have been stories published on individuals known as "toxic handlers," whom we might call compassion agents. These are salaried employees who regularly show compassion and kindness toward their colleagues, who relate to fellow employees having trouble at work, and who help soothe job-related conflicts and suffering. But there can be toxic handlers in any human group. In a natural way, these people give comfort and aid and spread compassion around them every day, in small doses, in a discreet manner. That comes pretty close to the "commonplace quality of goodness" that Matthieu often talks about. These people are often invisible, never recognized for the role they play as agents of compassion, because they don't do what they do to gain recognition or because it's their job, but just because it's their nature and they consider it normal.

Once we understand this idea and look around us, we see that there are lots of toxic handlers and that if they were to disappear, the groups that they take care of would fall apart. That's what happens when a toxic handler in a family dies. All of a sudden the unity of the family crumbles, and everyone begins fighting with each other.

The death of my grandfather, to whom I was very attached and who transmitted many of his values to me, brought about a kind of ecological disaster in our family on the relational and emotional level. Conflicts quickly emerged that have since never really disappeared. Similarly, in a hospital where I formerly worked, a triage nurse retired, and her absence was clearly felt in the workplace atmosphere because she had been a major agent of compassion. She was the kind of person who, whenever anyone complained to her, would try to round off the hard edges rather than blowing on the coals.

ALEXANDRE Toxic handlers—through their backing, their attention, their presence, and through a word here and a word there—come to the aid of people who have despaired of the goodness of life. They help *progredientes* to set off on some dynamic process when discouragement and darkness are about to take over. I very much admire these everyday therapists, these rescuers of the soul, who day after day soothe, support, and sustain those who are on the brink of giving into the blows of fate.

All spiritual traditions encourage nonviolence, compassion, and absolute respect for otherness. This is in striking contrast with TV moderators— veritable snipers who are paid to provoke their guests.

CHRISTOPHE Compassion is difficult when dealing with people who are deliberately aggressive—for example, in order to build up their ratings on TV or gather a following on social media. What you said about TV moderators whose job is to say nasty stuff reminds me of the discussion we had on mind training. The problem of badmouthing and malevolence is that it gives us practice in seeing the bad side of people and thus trains us in a kind of maimed way of looking at things. We see only the bad side of others, their weaknesses, their faults. And seeing these faults, what do we do? We make fun of them, we mock them, we distance ourselves from them ("We're not like that, we're smart"), and finally we reject them. These programs are anything but harmless, and under the pretext of getting laughs or provoking some sort of pseudo-debate, they activate our worst aspects. As a result of not cultivating our compassion function, we are no longer capable of anything but exercising these bad sides of ourselves and only seeing the bad sides of other people.

MATTHIEU There is a kind of immediate gratification and perverse pleasure in this spectacle. It's what the Germans call *schadenfreude*: unwholesome satisfaction coming from seeing other people tormented, ridiculed, or even injured. There is a kind of voyeuristic and unspoken enjoyment, doubtless connected with a certain kind of cruelty latent in us, in seeing the humiliation, belittlement, or defeat of a scapegoat exhibited in this way. We try in this way to build up our own ego by nullifying the other. This is the opposite of the upliftedness we feel when we admire and wholeheartedly take pleasure in the kindness, generosity, and excellence of someone else.

The Gratuitousness and Delicacy of Compassion

ALEXANDRE A certain kind of compassion can contain a big dose of paternalism and lots of little tricks. When I am asked, for example, how to approach a physically impaired person on the street, I certainly don't have much to say. There are not many rules or protocols for how to lend a hand. The challenge is to be yourself as much as possible and remain attentive to the needs of the other without projecting. And if you happen to be unskillful, that is perhaps less damaging than the mechanical quality of someone trying to follow a protocol: "To aid people with disabilities, execute the following steps—point 1, point 2, point 3."

CHRISTOPHE I don't agree with you 100 percent, Alexandre. Sometimes getting some simple information about the needs of such and such a person in such and such a situation can be helpful and save us from making mistakes. Explaining to someone that when a person has cancer they are irritated by being asked, "How are you?" or that a physically impaired person appreciates it when people are spontaneous with them, can help us do things right—or at least not screw up on account of ignorance rather than malice or indifference. The idea is not to mechanically apply some protocol in which we are really not there for the other. Compassion begins with being there for the other, with the attention we pay to the person in front of us and not by projecting our own needs or our own worldview on them. There is also a need for delicacy in practicing compassion, so that it doesn't become paternalism, intrusiveness, or ultimately a lack of respect for the other person and his or her needs.

ALEXANDRE One thing is for sure: compassion, as you say, requires delicacy, infinite tact. We don't want to seem to be imposing help from on high in a way that can be perceived as a humiliation; what we're really trying to do is give ourselves completely and be there, open and available. The challenge is always to manifest the goodness of life in the thick of difficulty, to lend a hand or offer support, and then to tiptoe quietly away.

Our habitual tendency is often to look at people suspiciously, even judge them outright. Leaving behind the realm of self-interest and consumption and daring to have an attitude that's a bit more contemplative has nothing sappy or mushy about it. On the contrary, this rare approach requires lucidity, guts, lots of courage. It means seeing that life is tragic—that it involves a lot of loneliness, illness, and unfairness, and it ends in death—without losing your composure or becoming bitter. The answer to this tragic side is solidarity, something a lot different from recoiling, distrusting, and being suspicious. Taking this approach requires us to drop the security-oriented logic that makes us defend our territory tooth and nail. Our job is to apply these grand principles in the midst of daily life, and there it's a whole different story.

MATTHIEU Compassion can be exercised in two phases. Begin by approaching the other with a fundamentally compassionate attitude. Then pause inwardly to give your discriminating intelligence the time to ripen and understand what the most judicious way of bringing a bit of well-being to the person in front of you is without hurrying, without imposing anything on that person, and without invading their privacy.

Indifference and Ill Will

CHRISTOPHE Another way of understanding compassion is to ask ourselves what the opposites are. Ill will? Indifference? Perhaps the first way of not being compassionate is indifference or neutrality. A little bit of added audacity brings us to ill will, which focuses on what's wrong, in our opinion, with the other person and turns that into a pretext for not being compassionate toward that person.

MATTHIEU The opposite of compassion is clearly ill will, the desire to harm somebody. Indifference is not exactly the opposite of compassion, even if, as Martin Luther King Jr. said, "Man's inhumanity to man is not only perpetrated by the vitriolic actions of those who are bad. It is also perpetrated by the vitiating inaction of those who are good."[1] The opposite of indifference is caring about the situations of others. The indifferent person has little or no concern for those who are not part of his own group, for society in general, and even less for those who live far away from him elsewhere in the world. One of the motivating forces of compassion is valuing others. Persecutions and genocides begin with the devaluation of the people you want to eliminate, followed by dehumanizing them altogether. They are called "a pestilence," "vermin," "cockroaches." This is the same as when we regard animals as things so we can see them as objects of consumption, as sausage-making machines.

CHRISTOPHE Yes, indifference often comes from not valuing others enough. But I think that there is also a kind of indifference that arises from impotence. For example, after a while, one is no longer able to relate to all the people in the street who are asking for money. Some days, thinking I'm wrong the whole time and that I should give them all a bit of money, I tell myself that that's not the solution, that there's no end to it. So all of a sudden I feel impotent, and I take refuge in a kind of indifference. I don't believe that I'm valuing them less, but I am definitely making a mistake. We should not leave off tirelessly doing our part just because poverty and distress are endless.

Navigating Between the Unpleasantness of Adversity and the Somnolence of Well-Being

ALEXANDRE   A big step toward freedom is daring to make inner peace, and this means throttling any warlike tendencies we might have and identifying the civil wars that are raging inside us. How do we vaccinate ourselves against the need for adversity, for an enemy, that's nesting in the depths of our personality?

In Korea, I had the good luck to encounter a Zen nun. Suffering from an incurable cancer at the age of forty, she radiated a sparkling sense of joy. Greater health was flourishing in her even though, physically, she was dwindling day by day. She told me that for a long time she had considered illness an enemy to be defeated. Headed straight toward exhaustion, she lived only to struggle, to beat the disease, until the day she decided, she told me, to make peace with it. Changing her outlook — to stop regarding her condition as an enemy, but instead to see it as the ground for a possible transformation — she relieved herself of a tremendous burden. This didn't mean that she resigned herself and abandoned all treatment, but she worked in the direction of health without battling an adversary morning, noon, and night.

CHRISTOPHE   In our lives, it's more often problems and adversity that cause us to progress on the path rather than success and ease. This is a pity, but that's the way our minds work. We need success and comfort because they are satisfying and feed us with pleasant emotions like a sense of well-being, self-esteem, and gratitude. But our successes do not necessarily lead us to call into question what we are and what the world is. For that we need the sting of failure or helplessness. The *occasional* sting of failure, not the constant tyranny of it!

We have to navigate between the unpleasantness of adversity and the somnolence of well-being. The ideal of wisdom and inner freedom is indeed, as you say, Matthieu, to continually find the way to our inner freedom between two dangers: enslavement to the wretchedness connected with adversity (despondency or anger) and habituation to, and then dependence on, the comfort connected with the absence of adversity.

MATTHIEU Buddhism tells us that we must also identify the right enemy. If somebody hits you with a stick, you don't get angry at the stick but at the person holding it — not realizing that the person is manipulated by animosity just as the stick is by their hand. The true enemy here, the only one toward which we can be merciless, is hatred, or in other cases, greed, jealousy, and pride. The war against them aims at triumph over suffering.

CHRISTOPHE But do we have to talk about war or struggle? Is "enemy" the right word? In medicine, for example, the war metaphor is frequently used: "fighting against disease," "the war against cancer." I'm always uneasy with this way of talking and the view that underlies it. It seems to me that it skips over a number of truths: illness is not an enemy or an adversary but rather an unbalance, a disturbance in the subtle mechanisms that maintain health in us. The idea of taking care of oneself, of pacifying one's emotions of fear or anger, seems more apt to me than waging a stressful war against an imaginary enemy.

MATTHIEU Nevertheless, isn't it legitimate to consider hatred an enemy? Unlike an ordinary adversary, who doesn't harm us continuously and might even become a friend, hatred, lust, and arrogance harm us all the time and totally: 100 percent. It's the enemy par excellence — the enemy of well-being, the enemy of goodness, the jailer of inner freedom.

Compassion Toward Oneself

MATTHIEU Compassion toward oneself is wishing to liberate oneself from the causes of suffering and wishing oneself well, which is not the same as egoism.

ALEXANDRE   Without being narcissistic, there's a lot of room left for this kind of self-love, this joyous acceptance of what we are in our basic nature. But it doesn't come condition free; it comes hand in hand with an urge toward self-development, a determination to uproot from our hearts all seeds of hatred, of self-centeredness, of egoism, and of war.

CHRISTOPHE   Compassion toward oneself consists in not adding an inner war to our external difficulties and in adopting a just attitude toward ourselves in which we are at once clear-headed and friendly in relation to our own person. A relationship of friendship is a compassionate one: Because we want what's good for our friends and they know it, they also are open to our criticisms and they understand that we're trying to help them, even by tampering with their comfort and certitudes. But we are open about these things with each other.

Compassion toward oneself has been identified as an essential element of self-esteem. It is what permits us to repair ourselves and move forward. And like compassion toward others, it is a very pragmatic attitude, not at all naive or ideological. It is the strict and secure framework that permits the most inner freedom. We are not afraid of either failing or disappointing—or at least we don't experience such fears in an obsessive or paralyzing way. This compassion must be unconditional and not concerned about any merits we may or may not be manifesting. Unconditionality is there first, in a prior position; compassion is there for me *a priori*. There are no malicious judgments (criticizing the person rather than their behavior) and no trying to reduce everything to one single right way of proceeding. Interest is there for what I do and who I am. Nevertheless, this unconditionality does not exclude *a posteriori* judgments and advice. (Once again, I am not talking about the absence of judgment but the absence of *a priori* judgment.)

What Is Unconditional Compassion?

CHRISTOPHE   Unconditional compassion is an ideal and a principle, like democracy or fraternity. Such ideals and principles still have to be actualized in the real world. For example, does the existence of a Hitler,

a Pol Pot, or other bloodthirsty tyrants challenge the pertinence, importance, and even the necessity of this ideal? I don't think so. Their coming to
power owes more to their political talents or to the difficult circumstances
that prevailed in their countries at that moment than to any naive or excessive compassion toward them.

MATTHIEU   Yes, it's political talent or Machiavellianism devoid of
any form of empathy or compassion. Syria's Bashar al-Assad is an abom-
inable fellow. Compassion does not consist in saying to him, "You're a
fine fellow. Keep it up!" It consists in looking at him the way a medical
expert would who was completely aware of the total madness of his
patient. He would begin by preventing him from doing further harm,
then he would look for a means of treating him. The best thing we could
wish for such an ignoble individual is for him to cease his horrendous
activities.

If we are free from hate ourselves, we will be able to envisage the best
means of minimizing suffering both in the short and long term. In the long
term that means various forms of assistance to improve education, standards of living, the status of women, and respect for personal rights. In other
words, we have to neutralize evil and heal its causes without indulging in
hate, revenge, and other forms of the desire to cause harm. This approach is
not one of weakness or negligence.

Universal or unconditional compassion is not a noble, utopic notion.
All beings without exception want to avoid suffering. If we wish from
the bottom of our hearts for this aspiration of theirs to come true, our
compassionate motivation becomes universal just by that. So unconditional compassion consists simply in not shutting anyone out of one's
heart. The circle of compassion begins by expanding, and its boundaries
end up fading out and becoming like the space that contains all beings.
Even if on a concrete level we can't bring benefit to all, every being
who appears in the field of our attention becomes the object of our
compassion.

Certain philosophers I have talked with, Jonathan Haidt in particular, think that this is too angelic a position. Haidt said he thinks that

compassion should apply to the people we're close to, and it is meaningless for it to extend to all beings. However, in extending our compassion to all, we don't love the people we are close to any less; rather, we become better at loving them because our compassion becomes much more refined. A person who loves only a small fraction of beings possesses only partial, truncated compassion. Moreover, when the circumstances of life place certain beings closer to the sun of our compassion, as though they were physically nearer to our star, those few naturally receive more light and warmth. But that never occurs at the price of exclusion. Thus, what compassion does exclude is the partiality, sectarianism, dogmatism, and discrimination that are the ills of our society.

Toolbox for Unconditional Compassion

CHRISTOPHE

Compassion is like little stalks of grass that manage to poke up in the cracks of the pavement: even if it seems like there's no room for them, they always win out in the end.

It is of the utmost value to dissociate compassion from our judgments. All human beings deserve our compassion. It's not a reward but a recognition of their humanity. Let's be as compassionate as we can, even with people who are different from us, even with people we consider to be wrongdoers. Compassion will only awaken or reawaken their humanity—as well as their sense of guilt.

Let's be toxic handlers as often as possible. As best we can, let's spread looks, gestures, and words of compassion through our days and encounters. When trees produce oxygen, and when humans produce compassion, the earth and humanity are better for it.

MATTHIEU

Let's make an effort to continually enlarge the circle of our compassion, so as to include the greatest number of beings possible. Let's wish for the day to come when no being will be excluded from our heart.

Unconditional compassion is not out of our reach. All beings desire to avoid suffering and achieve happiness. For this compassionate aspiration to be extended to all beings, it's enough to sincerely wish for it to be fulfilled.

Turn compassion into action. At the same time, let us gradually increase the expression of this compassion in our words and deeds.

ALEXANDRE

Compassion is a gift, freely given. True love doesn't impose anything on us at all; it requires nothing else of us but to be the way we are in our deepest nature. Being compassionate is trying to do good for others without trying to squeeze them into the mold of my preconceptions, never laying a finger on their freedom, and having the utmost respect for their uniqueness, their difference. In no case does it mean imposing a view of the world or a particular approach to life on them. Helping my neighbor is extricating myself from my projections, giving myself outright, and making myself totally available without judging or asking for anything in return.

Compassion is subversive. There's a mighty element of subversion—even rebellion—in compassion. We have to put an end to all tendencies toward violence, vengeance, domination, and authoritarianism and never let these sad passions govern our lives. This takes audacity, fundamentally active and shrewd, which ceaselessly invents and innovates without ever imposing anything. It lends its ear to everyone's genuine hopes and expectations and profound aspirations with radical acceptance. This woman, that man whom I am encountering right now—what do they really need? What do they desire from the bottom of their hearts?

Compassion gets things clean. Chögyam Trungpa tell us, "Dirt never comes first."[2] Dirt, trauma, wounds, brutality, malice, hostility are never the first things in a heart. Compassion gets things clean; it gently removes all intruders, all parasites gnawing on our being.

Compassion is not for dummies. Lending a hand, offering support to a person, calls for tact, delicacy, and infinite respect. The moment of expressing solidarity is not a time for crude gestures. It is a moment far from paternalism and condescension. Generosity arises from an intelligence of the heart, from perceptiveness, from a sense of lightness.

Conclusion

Were the Fruits of the Harvest Good?

MATTHIEU   It seems to me that we agree that the full attainment of inner freedom can only have wholesome consequences for ourselves and others. In freeing ourselves from the web of ignorance, confusion, and mental constructs, which brings nothing but misery and distress, we also are looking for the best possible harvest in the manner of a farmer who loves his work. This harvest is not one derived from an intellectual monoculture; it is born from the seeds of many human qualities that flourish thanks to the fertile ground of potential we have in us, from the water of compassion and the sun of perseverance. And the excellent harvest is one of wisdom, joy, inner freedom, and fulfillment that allows us to appreciate each passing moment.

ALEXANDRE   As Chögyam Trungpa reminds us, many of our torments and sufferings come from our inability to let go, from our refusal to see the world as it is, and from the bundle of neuroses that keeps recycling in us every moment. We always need reference points, the hope of being able to get out of this chaos, of reaching solid ground. However, ultimately it's in our daily life, with our currently available resources, when everything is shifting and tilting around us, that we have to learn to dance, to experience the feeling that we're making some headway in the very ground of our being.

To make the big leap, to give ourselves over to life and open ourselves to freedom, far from all fears, traumas, and mental obscurations, we definitely need a boost—some helping hands, ears that listen, friends in the good. Solidarity—that's what sets us free.

At the temporary end of our warm exchange, I would like to thank all those who help me continue this journey toward liberation. For the time being, with my infinite gratitude, I would like to offer them this little viaticum from Master Trungpa: "When a person develops real compassion, he is uncertain whether he is being generous to others or to himself because compassion is environmental generosity, without direction, without 'for me' and without 'for them.' It is filled with joy, spontaneously existing joy, constant joy in the sense of trust, in the sense that joy contains tremendous wealth, richness."[1]

CHRISTOPHE   I hope with all my heart that these amicable, spontaneous, and sincere exchanges of ours will be received by readers as though they were also part of our circle of friends. I hope we have inspired in them a desire to continue to advance on the path of inner freedom and solidarity. I hope that we have been able to show that being on that path is not only enriching but also accessible and exciting.

A little while ago, I was chatting with my youngest daughter about her professional future. I relayed to her this piece of advice from I don't remember which CEO of a big company, which is often cited as an example in schools of business and management. What he essentially said was that the secret of success was working hard and being nice to people. I believe that that is also the secret of a good life, a life that is wise, happy, and generous. Work on yourself and do good around you.

MATTHIEU   The time has come to share the fruits of our harvest with those with whom we share our lives. Let us dedicate to them the good we have been able to come up with in the course of these sessions, and to all the deeds of compassion we have done in the past and may do in the future. May these fruits help to soothe the sufferings they are enduring at present and root out the causes of their sufferings long term: ignorance, hatred, and the other mental toxins. Let's hope these benefits — seeds cast onto the fertile soil of the infinity of beings — will last for a very long time!

Notes

Epigraph

1. This passage is from writing dated November 1, 1928: "Freedom to the Free." In Mahatma Gandhi, *Young India: 1927–1928* (Triplicane, Madras: S. Ganesan, 1935), 901–902. Available online at archive.org/details/HindSwaraj.yi.10973.33464/page/n949.

Preface

1. Translator's note: The term "sad passions" comes from the Dutch philosopher Benedict de Spinoza, who divided all affects into those of sadness and those of joy. The affects of joy lead in the direction of greater self-perfection; those of sadness lead in the direction of less.

Introduction: What Is Inner Freedom?

1. Letter from Benedict de Spinoza to G. H. Schaller, The Hague, October, 1674. In Benedict de Spinoza, *On the Improvement of Understanding/The Ethics/Correspondence,* trans. R. H. M. Elwes (New York: Dover, 1955).
2. Benedict de Spinoza, *The Collected Works of Spinoza: Volume I,* ed. and trans. Edwin Curley (Princeton, NJ: Princeton University Press, 1985).
3. André Comte-Sponville, *The Little Book of Atheist Spirituality,* trans. Nancy Huston (New York: Penguin, 2008), 187.

Chapter 1: Akrasia: Weakness of the Will

1. Romans 7:19 (New International Version).
2. Oscar Wilde, *Lady Windermere's Fan* (1892), act 1, scene 1.

Chapter 2: Dependency

1. Jean-Jacques Rousseau, *Émile, or On Education,* trans. Barbara Foxley (Auckland, New Zealand: Floating Press, 2007), 404.

Chapter 3: Fear

1. Ramuz, Charles Ferdinand., and Bertola. *Le Gros Poisson Du Lac.* Genève: La Joie de lire, 2005. No English translation of the book has been published.

Chapter 4: Discouragement and Despair

1. Samuel Beckett, from the novella *Worstward Ho,* republished with two other novellas in *Nohow On: Company, Ill Seen Ill Said, and Worstward Ho* (New York: Grove Press, 1995), 89.
2. Jean de La Fontaine, "The Wagoner Stuck in the Mud," in *The Complete Fables of Jean de La Fontaine*, trans. Norman R. Shapiro (Urbana: University of Illinois Press, 2007), 147.

Chapter 5: Egocentricity

1. Jean de La Fontaine, 6.

Chapter 8: An Ecology of Relationship

1. Benedict (Baruch) de Spinoza, "Political Treatise [Tractus Politicus, 1677]," in his *Complete Works*, ed. Michael L. Morgan, trans. Samuel Shirley (Indianapolis, IN: Hackett Publishing, 2002), chapter 1, section 4.
2. François de La Rochefoucauld, *La Rochefoucauld Maxims*, trans. John Heard Jr. (New York: Dover, 2006), 4.
3. Jean-Paul Sartre, *No Exit*, trans. Stuart Gilbert, in *No Exit and Three Other Plays* (New York: Vintage International, 1989), 45.

4. Chögyam Trungpa, *Transcending Madness: The Experience of the Six Bardos* (Boston: Shambhala Publications, 1992), 34.

5. Marcel Proust, "The Prisoner," *In Search of Lost Time: Volume 5*, ed. Christopher Prendergast, trans. Carol Clark (New York: Penguin Classics, 2019), 244.

6. Les Journées Émergences is an annual cultural gathering mainly comprising presentations by cultural figures of note with an eye toward positive social change.

Chapter 9: The Impact of Our Cultural Environment

1. Lucretius, *On the Nature of Things,* trans. Martin Ferguson Smith (Indianapolis, IN: Hackett Publishing, 2001), 98.

2. Michel de Montaigne, *The Complete Essays of Montaigne*, trans. Donald Frame (Stanford, CA: Stanford University Press, 1958), 178.

3. Ayn Rand, *For the New Intellectual: The Philosophy of Ayn Rand* (New York: Signet, 1963), 179. See also *The Virtue of Selfishness* (New York: Signet, 1964).

Chapter 10: The Horizon of Effort

1. Michel Foucault, *The History of Sexuality, Volume 3: The Care of the Self,* trans. Robert Hurley (New York: Vintage, 1988), 46.

Chapter 11: Difficult Effort, Joyous Effort

1. Albert B. Hakim *Historical Introduction to Philosophy* (Boston: Pearson/ Prentice Hall, 2006), 281.

2. Christian Bobin, *Les Ruines du Ciel* (Paris: Gallimard, 2009). No English translation of the book has been published.

Chapter 12: Training the Mind

1. Leo Tolstoy, *Anna Karenina,* trans. Richard Pevear and Larissa Volokhansky (New York: Penguin Classics, 2004), 1.

Chapter 13: Meditation

1. Bobin, *Les Ruines du Ciel.*
2. Simone Weil, *The Notebooks of Simone Weil,* trans. Arthur Wills (New York, Routledge: 2004), 30.

Chapter 15: Inner Pacification

1. Epictetus, *The Handbook (The Enchiridion),* trans. Nicholas P. White (Indianapolis, IN: Hackett Publishing, 1983), 19.

Chapter 17: Dealing with Death

1. Montaigne, *The Complete Essays of Montaigne,* 62.
2. Benedict Spinoza, *Ethics,* trans. W. H. White and A. H. Stirling (Ware, Hertfordshire, UK: Wordsworth Editions, 2001), 212.

Chapter 18: Ethics

1. André Comte-Sponville, *A Small Treatise on the Great Virtues: The Uses of Philosophy in Everyday Life,* trans. Catherine Temerson (New York: Metropolitan Books, 2001), 226.

Chapter 19: Unconditional Compassion

1. Martin Luther King Jr., *King Papers*, Chapter 21, Death of Illusions, part of the Martin Luther King Jr. Research and Education Institute at Stanford University. https://kinginstitute.stanford.edu/chapter-21-death-illusions
2. Chögyam Trungpa Rinpoche, "The Shambhala Warrior Slogans," in *The Collected Works of Chögyam Trungpa, Volume Nine*, ed. Carolyn Rose Gimian (Boulder, CO: Shambhala, 2017), 298.

Conclusion: Were the Fruits of the Harvest Good?

1. Chögyam Trungpa, *Cutting Through Spiritual Materialism* (Boston: Shambhala Classics, 2010), 115.

Acknowledgments

We fully acknowledge the debt of gratitude we owe to Catherine Meyer for her patient and expert re-readings of various versions of this manuscript. She helped us a great deal to put our ideas in order and to improve the quality of presentation of our text considerably.

Wholehearted thanks to Delphine, who twice hosted us so warmly in the Swiss mountains, permitting us to carry on our dialogue in the most joyous serenity, as well as to Pauline, who received us very kindly at Saint-Maurice for one session of our talks.

Our thanks go also to Sandra and Aurélie for having carefully transcribed the recordings of our dialogue, and to Bertille for her efficient aid with proofreading.

We send them also to Carisse Busquet, who attentively reviewed our manuscript and made many highly pertinent suggestions.

Finally, we cannot express enough the gratitude we feel toward our editors, Sophie de Sivry, Nicole Lattès, and Guillaume Allary, who followed us with their compassion all through this work, as they have done for our previous publications, and also toward the teams at L'Iconoclaste and Allary Éditions who worked on the production of this book.

Alexandre particularly wishes to thank Corine Jollien, Romina Astolfi, Bernard Campan, Fréderic Rauss, Olivier Rogeaux, Jean-Bernard Daeppen, Firmin Manoury, and Mathieu Blard for their daily help.

The Matthieu Ricard Foundation for the Advancement of Altruism in the World

Matthieu Ricard donates all of his revenues—from photography, lectures, and the royalties of all his books—to Karuna-Shechen, an organization that has been providing support for more than twenty years to the most disadvantaged people of India, Nepal, and Tibet, with more than 380,000 beneficiaries yearly.

On a practical level, the book you are holding in your hands will permit a child in Nepal to go to school for a week, two people with physical disabilities to receive one medical treatment, and an Indian family to enjoy the benefits of an organic vegetable garden for one season.

You also can support the activities of Karuna-Shechen (karuna-shechen.org)

About the Authors

MATTHIEU RICARD is a molecular geneticist turned Buddhist monk, humanitarian, and author of several books, including *Happiness: A Guide to Developing Life's Most Important Skill*, *The Art of Meditation*, and *Altruism: The Power of Compassion to Change Yourself and the World*. A major participant in the research collaboration between cognitive scientists and Buddhist practitioners, Ricard also published several volumes of translations from Tibetan and several albums of photography. He founded and oversees humanitarian projects in India, Tibet, and Nepal. For more information, visit matthieuricard.org.

ALEXANDRE JOLLIEN is a philosopher and writer who spent seventeen years in a home for people with disabilities. His books, published in many languages, include *In Praise of Weakness*. He lives in Switzerland. For more, visit alexandre-jollien.ch.

CHRISTOPHE ANDRÉ is a psychiatrist specializing in the psychology of emotions. His books include *Imperfect, Free, and Happy* and *Meditating: Day After Day*. He lives in France. Visit his website at christopheandre.com.

About Sounds True

Sounds True is a multimedia publisher whose mission is to inspire and support personal transformation and spiritual awakening. Founded in 1985 and located in Boulder, Colorado, we work with many of the leading spiritual teachers, thinkers, healers, and visionary artists of our time. We strive with every title to preserve the essential "living wisdom" of the author or artist. It is our goal to create products that not only provide information to a reader or listener but also embody the quality of a wisdom transmission.

For those seeking genuine transformation, Sounds True is your trusted partner. At SoundsTrue.com you will find a wealth of free resources to support your journey, including exclusive weekly audio interviews, free downloads, interactive learning tools, and other special savings on all our titles.

To learn more, please visit SoundsTrue.com/freegifts or call us toll-free at 800.333.9185.